SPANISH CATHOLICISM

SPANISH CATHOLICISM
An Historical Overview

STANLEY G. PAYNE

The University of Wisconsin Press

Published 1984

The University of Wisconsin Press
114 North Murray Street
Madison, Wisconsin 53715

The University of Wisconsin Press, Ltd.
1 Gower Street
London WC1E 6HA, England

First printing

Printed in the United States of America

For LC CIP information see the colophon

ISBN 0-299-09800-1

"La historia hispánica, al menos en lo esencial, es la historia de una creencia y de una sensibilidad religiosa."

—*Américo Castro*

Contents

Preface

THE IMPORTANCE of religion in Spanish history, medieval or modern, would seem to require little demonstration. That constitutes the primary motivation for this book. The bibliography in Spanish is of course so enormous that it could scarcely be thoroughly digested in a lifetime, and yet the theme draws comparatively little attention from foreign Hispanists, primarily concerned with political and socioeconomic issues. The present study is the product of an effort to gain a degree of comprehension of this most controversial area, in both its traditional and modern dimensions. If it proves of some utility to others, the temerity of undertaking such a modest work on such a major topic will in some measure be justified.

I should like particularly to express my gratitude to Luis Apostua Palos, Subdirector of *Ya*, José Andrés-Gallego of the University of Léon, José Manuel Cuenca Toribio of the University of Córdoba, Fernando García de Cortázar, Dean of Philosophy and Letters of the University of Deusto, and Francisco J. de Lizarza Inda for their assistance with bibliography and other materials. Joaquín L. Ortega, Director of *Ecclesia*, Francisco de Azcona, Director of the Oficina de Estadística y Sociología of the Conferencia Episcopal Española, and Gustavo Suárez Pertierra, Director General de Asuntos Religiosos in the Ministry of Justice, were most generous in helping to provide current statistical data. Maureen Flynn was of great assistance developing reference material and also prepared the index. Joan Connelly Ullman of the University of Washington improved the manuscript considerably with very careful reading and many suggestions, and José M. Sánchez of St. Louis University also provided helpful criticism.

Thanks are also due to Karen Delwiche, who typed much of the manuscript, to Mary Maraniss, who edited the entire work, and to the Institute for Research in the Humanities at the University of Wisconsin, whose fellowship provided me with the opportunity to complete this study.

Stanley G. Payne
Madison, Wisconsin
June 1983

Introduction

THE RELATION between religion and culture is always a major problem for the study of religion, and nowhere in the western world has this been more salient than in the case of Spain. Though always fully orthodox in its formal doctrines, Spanish Catholicism is the product of a unique historical and cultural experience. The peculiar conditions of its history, together with the emphatic qualities of Spanish culture, have given a tone to Spanish Catholicism that is recognizably distinct, however unexceptionable its theological foundation.

Religion played a much more direct role in the original definition of a Spanish identity and culture than was the case in most western countries, sheltered from the onslaught of a different religion and an oriental culture during the Middle Ages. The subsequent history of Spanish Catholicism cannot be understood fully without a grasp of the manner in which this identity was forged during the Middle Ages. While interpreting their religion in large part through the common western medieval culture, the Spanish principalities also gave to their relationship with Christianity a special role that did not merely coincide with that of Europe as a whole.

The great criticism of Spanish Catholicism, since about 1965 frequently echoed by Spanish Catholic writers themselves, is that its religiosity has been highly "baroque," external, extravagant, given to form, display, and convention but lacking in personal religious experience or commitment, internal spirituality, or sober, sustained inquiry. This conventional criticism is correct as the description of a general tendency, but it is also to some extent a caricature, since it obviously does not constitute the whole truth.

This was also to some degree probably true of medieval Christianity generally. For reasons that will be touched on during the first two chapters, Spain found it more difficult than did most of western Europe to transcend the medieval structure of western culture. Thus the glories of the Spanish Golden Age of the sixteenth and seventeenth centuries to a large degree represented further development of the traditional culture and traditional Christianity, though admittedly with certain new features.

It is nonetheless a mistake to dismiss Spanish Catholicism as a traditional community or national cult without deep spiritual force or creative power. The expression of such spiritual force may be seen in all the manifold achievements of Spanish Catholicism, intellectual as well as spiritual, during that era. The redevelopment of Christian missions in the late Middle Ages was a part of this, just as the subsequent massive effort to evangelize the empire and certain other parts of the outer world represented a religious enterprise of unique proportions and scant precedent. That it ended in relative failure, even within Spanish America—which has never been transformed into a Catholic society on the European scale—ought not to diminish appreciation of its originality, scope, or intensity.

At the same time, considerable verbal ambiguity about religion can be found in the common cultural expression of this formerly most Catholic of peoples. The virtual ubiquity of formal sacralization in the traditional culture may also to help to explain the fact that Spain is also the classic land of blasphemy. On the popular verbal level Spaniards have always been quick to recognize the gulf between spiritual theory and personal and social practice, reflected in a host of popular sayings.

Related to this is the practical question of exactly what Spanish religion, embedded as it has largely been in a specific kind of religious culture, has meant in terms of social mores and the institutional development of society as a whole. Compared with north European Protestantism, it has failed to develop a keen sense of individual ethics and responsibility, for Spanish morality, like that of much of southern and eastern Europe, has been geared in considerable degree to group, subgroup, or familial behavior. In a different socionational context, such behavior has been termed "amoral familialism," broad aspects of which have certainly been present in Spain. Once more, however, it is important not to oversimplify, and thus Gerald Brenan's flat statement that "the Spanish have no sense of equity," while referring to genuine shortcomings of Spanish society and history, is much too extreme a generalization.[1]

The modern institutional transformation of Spain generated more intense conflict in church-state relations over a longer period than has existed in any other country in the world. This has variously been imputed to the peculiar nature of Spanish Catholicism, the weakness of Spanish liberalism, and the lag in socioeconomic development compared with northwestern Europe. None of these causal references is inapplicable, but each is altogether incomplete by itself, for the turmoil of

---

1. Brenan goes on to add (writing about 1950): "They live by a tribal or client system, which makes it a moral duty for them to favor their friends at the expense of the State and to penalize their adversaries. This is the first law of this country, and it was as much observed during the rule of the Republic as it is today. Three quarters of the endemic revolutionary feeling in Spain is caused by it." *The Face of Spain* (London, 1950), 227.

modern Spanish religiopolitical conflict has derived from the full complexity of Spanish history and the manifold cultural and institutional influences involved. In the abstract, the Spanish pattern has been like that of most Catholic countries, but in much of its rhythm, features, and intensity it has stood alone. The Carlist reaction, more vigorous and lasting than in any other European land, was a phenomenon that went well beyond the religious dimension, highly important though that was. The Catholic revival of the later nineteenth century was broadly paralleled in some other Catholic countries, though its exact timing and features were in some respects unique to Spain. Similarly, the reactionary Franquist essay in national Catholicism found ready parrallels in central and eastern Europe (Austria, Poland, Lithuania, Croatia, and Slovakia), but its scope and duration were particularly Spanish.

Spanish Catholicism has frequently been accused of being theocratic, of dominating the state, whereas it is much more nearly true that in major periods of Spanish history the Church itself has been dominated by an officially ultra-Catholic state. While the Church leadership was never willing to accept the principle of full religious liberty in Spain until about 1970, conversely the more radical of the new liberal regimes of the nineteenth and twentieth centuries did not offer the alternative of a fully free church in a free state. They attempted to combine special restrictions and discrimination with representative government and not surprisingly failed in such a self-contradictory enterprise.

The dominant cultural forms of Spanish Catholicism did not take full shape until the sixteenth century, but they endured for four centuries, until the later years of the Franco regime. The broader history of Spanish Catholicism should be seen not merely in the spiritual life of the clergy and laity or in the general expression of their religious culture but also in the interaction with national institutions and society throughout this period.

SPANISH CATHOLICISM

1

Religion and Identity in Medieval Hispania

THE HISTORY and culture of no other people in the world are more totally identified with Roman Catholicism than those of the people of Spain. This special identity stems not so much from the early centuries of Christian experience in the peninsula as from the great historical watershed of the Christian Reconquest. It is much more a product of the Middle Ages in all their complexity than of late classical or Roman Christendom. The history of the Catholic Church in the peninsula extends far back into the Roman period, yet though the Church achieved great prominence and full official status in late Roman and Visigothic times, the early history of Catholicism forms only a prelude to the main line of development of religion in Spain.

The special character of Spanish Catholicism stems first of all from a paradox, for it developed in eventual response to the Church's greatest catastrophe—the triumph of Islam in most of Spain after 711. Spain alone of all territories conquered by the Muslims and subsequently Islamicized managed not merely to throw off Muslim political and military dominance but to re-Christianize its land as well. The primary development of Spanish culture and institutions stems from a Christian resistance society in the northern hill and mountain districts of the peninsula during the eighth and ninth centuries, which in turn was associated with the first crystallization of the new civilization of western Europe during the same era.

The sudden and stunning Muslim conquest of most of the peninsula in 711–14 is to be explained primarily by political weakness, but evidently not by any comparative shallowness or debility of Hispanic Christianity in general during the Visigothic period. Indeed, the Hispanic Church was one of the more vigorous segments of Latin Christendom in that era. During the fourth century it had counted among its leaders Bishop Osio (Ossius) of Córdoba, chief religious advisor to the emperor Constantine and the head of the Council of Nicaea (325), one pope, Dámaso (366–84), and two major Latin Christian poets, Juvenco and Prudencio. Thence it

3

developed further, reaching its full cultural flowering in the seventh century.

After conversion of the Arian Visigothic dynasty in 587 there developed a greater degree of interpretation between Church and state than in any other west European kingdom of that era. In this relationship the stronger hand was held by the crown, contrary to vague notions about the origins of a supposed "Spanish theocracy" in the Visigothic period. The Church hierarchy also exercised major influence, however, participating decisively in key areas. The Church managed to establish a formal structure of law for a state in which such relations had been limited and fragmentary. The monarchy thus became subject in some respects to the higher laws of the realm, and its elective succession was normally ratified by the Church councils held at Toledo, the capital and senior metropolitanate. These councils came to define a specific national religious policy vis-à-vis the crown, questions of war and peace, and the only significant religious minority, the Jews. Outstanding leaders such as St. Isidoro of Seville defined the moral function of state power and gained at least nominal theoretical acceptance of the doctrine of power transmitted from the people through the crown. Conversely, it was the crown which designated appointees to the Church hierarchy, in nominal consultation and accord with the metropolitans, and in the great majority of political and administrative issues involving the Church it was the will of the crown which prevailed.

The Hispanic Church under the Visigoths was one of the better-educated sectors of Latin Christendom. Its condition in this regard was superior to that of Merovingian France, which would later receive several major Hispanic Church leaders to assist its own development after the Visigothic collapse. The Hispanic luminary was of course the great Isidoro, Europe's outstanding polymath in the seventh century. The twenty volumes of his *Etymologies* recorded much of the knowledge of the classical world and were reproduced by hand, and later in print, for nearly a thousand years. St. Isidoro wrote the first Hispanic history, the *Historia Gothorum*, and the "De laude Spaniae" with which he began this work has earned him the reputation of being the first conscious all-Spanish patriot, or at least patriotic publicist. The Church was undoubtedly the most important institution in the lives of the Hispanic common people, and it functioned as their representative and intercessor to a far greater degree than any of the organs of state.

It cannot be held, however, that the moralizing of St. Isidoro and other Church leaders had more than a modest effect on the behavior of the Visigothic monarchy and elite. Though conditions did improve in the final Visigothic century, more Visigothic rulers had been murdered before 610 than died natural deaths. Persistent internal strife among the elite was the primary cause of the final overthrow of the kingdom. Nonetheless, the Catholic monarchy did become slightly better institutionalized and rather more acculturated (as well as somewhat less violent) than its Arian predecessor.

The entire process of the Muslim conquest, whether in the greater Middle East or specifically in Spain, remains obscure. A standard explanation refers to the "rottenness" of Visigothic institutions, yet it is not clear that the institutions of the Hispanic kingdom were in generally worse shape than those of Merovingian France or Anglo-Saxon England at approximately that same time. We know more about Hispano-Visigothic shortcomings simply because more records have survived in the peninsula. Furthermore, the intense religious rivalries and antipathies between the several Christian churches of the east Mediterranean that are sometimes held to have facilitated the Muslim triumph there had no counterpart in Spain. Even the Muslims were astounded and deeply impressed by the relative ease with which most of the peninsula fell to their modest forces, a process which they could explain only as the inscrutable will of God.

The failure of the Visigothic elite was evidently decisive. Foreign intervention was no novelty: Byzantium had earlier held the southeastern corner of the peninsula for some time, and there had been several Frankish invasions as well. The subversion of the Witizan clan, which had recently lost the monarchy to a rival, was central. One of their members, Bishop Oppas of Seville, played a leading role in trying to discourage further resistance after the initial Muslim victories. Though such maneuvers ultimately ended in disaster, various combinations of treachery and opportunism among the Visigothic aristocracy were the probable key to the Muslim triumph.

The notion that Visigothic Spain fell before an overpowering onslaught of Islamic fervor and might is probably no more convincing in the spiritual than in the military realm. By 711 Islamic expansion was nearly a century old, and we do not even know for sure that the first wave of North African invaders was fully converted to the new religion, since most of them were recruited from the formerly Christian kabyles of northern Morocco. The function of religious fervor in the Islamic invaders should not of course be discounted, but their initial policy of religious tolerance was equally or more important. Ordinary Hispanic Christians may at first have had difficulty in viewing Islam as more than a kind of nonmalevolent heterodoxy. (Indeed, for centuries it was fairly standard for Christians to view it as heresy rather than as a completely different religion.) Most of the peninsula's population failed to glimpse the decisive importance of what at first appeared to be a rather superficial politico-military takeover. The Muslims were so few in number, and the genuine Arabs fewer yet, that they could not easily have been recognized as the vanguard of a definitive change in culture and civilization. It should be remembered that in the eighth century, before "western civilization" had really begun, there was considerably less difference in technology, culture, or general style of life between a west Mediterranean Catholic and a North African or east Mediterranean Muslim society than there would be between, say, Spain and the Maghrib or the Near East by the close of the Middle Ages.

The ordinary Catholic population was not yet used to resisting military overlords. Other small bands of Visigoths or Suevi had earlier wandered across the peninsula virtually without opposition; after the breakdown of the elite and of their military power, resistance from the Christian population had disappeared. Moreover, there were certain apparent advantages for the common people in Muslim rule. The initial tax on unbelievers levied on all Christians apparently began at a figure below the levies exacted by the Visigothic system. The Jewish minority, who had sometimes been severely persecuted under the Visigothic Catholic state, could apparently only gain from the Islamic system of domination.

The subsequent process of Islamic and oriental acculturation that took place in the peninsula between the eighth and tenth centuries is one of the most fascinating if obscure developments in all Hispanic history. It was accomplished, first of all, by means of cultural diffusion and conversion, not by mass immigration. Demographic movement from the Levant to the Hispanic peninsula continued over three centuries, but the numbers involved were slight. Most Islamic immigration came from the North African Maghrib, which had absorbed little of the high culture and technology of the Muslim east Mediterranean. The orientalization of most of the native Hispanic population was not immediate, and the old image of the people going over to Islam en masse within a generation or two is probably mistaken. Major cultural orientalization began only with the establishment of the independent emirate by Abd al-Rahman I (756–88), but consolidation of the new Islamic system, even in political and administrative terms, was not completed until the reign of the Emir Abd al-Rahman II (822–52), by which time at least a significant minority of the native population had been converted. Though Muslims were at first but a handful of the population, the new realm of Al-Andalus (Arabic for Hispania) had little to fear from internal Christian rebellion. With Muslims holding a semimonopoly on military power, internal strife was at first almost exclusively intra-Islamic, as in the Near East. The ordinary Hispanic population had done little to oppose the Visigoths, and we have almost no evidence of anything other than submissiveness so long as the original terms of capitulation were honored. Once the emirate was fully consolidated, however, taxation and other pressures tended to increase, and the rate of conversion commenced to accelerate. Broad patterns of cultural diffusion radiating from the Arab Near East expanded more rapidly and intensively. By the middle of the ninth century, a new oriental society was developing in the southern, eastern, and central parts of the peninsula. Accelerated Islamicization was probably responsible for provoking the "martyrs of Córdoba" movement of 850–59, in which several score Christian spokesmen were put to death for challenging Islam directly. Such religious confrontation was soon brought to an end through a combination of Muslim repression and dissuasion by local Christian leaders, while the Islamicization of Andalusi society steadily advanced.

The future of Hispanic Catholicism lay not with the Christian majority in Al-Andalus, even though it would remain the majority for nearly two centuries, but with the independent resistance society that sprang up almost immediately in the mountains of the north. Much of this territory was and is relatively bleak and inhospitable—though not without scenic grandeur—and save for the coastal and semiurban areas of Galicia had achieved little importance or prosperity in Roman or Visigothic times. Again with the exception of Galicia, it was the least formally Christianized region of the peninsula. Those very factors of geography and logistics that made the conquest of the northern heights difficult and unattractive for the new Muslim overlords had discouraged their full incorporation in the earlier Hispano-Christian culture and polity. We know very little of the exact conditions of this resistance society in its first generations, but a remarkable new symbiosis developed between the largely free native inhabitants, groups of émigré Visigoths who clung to independence, and Christian refugees from the south. Almost from the beginning it was militantly Christian, and indeed, its Christian faith proved essential to the preservation of its freedom and determination amid the harsh trials of the next three centuries.

Within a single generation, the key resistance nucleus formed in the northwest as the kingdom of Asturias. As early as the middle of the eighth century, Asturias took advantage of the first major civil war among the Islamic invaders to extend its borders into the more-exposed southern foothills, and to incorporate Christian refugees from the border districts and probably even from the heart of Al-Andalus.

The Asturian Church never recognized the overlordship of the metropolitanate of Toledo, living under Muslim rule. Outright antagonism between the politically independent and dependent sectors of Hispanic Christianity developed by the end of the eighth century in the form of the Adoptionist controversy. Perhaps hoping to refute Muslim charges that Christians worshipped three different Gods, the metropolitan of Toledo, when referring to the two natures of Christ, spoke of his "natural filiation" to the divine and of his "adoptive filiation" to the human, differing from the unified interpretation that had become orthodox in Latin Christiandom. Small and weak though the Asturian culture was, it soon forged links to the main centers of western Christian culture in France and Italy. Its leaders prided themselves on Latin Christian orthodoxy—doubtless not least in contradistinction to Islam and its dependencies—and carried the Adoptionist issue to Rome for resolution, possibly the first such invocation of papal authority by Hispanic Christians. In 794 Rome excommunicated the metropolitan of Toledo. Under Alfonso II the Chaste (791–842), the Asturian monarchy created a separate ecclesiastical system independent of Toledo, thereby affirming the special identity of Asturias and the legitimate authority of its institutions as heirs to the Visigothic realm.

Relations between the monarchy and Church in Asturias were extremely close, with the crown predominating to an even greater extent than in the preceding Visigothic kingdom. This was so much the case that the leading specialist in the period, Claudio Sánchez Albornoz, has suggested that it would be more accurate to speak of the monarchy's administration of the Church than of Church-state relations. As in contemporary Carolingian France, it was accepted that the role of the Christian king was active leadership and reform in the affairs of the Church whenever that was needed. Thus early was established a practice that with varying degrees of zeal would be followed by the Spanish crown for a full millennium.

It was not possible to sustain the wealth, sophistication, or learning of the Visigothic Church in the small, backward realm of Asturias-León, but the intensity of religious faith among the early Asturians does not permit of doubt. This took the form of a simple, martial, prenational kind of faith that involved no hesitations but also permitted no exceptions. There is some indication that in early centuries Asturians and Leonese were more demanding of their clergy than in the later period. Several instances may be documented from early chronicles in which ordinary townspeople or peasants joined together in attacking or punishing monks or nuns deemed guilty of loose or immoral conduct.

The Asturian clergy did produce one figure who can in a sense be called the first Spanish intellectual of note, the monk Beato de Liébana, born about the middle of the eighth century. Beato was the most vigorous spokesman for the Asturian position in the Adoptionist controversy, adopting a rough and brutal polemical style that denounced the metropolitan of Toledo as the "testicle of Antichrist." He also wrote the first Spanish bestseller, medieval style, for his *Commentaries on the Apocalypse* were copied many times in Asturias-León during the next two hundred years. The vision of harsh trial and eschatology came readily to the militant Christian frontier society, subjected to frequent trauma by Muslim attack. Beato's *Apocalypse* was apparently much less successful among the more sheltered and sophisticated population of Galicia. This learned monk collected a sizable library for his day and achieved broad erudition. He helped to inspire a school of miniature manuscript illustration that later exerted some influence in France and western Europe. Ever an ardent Catholic patriot, Beato sharpened a special sense of Christian identity and antagonism against the Muslims. He also helped prepare the way for the adoption of Santiago as the new national patron saint, probably composing "O Dei verbum," the first major hymn in his honor.

ORIGINS OF THE SPANISH IDEOLOGY

During the early ninth century, in the reign of Alfonso the Chaste, there emerged the first direct expressions of what was to become the millennial Spanish ideology of patriotic Catholicism, reconquest, and expansion. It is not possible to specify the exact terms in which this was first defined, but the Asturian monarchy early adopted as its goal the regaining of political independence for as much of the peninsula as possible and the restoration of its Christian identity. Even as early as 760, after increased Christian immigration into Asturias and the first generation of successful counterattacks, there were glimmerings of the "neo-Gothic" idea of restoring the independent Hispano-Christian monarchy of the Visigoths. This concept also identified the political and military mission of the society with its religious beliefs, and by the ninth century, chronicles would speak of religious strife with the Muslims as the main motive of the frontier struggle.

Another dimension was added with the discovery of an impressive tomb in central Galicia early in the ninth century. This provided the kingdom with a special spiritual patron, for it was soon labeled the sepulchre of "Santiago"—St. James, the brother of Christ—subsequently adopted as patron and protector of Asturias-León. The special function of St. James lay in his metamorphosis as "Santiago Matamoros"—St. James the Moorslayer—spiritual leader of the struggle against the Muslims, to the extent that Américo Castro has viewed the

Santiago cult as the creation of a special, supernatural "anti-Mohammed." As conflict sharpened, Santiago would later be depicted in the heavens mounted on a white horse, sword in hand, leading Christians to victory.

The cult of Santiago, centered on his shrine of Compostela, eventually created one of the major religious centers of western Christendom, target of one of the most heavily traveled international pilgrimages in Europe and the source of a special identity and pride for the beleaguered Christians of the northwest. Whereas leaders of the small Christian counties in the Pyrenees thought of themselves as minor parts of a broad political framework (the Carolingian empire), the rulers of Asturias affirmed for themselves a very special identity as heirs of the Visigoths charged with a broader mission and attended by a specific form of divine assistance.

This is not to assume that a doctrine of full reconquest became the immediate and conscious program of the Asturian monarchy in the ninth century. Such a pretension would have been unrealistic in the face of the crystallization of the powerful, wealthy, and sophisticated Muslim society of Al-Andalus. The resources of the Asturians and the tiny Christian hill principalities to the east of them were most meager by comparison. Such a goal emerged only at the very end of the ninth century when extensive civil war in Al-Andalus led to momentary expectations of a great reconquest. Apocalyptic expectation in both north and south in this period probably reached its height during the last two decades of the century.

The Spanish ideology thus achieved its first degree of plentitude during the reign of Alfonso III el Magno (886–911), apparently the first Hispano-Christian king to claim the title of emperor. If such a title was indeed used by Alfonso el Magno—and the sources are by no means unequivocal—it referred only to the lands of the Hispanic peninsula, held to be the legitimate patrimony of the Visigothic monarchy. From the time of Alfonso el Magno there was a conscious revival of certain Visigothic court forms, such as the traditional rite of royal consecration. This neo-Gothic and prenationalist Catholicism seems to have been particularly stimulated by immigrant clergy and monks from Al-Andalus, refugees from Islamic domination.

The neo-Gothic goal of reconquest and the revindication of Christendom was not, however, necessarily imparted to Asturian society as a whole, nor did it necessarily become the dominant motif in Christian-Muslim relations. It represented the doctrine of ideologically conscious elements at court and especially of some of the higher strata of the clergy, but at first may have been only minimally imparted to the common people. The border struggle with Islam may in many cases have been carried on from more simple motives of land or booty or mere self-protection. Nor was there in the ninth or tenth centuries any specific concept of a crusade, of a divine war for God per se, even though some such idea might be derived with little difficulty from a continuing conflict that was motivated in part by religious difference. The emphasis in the early reconquest was always at least as much political as religious, an emphasis on the legal right to regain territorial patrimony seized by force. Development of the Spanish identity was only beginning in this era. Its elaboration would be the work of the entire Middle Ages, and only in the sixteenth century would it reach its height, with the diffusion of the notion of the Spanish as the new chosen people of God, equivalent to the Hebrews of old.

THE MOZARABS

In contrast to Asturias and the northern regions, the original Christian majority in Al-Andalus underwent a steady decline, unable to resist political pressure and the influence of the new oriental culture. Islamic immigration, though limited in numbers, introduced new agricultural and hydraulic technologies, new craft industries, and Levantine techniques of shipbuilding. This was accompanied by an Arabic-language culture that brought with it the higher learning and science of the classical and postclassical Levantine world. The allure and glamor of this new cultural complex, combined with its almost complete political and military dominance, was difficult to resist. By the tenth century Christians in the Andalusi cities had begun to use Arabic, at least for certain purposes, and to take up Islamic economic and social styles. The Christians of Al-Andalus thus ultimately came to be known as "Mozarabs" (Sp. *mozárabes*), a name derived from the Arabic *musta'rib* ("Arabized").

With the crystallization of the new oriental high culture, pressures mounted steadily, for the Islamic system was one of discriminatory toleration at best. Christians never enjoyed equal rights in a Muslim conquest society, and their original guarantees, at first fairly broad, steadily diminished. They were still allowed to practice their own religion in private, but found their cultural autonomy increasingly reduced. Mozarabs inevitably lost more and more status, but they long maintained their dignity and the integrity of their culture, and they never entirely lost personal and cultural contact with the Christian West. Heterodox features of their culture inevitably became more prominent, however. Christian women often married Muslim men; their children were raised as Muslims. Even within Mozarab families, legal divorce eventually came to be practiced along Islamic lines. Ordination of the clergy ultimately drifted far from canonical norms, and concubinage and fornication among the clergy may have been more widespread than in most parts of western Europe (though the main testimony to this came from hostile Muslims).

Mozarabs did join in the many regional revolts that formed the great *fitna* (unrest) of the late ninth century, but ultimately their only salvation lay in emigration to the Christian north. The exodus of Christians from Al-Andalus was fairly steady, though especially strong at various times in the ninth and early tenth centuries. This further reduced their numbers in Al-Andalus. By the time that the Andalusi emirate was firmly reestablished and developed into the greatest power of the west Mediterranean under Abd al-Rahman III (912–61), Muslims made up the great majority of the population. This expansion had come about through conversion and absorption and only secondarily through immigration. The remaining Mozarab minority shrank into an increasingly fossilized remnant.

GROWTH OF NORTH SPANISH CHRISTIANITY

Though impossible to quantify, immigration of Mozarabs from the south was probably a significant factor in the growth of the Christian principalities of northern Spain. For most of the ninth and tenth centuries, north Spanish Christian culture was stimulated, probably dominated, by the learning of Mozarab immigrants, who helped to accentuate its Christian identity and apparently played a major role in development of the Spanish Christian ideology.

Christian immigration stemmed not only from Al-Andalus but also, at least a little, from the remaining Christian population of northwest Africa as well. There is some archeological evidence that the latter immigration was particularly concentrated in the eastern territory of Asturias-León—the frontier region of Castile—and it has been conjectured that this had some influence in shaping the militant Castilian character.

From the ninth century on, monasteries played a vital role in both the religious and secular affairs of the Hispanic kingdoms. Much time was devoted to prayer and contemplation, their primary function, and also to scholarly and educational activities. But monasteries were also of prime importance to the social, economic, cultural, and even military affairs of the Christian kingdoms. Amid an almost unrelievedly rural society, they carried out the functions of towns, fortresses, and market centers, and even became centers of technological diffusion, promoting new grape culture and wine production and helping to introduce improved agrarian techniques and irrigation. Though monasteries in Spain, like medieval

Spanish society in general, were less innovative than those in some other parts of western Europe, their influence was broadly felt in the practical as well as spiritual domain. In this respect they were typical of the western form of Christian monastic life, which differed greatly from the eastern, with its almost exclusive devotion to contemplation and withdrawal.

Church wealth in landed endowments grew steadily, with the greatest concentration of Church land in Galicia. Some contrast existed in the social and economic pattern of Castile, where endowments, though large in number, tended to be proportionately much smaller, and ecclesiastical leaders had a rather less imposing place in public councils than in Galicia and León.

A distinctive church architecture began to emerge in Asturias by the second half of the ninth century. The palace of Santa María de Naranco and the church of San Miguel de Lillo, near the capital of Oviedo, are the best surviving specimens of what has been called the Asturian pre-Romanesque, noteworthy because of an emphasis on the vertical, novelties in arch construction and in the design of transept and apse, and the early use of buttresses.

In contrast to the regionally semiautonomous and somewhat archaic Church in León, the Church in the Catalan countries, from the end of the eighth century, was organized directly under the administrative system of Rome. The native Hispano-Visigothic liturgy and forms persisted in León, but in Catalonia, which did not obtain a cis-Pyreneean metropolitanate of its own until the eleventh century, they gave way almost immediately to the more typical Roman rite. The economic endowments and political influence of the Church in Catalonia were more typically feudal. There, too, the Church soon amassed considerable wealth, and enjoyed a greater local autonomy because of the decentralization of political authority. Propertied monasteries in Catalonia remained strong supporters of the Carolingian crown even after its decline, in opposition to the local power of the counts and other overlords. Church-state tensions were more extreme in Catalonia than in León. Perhaps the most atrocious example was the fate of Arnulf, archbishop of Narbonne, who in 912 excommunicated Count Sunyer II of Ampurias (a district in northeast Catalonia). The count's henchmen waylaid the hapless archbishop, blinded and mutilated him, and tore out his tongue before he died.

Between Catalonia and Castile-León, a partly pagan territory existed for some time, since the Christianization of much of the Basque population did not get underway until the tenth century. By the end of that century most of the Navarrese had been converted, but the inhabitants of Vizcaya and Guipúzcoa were not brought fully within the sphere of

Christianity until after the establishment of the bishopric of Alava in the eleventh century. The seizure of power in the principality of Navarre by a new Christian dynasty in 905 oriented that state to a policy of expansion against Islam, and Navarre's conquest of part of the Rioja district (modern Logroño province), was one of the few Christian territorial advances of the tenth century.

THE GREAT RECONQUEST

The years immediately following the end of the first millennium A.D. marked a decisive turning point in peninsular history, for the power of the Cordoban caliphate collapsed within two generations after reaching its zenith. The politico-military implosion of Al-Andalus is only slightly less difficult to explain than the overthrow of the Visigothic state. During the tenth century, Al-Andalus moved swiftly toward a pinnacle of prosperity and sophistication that was readily translated among the ruling strata into a love of ease and indulgence bordering on outright decadence. Degeneration of the ruling dynasty encouraged military usurpation within the Muslim system that soon undermined its central institutional structure. The usurper, Al-Mansur, eschewed the traditional military forces and tried to form a new armed elite in rejection of the established system. Immigration of new Berber elements, especially military forces, created intense friction with the main body of Hispanic Muslims. The attempt to paper over differences with a call to *jihad* (Muslim holy war) in an army that also included Andalusi Christian mercenaries did not disguise the fact that the Cordoban government had lost traditional (and also religious) legitimacy, relying on naked force. After the death of Al-Mansur's son in 1008, this semicentralized despotism resting on a rather fragile regional and ethnic balance soon shattered into pieces.

Even at the time of the final Muslim collapse, the territories that remained to Al-Andalus were superior in wealth and many aspects of sophistication, but their rulers had lost the capacity to defend themselves and faced the dire alternative of certain conquest by hard, militant, militarily vigorous Christians or total subordination to the fanatical Moroccans whom they reluctantly called to their aid. The predicament of Andalusi society was remarkably like that of contemporary western Europe, which is economically and technologically superior to the Soviet Union but militarily inferior.

The major Christian reconquest occurred during a period of about two centuries between approximately 1035 and 1250. Nearly 80 percent of the territory of the peninsula was reoccupied during this period, which was divided by the major Moroccan invasions of Almoravids and Almohads (1086–1212) into two principal phases, that of the eleventh and that of the thirteenth century. By the middle of the thirteenth century, the Hispanic peninsula had largely been restored to Christendom. Only one Muslim state remained, the prosperous and sophisticated emirate of Granada in the southeast, and it would more often than not make regular tribute payments to the crown of Castile to guarantee its survival.

THE ELEVENTH-CENTURY EUROPEANIZATION

The eleventh century was an era of major expansion not only for the Hispanic kingdoms but also for western Europe in general. Whereas the Hispanic expansion was first of all military and geographic, the growth of western Europe was originally most marked in religious, cultural, economic, and demographic development. This can be called the first century of the "take-off" of western civilization, and it influenced the Hispanic kingdoms and their religious life decisively. Within western Christianity as a whole it was a period of spiritual renewal and conversion, represented especially by the Gregorian reform movement in France and Italy, which aimed at the moral conversion of all nominal western Christians. Institutionally, it was an era of administrative centralization and liturgical unification under the papacy, which sought greater internal cohesion within the west even as the west expanded through the Mediterranean.

The full institutional authority of the papacy was first introduced by way of southern France and Catalonia, where papal influence had proved particularly useful at the time of the tenth-century Cordoban offensives. The counts of Barcelona entered into regular relations with the papacy from the third quarter of the century, and were followed a generation later by Sancho the Great of Navarre, whose political hegemony in northern Spain was assisted to some extent by papal diplomacy.

The effect of papal influence on the politics of the Hispanic kingdoms was both centripetal and centrifugal. The papacy did sometimes effectively promote Hispanic unity and cooperation against the Muslims, but it occasionally attempted to divert Hispanic resources to the central crusading effort in the Holy Land, as well. It also sometimes encouraged the independent ambitions of the several kingdoms in order to increase its own influence and gain larger financial contributions. Pope Alexander II (1061–73), for example, used his authority to ratify the independence of the kingdom of Aragon, whose rulers were willing to recognize papal suzerainty. A similar relationship developed with the crown of Portugal in the twelfth century.

Rapid growth of European influence in the peninsula during the eleventh century led to full incorporation of the Castilian-Leonese Church in the papal network. Uniform liturgical practice was a major goal of Romanization, as was full acceptance of the Benedictine monastic rule, which stressed the reform of behavior, new and more efficient administrative practices, and clear jurisdictional demarcations between monastic life and other institutions. Together with these and other reforms, the Roman rite was officially adopted for Castile-León at a Church council in 1080. Though local practices would continue to vary considerably for at least five hundred years, the common use of the historic Hispano-Visigothic liturgy, for centuries a religious bond between Christians throughout the peninsula, was ended.

The beginning of full Romanization also introduced standard features of Roman iconography such as the cult of images, heretofore little practiced in the peninsula. This resulted in a new Christianization of the landscape of northern Spain during the eleventh and twelfth centuries with the erection of many new shrines and chapels sheltering images. Many of them at first honored local saints or central Church figures in the beatific tradition, but later came more and more to center on various representations of the Virgin Mary.

Perhaps the most important agents of the Roman reform were French Cluniac monks, who entered Castile-León in significant numbers during the second half of the eleventh century. Encouraged by the crown, they quickened cultural life, raised administrative standards, and were especially concerned to purify morals. By the close of the century, many bishoprics in León, Galicia, and Portugal were occupied by members of the order. Their advancement was the more easily accomplished because Hispanic rulers in many cases continued, at least indirectly, to control appointments to the hierarchy.

The role of the Cluniacs was subsequently assumed by the next major European monastic reform movement, the white-robed Cistercians (from Citeaux in Burgundy) of the twelfth century. The Cistercians concentrated on the reform and development of monasteries, and to some extent also endeavored to broaden learning. For a century or more they were able to enforce relatively uniform standards.

FROM RECONQUEST TO CRUSADE

The era of major reconquest and Europeanization also resulted in a new hardening of attitude toward the Muslims and in the introduction of a new institution—the crusade. Cause and effect are not easy to determine in these developments. Though the Spanish are sometimes said to have invented the practice of crusading, the institution was technically a

European, specifically papal, invention of Gregory VII. As indicated earlier, it is doubtful that early Hispanic campaigns against the Muslims were conceived of as religious enterprises per se, even though they were usually associated with religious goals. The specific concept of warfare as a religious instrument to liberate the peninsula and, more important, the Holy Land, was a product of the eleventh-century papal revival, though it was also stimulated by the emergence of a dominant new aggressive Muslim force, the Seljuk Turks, in the east Mediterranean. With the institution of the crusade came a variety of special taxes, Church subsidies, and new income-producing religious practices such as the indulgence, to finance campaigns.

It was first officially essayed in the peninsula and took hold immediately, introduced in Aragon for the campaign against Barbastro in 1064. Thenceforth, for the next four hundred years, the crusade as a matter of course accompanied major campaigns of defense and reconquest. It became a more consistent feature of Hispanic life than any other part of Christendom because of the obvious fact that only in the peninsula did the Muslim frontier lie at hand. Hispanic volunteers were normally not recruited for the long-distance crusades to the Holy Land, though on occasion thousands of non-Spanish Christians (primarily French) took part in peninsular crusades.

The development of such religious military orders as the Templars was typical of the era of the crusades throughout western Europe, but only in the Hispanic peninsula and east Germany were separate monastic fighting orders established specifically to combat infidels along the national frontier. The three key orders of Calatrava, Santiago, and Alcántara were founded in the third quarter of the twelfth century. During the broad thirteenth-century reconquest they received large endowments of land in Extremadura, La Mancha, and Andalusia, where they became responsible for local civil and economic administration in sizable districts. Until their endowments were taken over by the crown at the end of the fifteenth century, they played a role in the affairs of southern Castile that had no European counterpart save on the German-Baltic frontier.

In some ways the institution of the crusade thus seemed ideal for peninsular conditions, and nowhere else was it so widely practiced for so long. Yet it is easy to exaggerate the degree of change, for the crusade was adapted to the specific circumstances and cultural relations of the peninsula. Earlier attitudes toward reconquest that viewed it in considerable measure as a practical, political, and economic enterprise as well were not eliminated by the institution of the crusade. Though the crusade was adopted as a means of stimulating the reconquest, the relationship of

Christian and Muslim was only partially changed, even after the great Moroccan invasions, and remained more practical and humane than was often the case with trans-Pyreneean crusaders. Hispanic crusaders were distinguished by greater tolerance as well as by a somewhat more calculating and businesslike approach to both war and peace in their relations with the Muslims.

The complexity of the Hispanic approach is best exemplified by the prototypical figure of the age, the all-time Hispanic hero Rodrigo Díaz de Vivar, known as El Cid, who died in 1099 at the close of a century of momentous change. The Cid was devoted to fundamental Christian reconquest, but he was nonetheless not a crusader in the European sense, for he maintained excellent relations with friendly Muslims and included Muslim volunteers in his own forces. The name by which he soon became known to history is Arabic, derived from the title *sidi*, "lord," used by his Muslim followers. The Cid served for a brief period as leader of the military host of the Muslim emir of Zaragoza against the advance of the Aragonese. In this he was not abandoning the Christian cause, as some have suggested, but rather remaining faithful to the military and foreign policy of Castile. The emirate of Zaragoza was tributary to Castile, and from the Castilian point of view the Aragonese advance against the Muslims of Zaragoza infringed on the Castilian sphere of reconquest. When Castile itself marched directly on Zaragoza, the Cid abandoned Muslim service. Something of a military genius, he inflicted the first two defeats ever suffered by the advancing Almoravids, and despite his general tolerance of Muslim underlings, adopted a sterner policy of reconquest than some of his predecessors. He did not hestitate to expel disloyal Muslim subjects and introduce a new pattern of direct Christian resettlement.

Institutionalization of the crusade did not put an end to the practice of individual Christian soldiers serving as mercenaries in the forces of Muslim rulers, even while sometimes retaining their Christian identity. Though this practice became less and less frequent, it persisted into the fifteenth century.

HISPANIC CHRISTIAN CULTURE AND ISLAM

From the very beginning there seems to have been suspicion among west Europeans that Hispanic Christians were in some fashion contaminated with Islam and Judaism, despite their strict theological orthodoxy. This attitude was later accentuated in pejorative epithets against the domineering Spaniards of the sixteenth century, and in modern times has generally been transformed into a vague notion of the cultural influence of Islam in Hispanic history and society. More recently, Américo Castro has contended that centuries of contact with Muslims and Jews deeply influenced Spanish culture and religion. For Castro, this helps to explain the thoroughness and intensity with which religion came to be identified with nearly all aspects of Spanish life, leading to the ultimate rejection of tolerance and religious pluralism. Castro's pronounced tendency toward both vagueness and hyperbole have weakened his case, and yet there is no doubt that he has correctly pointed out certain cultural and esthetic transfers, even while sometimes exaggerating their character and significance.

Centuries of confrontation with Islam obviously had deep and fundamental effects on Spanish culture, though that must be distinguished from direct absorption of the most fundamental Muslim values and practices. The ultimate consequence was of course much more an attitude of rejection than a process of assimilation. It should always be kept in mind that the basic social structures of the two cultures were entirely differentiated according to western and oriental patterns. Hispanic society was exogamous rather than endogamous (it did not marry exclusively with clans), lineage and property inheritance were bilateral rather than agnatic (through the male line alone), the sense of honor pertained to individual and nuclear family status and virtue, not to those of the clan, and the society recognized certain specific rights of women. Indeed, the individualistic, semiegalitarian, and nuclear, unsegmented structure of Hispanic society ultimately endowed it with certain political and military advantages, probably giving it greater long-term cohesiveness and enabling it to advance southward and to reproduce organic relationships in new territory.

Nowhere is the difference between the two cultures more manifest than in marriage and the family. The Koran ignores the question of the family and has no particular doctrine of marriage. The original Islamic conquests permitted the development of an enormous female slave society, with the consequences that Islamic slavery has been above all domestic rather than economic as in Rome or the Americas. In contrast, Hispanic institutions adhered fully to the western structure of conjugal society, based on bilateral alliances, equal inheritance, and the patrimonial rights of women.

It is sometimes contended that relations were reasonably good between Hispanic Christians and the bulk of the Andalusis, since the majority of the latter were converts or *muwalladun*, ethnic Spaniards of the same racial background and for a long time even of the same speech (given major differences in dialect). It is true that the muwalladun seem commonly to have hated Moroccan Berbers and that they often lived in a state of extreme tension with the Andalusi Arab aristocracy, who persisted in referring to them as "sons of slaves" or "sons of white women." Yet the common Hispanic identity of Christians and muwalladun is often exaggerated. The former felt it absolutely inperative to triumph over the latter, while the Andalusi leaders, pressed by a growing religious revivalism, even fanaticism, among their people, showed where their ultimate identity lay by bringing in the rigidly Muslim and fiercely barbarian Almoravids of Morocco to stem the reconquest in 1086.

A certain change in attitude does seem to have occurred by the twelfth century. This is commonly attributed to the influence of the new institution of the crusade among Christians and the fanatical policies of holy war that motivated the new Moroccan invasions of Almoravids and Almohads. It is true that by the early twelfth century Castilian raiders sometimes drew distinctions between Almoravids and *faqihs* (jurists and Islamic leaders) as distinct from ordinary Hispanic Muslims, slaughtering the first and treating the second with relative leniency. In the second half of that century, fanaticism was further incited by the Almohads, who virtually did away with the remaining Mozarab population through forced conversion, imprisonment, slaughter, and emigration.

All this throws doubt on Castro's concept of the *convivencia* (coexistence) of Christians and Muslims. There was, first of all, little physical convivencia. North Spanish Christians lived quite apart from Muslim society until the major reconquest of the eleventh and thirteenth centuries, and even then it was only the southern and eastern sectors of Spanish society that had a certain amount of regular contact with Muslims. At no time was there a coexistence of equals, the full tolerance of a twentieth-century liberal democratic society. Christian policy, like that of Islam, was one of discriminatory and limited toleration.

Tolerance, to the extent that it existed, was above all a matter of official policy; much of the time the common people, both Christian and Muslim, were intolerant. The official position of the Church was to accept the guarantees of toleration extended by the Hispanic kingdoms of the reconquest but at the same time to pressure the royal governments for a somewhat more militant policy. Certainly the attitude of the Christian clergy itself became increasingly militant from the eleventh century onward.

Convivencia, in so far as it can be said to have existed, represented the period of the later Middle Ages, from the thirteenth to the fifteenth century. During that time, the Christian hegemony was firmly established and sizable minorities of *mudéjares* (subject Muslims) had been incorporated in the south and east. The main Islamic influence in Spanish society and culture was exerted during this period, especially during its first phase. This involved integration of certain economic techniques and institutions on the one hand and esthetic and stylistic influences on the other. In some areas the Muslim systems of local market organization and irrigation were broadly copied, while public baths flourished more than anywhere else in Christendom. Andalusi techniques in construction and steelworking were widely diffused. Muslim interior decoration and architectural styles, commonly known as Mudejar, became predominant motifs in Castile during the fourteenth and fifteenth centuries. After all danger from Africa had passed, Islamic society was even sentimentalized among the upper classes, who took to wearing articles of Muslim clothing. Moreover for several generations after the reconquest in formerly orientalized regions such as Toledo where numbers of Mudejars or resident Mozarabs remained, some Christian women wore veils.

Arabic influence on the Castilian or Spanish language, though certainly present, is often exaggerated. The language was well established before it entered into very extensive or intimate contact with Islamic culture, and Arabisms count for less than one-half of one percent of the total vocabularly. According to one study, the majority of such terms (71 percent) entered Castilian during the course of the thirteenth-century reconquest.

The most important aspect of Islamic culture for the West lay in its preservation and development of the science and philosophy of the classical and Byzantine worlds. As soon as such Middle Eastern culture had crystallized in Al-Andalus during the tenth century, it began to be acquired and transmitted by the Hispano-Christian principalities, first at the Catalan monastery of Ripoll and then at other centers in Castile, Aragon, and Navarre. Already by the second half of the eleventh century, however, scientists in the West equalled in number those in the Islamic world, and their work was of equal quality. The first phase of the diffusion of Muslim knowledge was completed during the twelfth century, when western science and philosophy began to register significant advances of their own. The famed "translators' school" of Alfonso el Sabio in the thirteenth century only provided better quality translations and wider diffusion for a corpus of knowledge that had already been transmitted. As far as Hispano-Christian culture was concerned, it was little more than a transmission belt in the process. Hispanic society was one of frontiersmen and warriors. In the organization of schools and universities it did not begin to catch up to western Europe until the sixteenth century. Muslim learning exerted much more influence in Paris and Oxford than at Salamanca or Valladolid, where it was viewed with deep suspicion and normally accepted only after it had been worked into a new Christian synthesis by Frenchmen, Englishmen, or Italians.

Hispanic Christians never proposed to exterminate Muslims, but neither did they wish to live freely with them in peace, treat them as equals, or in general, accept their ways. The author of the only general history of the reconquest, in describing the main period of so-called convivencia, emphasizes

> . . . The endemic and popular nature of Christian-Muslim warfare, for in this period [1086–1340], despite royal truces, the ordinary Christians fought continuously against the Muslims. The few traces of peaceful traffic across the frontier are far outstripped by the plundering raids and acts of violence; and though some peaceful contacts may have occurred at governmental level, the masses were as permanently and irreconcilably hostile as the frontiersmen and Indians of nineteenth-century America or Argentina. One must discount the view that peaceful co-existence of the ordinary people was occasionally disturbed by warfare provoked by the religious and political establishment; it would be truer to say that the kings made occasional ineffectual attempts to limit the endless warfare enjoyed by their subjects. . . . The concepts of Reconquest and Crusade may have originated among the leaders of Christendom; the practice of permanent warfare against the Muslims was a creation of the people. And, despite the gaps in our evidence, it seems clear that even these concepts of Reconquest, Holy War and Crusade became widely diffused and accepted among the lower levels of society.
>
> Another characteristic of the Berber period is the religious fanaticism [which] can be seen much more clearly . . . than in the Umayyad period; but this may simply be the result of the greater accessibility of the sources. . . . The characteristics of the Berber period may have been present before 1086. Certainly one cannot assume from the silence of our Umayyad sources that endemic popular warfare and religious fanaticism were unimportant then. . . .[1]

HISPANIC CULTURE AND THE WEST

Conversely, the Hispanic society of the Middle Ages exemplified nearly all the distinctive institutional and cultural traits of the Latin west. The west European political principle of monarchy was fully developed, in fact overdeveloped, in the peninsula. Western emphasis on the nuclear family and the individual was fully paralleled as well. The Hispanic kingdoms were leaders in the western process of developing institutional pluralism and balanced representation through constitutional mecha-

---

1. Derek W. Lomax, *The Reconquest of Spain* (London, 1978), 174–75.

nisms and parliamentary assemblies. Hispanic religion was scrupulously orthodox, and Hispanic culture paralleled the development of western science and universities in so far as it was able. Hispanic society was perhaps most typically western in its contradiction between the spiritual principles of Christianity and the practice of self-assertiveness and pursuit of power.

In its relation to science, economics, and practical affairs, Hispanic culture probably least resembled either the general western culture of which it was a part or the Islamic culture which it combatted with such determination. North Hispanic society was at first somewhat overawed by the economic achievements and splendors of Al-Andalus, with which it could not hope to compete. Yet before the end of the Middle Ages the new western society had begun to surpass the Muslim culture in its development of science, technology, and economic growth. Hispanic society did not fully participate in this dimension of western development, either.

The Castro intrepretation would explain this by means of the distinct caste identities of medieval society in the peninsula, according to which ordinary work and economics was the province of Muslims, advanced science and intellectual endeavor that of Jews, and true religion, military affairs, and the fruits of dominion that of Christians. This is by no means altogether incorrect, though like most of Castro's theories it oversimplifies. There is little doubt that the Hispanic outlook and value system tended to differ from most of western Europe in this regard, though the differences were somewhat less and certainly more subtle than normally represented.

The principal effect of the Islamic confrontation with Hispanic Christian society was not any orientalization of that society but rather the development of a distinct Hispano-Christian subculture within western civilization, a subculture whose attitudes and values were shaped not by Islam but by a centuries-long process of warfare and confrontation. This resulted in a kind of exaggeration of typically medieval qualities in Hispanic culture. All medieval societies in western Europe were dominated by aristocracies geared to military leadership and ruled by codes of behavior that emphasized honor and status. This did not altogether change until the entire ancien regime was replaced by modern capitalism and liberalism. Hispanic society was thus not an exception but only a more extreme and narrow form of a common phenomenon. The frontier society of Castile, particularly, emphasized military status above all else. The role of the warrior aristocracy was ultimately more important in the peninsula than in almost any other part of western Europe. Aristocratic status was consequently more deeply honored, as well as more profoundly internalized by lesser members of society. Status and honor became proportionately even more important, for wealth was based on conquest, dominion, and subsequent status more than upon work and economic achievement. Thus the aristocratic society of honor and arrogance had deeper roots in the experience of Reconquest Spain than could be provided by the history of other more settled parts of western Europe.

With the exception of thirteenth- and fourteenth-century Catalonia, most of Hispanic Christian society could have been considered at least somewhat backward economically, even by medieval standards. At one point such differences, however certain, might have seemed slight and relative, for by the norms of preindustrial society the lag or variation between Hispanic economic performance and that of more advanced areas was considerably less than would be the case after the seventeenth century. Technological failure did not become apparent until the middle of that century,[2] and in the meantime Spanish scientists and entrepreneurs had far outdistanced their former Islamic superiors. Yet the difference in orientation was already there before the end of the Middle Ages. Spanish prototypes would be religious and military; ideals based primarily on economic performance would hold much less sway. The roots of Spanish difference, like so many other unique features of Hispanic history, date from the Christian Reconquest.

---

2. It is obviously a mistake to read too much of modern economic failure back into the Middle Ages, for "one could, in fact, make the case that the Christians of the High Middle Ages had a rather high value for technological expertise, to judge by the number of technologists who were canonized. Best known is Santo Domingo de la Calzada, who built the bridge over the Oja river with a timber framework and pillars of stone, as well as constructing hostels for pilgrims and repairing roadbeds along the pilgrimage route. His disciple, San Juan de Ortega, was also a builder of roads and bridges. The patron saint of Burgos, San Adelelmo or Lesmes, was best remembered for devising a sewage system for the town by diverting water from the Pico and Vena streams (affluents of the Arlanzón) through canals which he constructed down the centers so the streets. With an adequate drop, the water carried the sewage off. These conduits were called *esquevas* and were imitated in Valladolid and othe towns." Thomas F. Glick, *Islamic and Christian Spain in the Early Middle Ages* (Princeton, 1979), 247.

2

The Traditional Religion

THOUGH a special prenational identity of Hispanic society and religion took shape during the centuries of reconquest, the common culture and practice of religion adhered broadly to the norms of medieval western Europe. Indeed, reconquest Catholicism was in major respects more tolerant, at least with regard to non-Christian peoples, than was common in Latin Christendom. Popular behavior, whether of the clergy or laity, seems to have been about as latitudinarian as would have been found elsewhere.

The most distinctive historical traits of Spanish Catholicism were acquired during the fifteenth and sixteenth centuries, a time of fundamental change in religious policy and emphasis. The new direction was decisively influenced by conflict with the Muslim and Jewish minorities in the peninsula, followed by protracted international rivalry with the forces of the Protestant Reformation and the Ottoman Empire. During that age the Inquisition developed, and absolute religious unity and exclusiveness became hallmarks. While the esthetic and intellectual culture of Spanish Catholicism flourished into the early seventeenth century, its channels grew increasingly narrow.

It is important to understand that these fateful changes were also grounded in a major religious revival similar to the popular religious reburgeoning that in certain countries produced the Reformation. Spanish religiosity did more than change certain formal qualities; it also increased considerably in intensity, and produced an outpouring of new vocations that heightened the spiritual expression of the religion that carried out massive new evangelistic efforts in farflung parts of the world. The militancy of Spain's Catholic Reformation, together with its organizational growth and cultural activism, enabled Spanish clergy and laity to play the major roles in the primary phase of the broader European Counter-Reformation.

The apex of Spanish Catholicism can be divided chronologically into three principal phases. The first, from the late fifteenth century to about 1540, was a time of major reform and also of creative, diversified new

spiritual and cultural trends. Both the Inquisition and the purification of
Church institutions were deemed compatible with scholarly development
of a broadened Renaissance Catholic humanism and more sensitive
personal expressions of internal religiosity.

The central period of what is normally called the Counter-Reformation and struggle against Protestantism stretches roughly from 1540
to the close of the century, coinciding with the redefinition and retrenchment of Catholicism at the Council of Trent (1545–63) and the subsequent implementation of Tridentine reforms. It was marked by increasing rigidity that choked off some of the liberal trends of the preceding
generation. Despite the Church's paranoia and marked tendency toward
rejection of new currents, this continued to be a time of active reform and
major development of religious culture.

By the seventeenth century the traditional religion reached its full
flowering and entered a phase of decline. In many ways it had come to
represent the highest development of the Catholicism of the late Middle
Ages. It was culturally more sophisticated than it had been (though by
then declining in initiative), more intense, militant, and intolerant. Fully
unified in an ethnonational sense, it was divided internally only by fierce
jurisdictional disputes and rivalry between various groups of clergy.
Spanish Catholicism had developed a genuine tendency toward xenophobia that had generally been absent in earlier times, and a stiff, unbending
pride in its purity, orthodoxy, and unity. During this period the tendency
toward the development of a special "Spanish ideology," already forming
during the Middle Ages, reached its height. For several generations the
Spanish were inclined to view their religion as superior to other branches
of Catholicism and themselves as a kind of second Chosen People, until
the disasters of the seventeenth century finally shook their confidence.

THE LATER MIDDLE AGES

After the thirteenth century, Catholicism was secure and triumphant
within the Hispanic peninsula, excepting only Granada. For several
hundred years Hispanic religion and culture had been moving toward
fuller integration with western Europe, and the Church of the thirteenth
century was both wealthier and more sophisticated than in earlier times.
The peninsula was being restored region by region to Christianity, and
nowhere could the formal religious identity of the people have been said
to be stronger.

Yet the power and position of the Church in medieval society can be
easily misunderstood. Though papal influence increased through the
thirteenth century, it was the crown that normally held the dominant

voice in Church-state relations, both in the Hispanic kingdoms and most others. For example, at the height of nominal papal authority, the crown attempted to introduce the Patronato Real—the formal right of royal presentation to high Church offices—in Castile in 1236 and in Aragon in 1238.

It was certainly correct that the Church, or various sectors thereof, was nominally very wealthy. Completion of the Great Reconquest resulted in extensive new endowments of land in the south-central and southern parts of the peninsula, following centuries of generous endowments elsewhere. Various sees or other agencies of the Church by this time held domain over at least 15 percent of all the land in the Spanish kingdoms, with one-third of their total in the hands of the new monastic crusading orders founded in the twelfth and thirteenth centuries. Over half the northwest region, Galicia, the seat of Santiago de Compostela, was under Church domain. The Church was owed a tithe of all regular income and collected many other fees of varying kinds. The great Gothic cathedrals at León, Burgos, Toledo, and elsewhere that were begun at this time evidence the splendor of the thirteenth-century Castilian Church. Some hierarchs were even able to invest in the royal debt of the crown of Castile, and the kingdom's Cortes (parliament) repeatedly petitioned the crown to prohibit acquisition of more territories by the Church.

Yet the Church was at the same time much less wealthy than it appeared. Various of its divisions differed greatly in endowment and level of income. Certain large monasteries and central diocesan treasuries held considerable wealth, while many local parishes existed in relative poverty. A sizable portion of ecclesiastical income was alienated or drained off altogether, primarily by the crown. For example, from the tithes regularly collected, about one-third of the revenue was kept by local units and often no more than one-third went to the central ecclesiastical organization. Beginning in the mid-thirteenth century, the crown periodically gained the right from the papacy to sequester *tercias reales*, "royal thirds," for itself, and such government exactions grew more frequent and exorbitant. The Church had paid a large share of the heavy costs of reconquest and would be called on for similar payments in the future. It was in fact the most heavily taxed institution in Spain. Some abbots or prelates may have been moneylenders, but at the same time some of the major archdioceses in Castile were heavily in debt.

The Church does not seem to have been able to follow up the reconquest by extending parish organization adequately through the southern part of the peninsula. Whereas approximately twenty episcopal sees had existed in "Old Spain" north of the Duero River and approximately twenty new ones had been created for the new central or intermediate districts following the eleventh-century advance, only seven new sees were established for the south. Presumably the scant population of the new territories required less attention at first, but in some districts the thin parish and diocesan network was never adequately expanded. By the nineteenth century, certain areas of the south would stand out as the major unchurched districts of Spain.

The thirteenth and fourteenth centuries were an age of frequent and bitter jurisdictional conflict between various religious units and secular authority and sometimes within the Church itself. Local aristocrats, municipal governments, and sometimes even neighborhood peasants, in addition to the crown, struggled to reduce landed jurisdictions and income rights of Church units. In the Aragonese principalities particularly, landed domain brought full involvement in the responsibilities and politics of the feudal system, though there was a general movement to reduce feudal associations of Church establishments.

During the past generation, social historians have commented more and more on the superficiality of much medieval religious practice and on the frequent tendency to profane the sacred in those centuries. In a society thoroughly identified with religion, common association with religious objects had a tendency to trivialize the sacred and to bring contradictory juxtapositions of pious and highly mundane activities. The not-infrequent assaults on clergymen, desecration of churches for personal or political ends, and even avoidance of the sacraments normally had no theological implications in themselves. Though violence against clerics or churches was in most cases recognized to be sacrilegious, its practice in a society where religion was to some degree involved in almost everything was much more a matter of common criminality than an attack on religion itself.

The clergy were undoubtedly the most diverse sector of society. They were the only group drawn from all social classes, though the highest positions in the Church were normally reserved for those of aristocratic background. They were also the only group in some form of direct contact with all the population, attempting at least in theory and sometimes in practice to minister to the most diverse needs. They also exhibited the broadest range of knowledge and preparation and some of the greatest extremes of behavior.

Discussions by historians of religion in the Middle Ages almost invariably give the clergy low marks, which by every evidence they frequently deserved. Medieval clergy at most levels were ignorant and poorly trained. Parish priests ordinarily did not preach and often took little responsibility for religious instruction. They did not normally wear clerical garb but dressed in secular, often brightly colored attire and not infrequently wore beards. Much of the clergy behaved little differently from ordinary society, indulging in popular vices and excesses. Though the Spanish clergy did not have the reputation for drunkenness enjoyed by their counterparts in some other regions, they yielded to none in concupiscence. Concubinage and bastardy were common among parish priests and hardly unknown among monks. One medieval commentator observed that the clergy seemed to have about as many children as any other group in society.

Spanish frontier conditions may have made some problems worse in the peninsula than elsewhere. Clerics at all levels took part in military campaigns against Muslims, creating the famous typology of the medieval prelate "a Dios rogando y con el mazo dando" (praying to God and striking with the mace). Many of the Spanish clergy thought nothing of wearing weapons as part of their normal costume, a practice that took many generations to eliminate.

From the eleventh to the sixteenth century, efforts to reform and improve the clergy were almost continuous. Slightly more progress seems to have been made in improving education than in raising morals. In 1251, for example, Innocent IV had to revoke earlier sentences that automatically excommunicated priests who publicly kept women, because too great a cross-section of the European clergy was involved. An occasional reform census would reveal that in a given district the majority of secular clergy were publicly living with women. In 1351 the Cortes of Castile tried to take a hand, ordering *barraganas de clérigos* (concubines of clerics) to wear a distinctive head-dress, but this could not be enforced either. In fact, such practices as concubinage seem to have been tolerated by much opinion in ordinary society, and in the Basque region villagers were said to expect and indeed require that parish priests have a woman of their own, as a safeguard against misconduct with the wives of others. The church hierarchy was thus reduced to merely prohibiting wives and children of the clergy from helping in the service of the Mass, but even this stricture was not necessarily effective.

Behavior of the laity toward the clergy was in turn often disrespectful in the extreme, and a kind of anticlericalism can be said to have been a fundamental part of the common medieval culture. Hostility to the clergy had nothing to do with religious faith or its lack, but was expressed as an attitude toward fellow mortals often engaged in activities common to all society or guilty of outright malpractice and evildoing. Those in positions of power frequently sought to control local church administration and appointment, and efforts to evade tithes and contributions seem to have been common at all levels. There was (by modern or post-Reformation standards) curiously little sense of sanctity of churches themselves, in which both clergy and laity behaved profanely and which were occasionally invaded by outright violence.

Religious service was dominated by formality and ritual, and it was apparently not uncommon in some parishes for peasants to hear Mass from outside the church building itself. The concepts of Christianity taught the ordinary people seem to have been extremely legalistic, and yet there is impressionistic evidence that the quality of Christian education was slowly improving. Jocelyn Hillgarth has suggested that for the common people, the most tangible aspects of religious life were probably the parish system itself, formal services and the administration of the sacraments, the blessing of crops, the presence of vows and ceremonies at baptism, marriage and death, and the annual rotation of the church calendar and its festival days.

The three general reform movements in the peninsula during the later Middle Ages corresponded to those in Latin Christendom as a whole. The first was the papal and Cluniac reform that was mentioned in the previous chapter. The second was the reform movement of the thirteenth century, led by new orders such as the Dominicans, Franciscans, Carmelites, and Augustinians. The older monastic groups were already in decline, increasingly hard put to defend their lands and endowments. The new thirteenth-century orders of friars were quite different, composed in part of mendicants who worked directly among ordinary people. They emphasized preaching, social service, and genuine spiritual conversion, and their begging of alms represented a reaction against the materialism of some monasteries with concentrated endowments. The new approach was in fact a Spanish invention, for the Castilian Santo Domingo de Guzmán initiated the institution of preaching friars when he founded the Dominican order early in the thirteenth century.

This order was more closely identified with Spain than any of the others. The friars encouraged learning, often requiring serious study of their members, and played an important role in the development of the new universities. Yet even the mendicant orders began to amass property, and after several generations lost much of their zest for spiritual and intellectual renewal.

Their most remarkable figure was the thirteenth-century Mallorcan friar and autodidact Ramon Llull, arguably the most influential thinker in all Spanish history, bar none. Llull's passion was conversion of the Muslims, for which he learned Arabic as well as the conventional Latin. Llull wrote in both Arabic and Catalan and has the reputation of being the virtual creator of Catalan as a literary language. His concern to communicate with Islamic culture for purposes of conversion influenced his approach, and he is the only Spaniard who can properly be said to have created a significant and distinct theological and philosophical system, for his emphasis on extreme rationalism in theology and proof and demonstration went beyond standard medieval scholasticism. Among his 243 known works are major writings on theology, philosophy, moral counsel, two remarkable Catalan vernacular novels, a scheme for a practical utopia based on an international assembly, and significant expressions of mysticism, developed in original psychological terms. In his *General Art* Llull endeavored to outline a system of universal logic that would provide logical and arithmetical correlations of all knowledge and science, a sort of primitive philosophical computer. This remarkable Mallorcan thinker and mystic, who traveled throughout southwestern Europe and the Mediterranean, eventually died a martyr in Tunis at nearly eighty-four years of age in 1316. The "Paul of the Middle Ages," Llull was the prime symbol of a new missionary spirit, couched in apocalyptic terms, and had university followers in both Catalonia and France. Revived by champions of neoplatonic and antischolastic thought a century later, his work has been studied with interest by certain French and German philosophers since the time of Leibnitz. His voluminous writings are today the subject of a specialized journal published in Spanish and of a small Raimundus-Llullus-Institut at Freiburg University.

The last medieval reform movement was even more diverse and pluralistic and cannot be described in a simple phrase. It began somewhat sporadically in the late fourteenth century and did not gather momentum until about a hundred years later. One of its first manifestations was the attempt of leaders of the Castilian hierarchy in the 1370s and 80s to purify morals and expand education, and also to further encourage royal power in the hope that its authority would be used to reform certain sectors of the Church. A monastic movement of spiritual and moral revival known as the Observancia stimulated new evangelical concern among the mendicant orders. The rise of the Jeronymite order in the second half of the fourteenth century, encouraging a more contemplative, internalized religion, was another significant new expression. Late-medieval religious ferment, though certainly not involving most of the clergy and the faithful, was manifested in new ideals of interiorism and antisacramental mysticism, and also in a growing vein of apocalypticism. In addition to the Jeronymites, the Carmelites and reformed Franciscans were active in trying to encourage spiritual change and growth, playing a major role in the subsequent "Catholic reform" of late-fifteenth-century Castile.

Educational levels among the elite of Spanish society and among at least some of the clergy rose during the fourteenth and fifteenth centuries. Though none of the new Spanish universities was distinguished by the standards of Oxford, Paris, Bologna, systematic study began to develop, and by the beginning of the fifteenth century the existence of professional Spanish philosophers and theologians was no longer an absolute novelty, though few could have been considered influential.

THE INQUISITION

In the late Middle Ages, the Hispanic kingdoms were unique among western states in containing sizable ethnoreligious minorities. Since the thirteenth century, a subject Muslim population, the Mudejars, had lived in Castile, Aragon and Valencia, and increased considerably in size with the final conquest of Granada, the last remaining Islamic territory, in 1492. Equally important, during the Great Reconquest the Hispanic kingdoms had incorporated the bulk of the Jewish population, resident mainly in the southern and eastern parts of the peninsula. By the tenth century, Hispanic Jews had been culturally Arabized and for a long period seem to have had little complaint about Muslim rule, but as the power balance shifted, some Jews clearly favored the Christian side. A contingent of Jewish troops had fought with the Castilian forces in the eleventh century, and the fierce intolerance shown by the twelfth-century Moroccan invaders produced a considerable emigration of southern Jews to the Christian north. In the course of the next two or three hundred years, an enlarged Jewish community developed a pronounced new Castilian identity in the largest of the Hispanic kingdoms.

During the fourteenth century there was a fairly strong general climate of tolerance toward Mudejars. Some small Muslim groups were in the process of assimilation, and only in Valencia (and later Granada) was the use of Arabic effectively preserved. Attitudes toward the Jews were quite different, partly because there was less cultural distance. By the fourteenth century they played a more inportant role in Hispanic, especially Castilian, society than they had in any part of Europe. Jews constituted the major single group, though by no means the whole, of the Castilian financial class. Jewish scholars, physicians, and specialists composed a large part of the Hispanic intelligentsia. While most Jews were ordinary artisans and trademen in such offices as silkweaving, silversmithing, and shoemaking, a small number also performed major functions in royal administration, especially tax collecting, an activity much resented by the common people. By the late fourteenth century Jews had been expelled from most other parts of western Europe, but in Castile the upper class of Jewish society had become extremely wealthy and also apparently ostentatious. Intermarriage within the upper classes, and less official forms of sexual liaisons, had become common. Popular hatred of the Jewish community grew, but royal protection remained strong, at first, because of the importance of Jews to financial and administrative affairs.

Anti-Jewish riots by Hispanic townspeople became increasingly frequent during the fourteenth century and reached a climax in the great pogrom of 1391. This was precipitated by the combination of economic distress and religious revival in the southern districts of Castile that preached puritanism, strict religious observance, and restrictions on Muslims and Jews (a demand reiterated by the Hispanic clergy). A leading role was played by some of the friars, the mobs being primarily composed of urban middle class and lower class people. The initiative in suppressing Jewish communities amd placing heavy pressure on Jews to convert was actually taken in Catalonia, where they were less important in both numbers and influence. Practically the entire Jewish community in Barcelona was converted or forced to leave, and by 1435 this was true of Palma de Mallorca also. Almost equally heavy pressures for conversion were felt in Castile in the 1390s, and a second wave of semivoluntary conversions followed between 1411 and 1415, prompted by the evangelism of the Dominican Vicente Ferrer and by new anti-Jewish legislation. By the early fifteenth century more than half the original Jewish population of over 200,000 in the Hispanic kingdoms had become *Conversos*, converted Catholics either nominally or sincerely. This step was the easier for many because of the status of many Jews among the upper class and the opportunity for further advancement that conversion brought. Conversely, in the case of Aragonese Jews with more modest resources, conversion made it possible to escape heavier taxes.

Paradoxically, mass conversion was not a step toward solving the religious problem but only made it more intense. Suspicion and hatred of Conversos grew more intense as their positions and wealth increased; they were resented as opportunists and insincere Christians, an allegation true of some and false of others. Moreover, there were further demands that all Jews convert or leave, since it was maintained that Conversos would never become genuine Christians so long as a regular Jewish community remained as an incitement to "Judaizing." Major riots erupted once more in 1449, attended by new demands for a special tribunal or inquisition to prosecute crypto-Judaizers.

During the next quarter-century, feeling against Conversos spread among zealots in Church leadership, among some of their rivals in the middle and upper classes, and especially among much of the ordinary population inflamed against "false Christians" and genuine or supposed oppressors. The Conversos' enemies insisted that many of them secretly practiced Jewish rites and constituted an insidious element of subversion within Spanish Catholicism, corrupting the faith and conspiring with the enemies of a united Catholic state and society. More riots broke out in the 1460s, and in certain cities of Andalusia and New Castile, where the Converso and Jewish population was most numerous, conditions verged on local civil war. The Jewish question had become the principal source of internal discord in Castile.

Traditionally, Castilian Jews had relied on the support of the crown, but in the contest that brought Isabel of Castile and her husband Fernando of Aragon to power in 1478–79, uniting the monarchies of Castile and Aragon, most Conversos and Jews had supported the losing side. Two centuries earlier Fernando III el Santo had, despite his intense piety and persecution of Christian heretics, broadly termed himself "king of the three religions." Fernando and Isabel were determined to complete the final reconquest and would be hailed by the papacy as "the Catholic Monarchs," the much more exclusive name by which they are known to history. The rulers who forged the united Spanish monarchy could not conceive of unity and security, either spiritually or politically, in anything other than a staunchly, ultimately monolithic Catholic society. The existence of a powerful financial caste closely associated with influential (and potentially antagonistic) groups in the aristocracy, all the while vaguely identied with an alien religion, stood as a theoretical menace to political and spirtitual unity. Conversos were also a major part of the urban oligarchy, another special power group, and were on good terms with certain wealthy prelates. They were a sort of state within a state, but Fernando and Isabel would permit no more than one state and no more than one conceivable religious identification. After a ten-year campaign against Judaizing by the head of the Jeronymite order in Castile, and a new series of anti-Converso outbursts in Castilian towns in 1473, the crown finally acted on demands for an inquisition and applied to Rome for approval of a special ecclesiastical inquisition under the aegis of the monarchy.

Historical speculation about the motivation for the Spanish Inquisition has proposed highly diverse explanations. Among them are religious fanaticism, political state-building, the envy of the aristocracy, the rivalry of the middle classes, resentment of the lower classes against economic exploitation, the desire of the government to enrich itself by confiscating Converso wealth, and even the zeal of some genuinely converted Conversos to separate themselves from crypto-Judaizers by persecuting the latter. Probably none of these motivations was entirely absent, but the predominant cause seems to have been the religious ideals of the Catholic Monarchs and their closest advisers. In the long run, the tribunals of the Inquisition cost the state more money than was brought in through confiscation, while some members of the upper classes actually tried to protect the Conversos. It is certainly correct that the defense and purification of religious practice was seen almost universally in medieval and early modern Europe as necessary to developing a strong state. The Spanish crown insisted on royal patronage in naming the Inquisitional tribunal, rather than merely soliciting a branch of the medieval Church's papal inquisition, in part because much of the Castilian church hierarchy was deemed too corrupt and too political to be trusted on its own. Moreover, a royal-ecclesiastical institution would identify royal initiative more closely with the common people, whose antipathy to the Converso oligarchy was intense.

Pope Sixtus IV, favorably inclined toward the new Spanish rulers, authorized a royal Inquisition in 1478. The first ecclesiastical inquisitors were named two years later, and the work of the Holy Office, as it was termed, first got under way in Seville, a major center of Conversos. During the next eight years in that region, 700 Conversos were burned, either alive or after execution. During the aegis of the first grand inquisitor, Tomás de Torquemada (1483–98), some 2,000 Conversos were burned or otherwise executed and at least 15,000 subjected to lesser punishments. Large amounts of property were confiscated. In some cases entire families were wiped out, and most of those punished more lightly were reduced to the status of pariahs, living in perpetual uncertainty.

As a Catholic institution, the Inquisition held jurisdiction only over Christians, which Conversos were in theory if not always in fact. Regular Jews and Muslims were not subject to it. It was increasingly argued, however, that the Conversos problem could never be solved if Jews were still tolerated in Spain. All remaining Jews were therefore required to convert or emigrate in 1492, most accepting the latter choice. Religious toleration for the Muslims in southern Castile was withdrawn ten years later, and they too were required to convert. Similar terms were imposed on the Muslims of the Aragonese territories in 1525. Most of the Muslims lacked money or opportunity to emigrate, and as nominal Christians they were subsequently known as Moriscos—a large, only superficially converted, still basically Islamic minority in southern and eastern Spain.

The Inquisition has often been described as a popular institution, and so in many respects it was. Its work was obeyed and usually applauded by the population, and its elaborate ceremonies of sentencing and punishment, the notorious autos-de-fe, were remakable spectacles attended by vast crowds. The Inquisition also became the only unified Spanish institution, with branch tribunals in all the various kingdoms ad principalities of the monarchy. Yet its introduction was bitterly resisted in the Aragonese territories, and particularly in the Inquisition's bloodiest early years there were rather frequent complaints about injustice and corruption among the inquisitors themselves. Reforms correcting some of the procedural abuses were eventualy instituted in the sixteenth century. Thus although opinion generally approved of its work, the Inquisition was also recognized by many Spanish people, especially outside Castile, as a radical and potentially dangerous innovation.

The Inquisition became one of the most fundamental of Spanish institutions, lasting nearly 350 years. Though such a structure already existed in the Roman Catholic Church, the Inquisition of Spain was distinctively Spanish in several ways. As indicated, it was technically a royal as well as ecclesiastical tribunal, first designed for a peculiarly Spanish situation, and then subsequently used more broadly as an instrument of royal policy. It was occasionally employed for nonreligious ends, particularly in the Aragonese kingdoms, since the Holy Office was not itself subject to standard constitutional restraints on royal power.

Altogether, it went through four phases. The first, lasting until about 1520, might be called the Converso phase, when the Inquisition was directed almost exclusively against converts from Judaism and their descendants. From the 1520s on its work became more general and more intensively organized, dealing with potential heresy throughout society and increasingly with cases of vice and religious misconduct other than heresy. During this second phase there were proportionately many fewer executions, but there were severe repressions of suspected Protestants as well as Judaizers and to some extent Moriscos as well. After several generations, the Inquisition found fewer and fewer heretics, and devoted itself increasingly to the repression of vice and the reform of social and religious conduct. After the middle of the sixteenth century, most of those who appeared before it were accused of such sins as bigamy, sodomy, fornication, impious conduct, "palabras escandalosas" (scandalous words) and "proposiciones," false though not heretical statements about religion. For most of its life the Inquisition's primary goal was not so much the repression of heresy, which ceased to exist in Spain, as the proper formation of Catholic conduct, in which it also seems to have had considerable success. After the immigration of thousands of moneyed Portuguese Conversos into Spain, a new phase of prosecution of Judaizers ensued between 1640 and 1660. During the concluding phase of its last 160 years, the Holy Office became less and less active, but a final round of prosecution of descendants of Conversos took place as late as 1720–25.

It will never be possible to tabulate fully the number of the Inquisition's victims, since not all records have survived. At one time or another a total of about 50,000 Conversos—a large minority of the total Converso community—were condemned in one manner or another. The number of

"Old Christians" who incurred fines and light punishments in the latter phases was much greater. Altogether there were probably around 5,000 executions during the entire span of the Inquisition, mostly of Conversos and their descendants.

The Inquisition is usually considered the darkest, most destructive chapter of Spanish history, and this judgment is doubtless correct. Like all institutions, however, it must be seen in full historical perspective, and certain facts should be kept in mind. Even the most tolerant west European states of that era had tribunals for the repression of heresy and subversion. Spain happened to contain many more non-Catholics than any region up until the Reformation. Later, the number of Protestants killed in one day in France would equal the total number of Conversos burnt during the fifteen most severe years of the Inquisition. The total number of executions for heresy in the entire history of the Holy Office was not appreciably more than the number of people destroyed in Germany by Protestants and Catholics alike during the witchcraft craze of the seventeenth century. Moreover, on those occasions when witchcraft mania did break out in Spain—as in Navarre and Catalonia in 1527–28 and in Navarre in 1610—the Inquisition acted to calm the hysteria and accurately diagnosed this tendency to mass psychosis.

Twentieth-century commentators often liken the mass terror of modern totalitarianism regimes to the Spanish Inquisition. Without minimizing the horrors of the Holy Office, this is ignorant and inaccurate. First, the inquisitors did largely abide by their own rules, even though these were stacked against the accused. They did not prosecute people as a class or race, but on an individual basis. The majority of Conversos were not directly impugned. The majority of those arrested were not tortured, and while torture was normal practice in some judicial procedures in all countries of that era, the kinds of torture employed by the Holy Office were mild and restrained by comparative standards. Some of the accused successfully resisted the test of torture. Nearly all were permitted to name advocates, and a sizable minority were able to mount a successful defense. With respect to censorship, the Spanish Inquisition's own Index of Prohibited Books was administered with somewhat greater restraint than the Papal Index in Rome. The Spanish Index often did not surpress books in their entirety but published lists of excisions and corrections. It did not choke off new learning and reform in themselves, for the period of greatest liberalism in traditional Spanish Catholicism and of the greatest development in Spanish learning occurred in the century following the inception of the Inquisition.

Yet the destructive effects of the Inquisition on Spanish society and culture are obvious. It reinforced narrow ethnocentric values and discouraged, though it did not totally prohibit, dissent. Though the Inquisition was not alone responsible for the decline of Spanish culture in subsequent generations, it was later used to discourage nonconformity and new ideas of many sorts. An instrument and not an independent cause, the Inquisition nonetheless marked the beginning of a process of historic inversion that was paradoxically present *in ovo* at the beginning of Spain's Golden Age of cultural flowering.

THE GOLDEN AGE

When the Catholic Monarchs, Fernando and Isabel, unified the Spanish dynasties, they also embarked on a general program to revitalize some of the major institutions of their realms. Reform of the clergy and of ecclesiastical policy constituted primary aims. As in other European monarchies, this concern had political and nationalist dimensions as well as religious goals. Though the Catholic Monarchs recognized the pope's full spiritual authority, they were much more jealous of his temporal power. They constantly petitioned and protested to Rome concerning Church affairs in Spain, and occasionally even used force to contravene specific papal acts. For example, they strongly objected to large financial payments to Rome and to the appointment of foreign prelates, mainly Italian, to Spanish positions. They won from the papacy the right of *patronato*, or patronage of most ecclesiastical appointments, in the newly conquered territory of Granada (bull of 1486), a right subsequently extended to all Spanish America. During the reign of their grandson and heir, Carlos V, the crown in 1523 obtained the right of presentation (in effect, nomination) to all dioceses within Spain. Six years after that, the papacy recognized limited jurisdiction for a special Spanish court of ecclesiastical appeals, the *tribunal del nuncio*, that heard many ordinary ecclesiastical suits and petitions without need to refer them to Rome.

The question of royal authority and right of nomination was linked with spiritual reform, as well, for the religious zeal and vigor of the Catholic Monarchs was greater than that of most Renaissance popes. Fernando and Isabel were determined to appoint prelates who would improve the quality of Church life, and consequently royal authority was invoked by the most earnest champions of reform within the Spanish Church itself. The reign of the Catholic Monarchs thus crystallized the halting efforts at ecclesiastical reform that had been developing for more than a century. The greatest resistance to change came not so much from the hierarchy itself as from routinists and bureaucrats in the middle levels of the clergy.

Major reform of clerical conduct and organization in Castile was carried out in the 1480s by the Franciscan provincial of the kingdom, Francisco Jiménez de Cisneros, one of the outstanding figures in the Hispanic Church of the imperial age. Permission was then obtained from the pope to extend the reform to other orders and segments of the clergy, and in this enterprise Cisneros used a wide broom. Concubinage as a form of common-law marriage was so taken for granted that its abolition led to physical violence by the clergy in some towns; an undetermined number of friars apparently emigrated to Morocco and converted to Islam rather than give up their women. Abuses of privilege, dereliction of duty, and personal misconduct were so widespread that they would not be reformed overnight. At a church council in Seville in 1512, the presiding archbishop Deza simply recommended that local clergy at least try to give an appearance of chastity and virtue, abstaining from attending the marriages of their grown children or officially deeding their personal property to concubines. Most of these problems remained to be addressed by the more thorough-going Counter-Reformation reforms a half century later.

Sixteenth-Century Thought

During the sixteenth century, the Hispanic peninsula became the center of Catholic thought. This was due first of all to the remarkable expansion of education in Spain during that period. Six universities existed in Spain by 1450, but during the next century and a half twenty-seven new ones were founded. By the late sixteenth century, some kind of Latin school existed in almost every Spanish town of 2,000 or more, and approximately 5 percent of all adult males matriculated in a university, at least during the zenith of this expansion. For a brief period, Spain had proportionately the largest educated population of any country in the world.

The universities were not Church institutions, but the Church played a major role in them through its numerous residential colleges and faculty. Before the intensification of the struggle with Protestantism, the Spanish Church encouraged humanist scholarship as a major instrument of reform. Nearly all the leading Catholic scholars of the age held university positions, and a major ambition of Cisneros was to develop a new university that would not emphasize legal studies so much as the employment of Renaissance learning in the service of theology and the training of priests. This took full form in the new University of Alcalá de Henares, founded between 1502 and 1508 (the predecessor of the University of Madrid), which became a center for Catholic humanism.

A main feature of the new religious learning in Spain was Bible study, a Catalan translation of the Bible having been published in Valencia as early as 1478, the first full translation in any western vernacular. The principal achievement of early sixteenth-century Spanish scholarship was the University of Alcalá's Polyglot Bible, which published original and complete texts of both Old and New Testaments in all the classic languages in which they had been rendered, with vocabularies and analyses of grammar. The first volume of this work, the most complete comparative textual exposition of the scriptures ever made in Christendom, was published, paradoxically, in 1517, the same year that Luther nailed his ninety-five Bible-inferred theses on the church door in Wittenburg, starting the Protestant Reformation.

The principal foreign works of Christian devotion were eagerly translated and studied in early sixteenth-century Spain. During the 1520s, the Catholic humanism and moderate reformism of the Dutch scholar Erasmus enjoyed great vogue among Spanish scholars and religious leaders, inspiring the main new current of Spanish Catholic thought in that generation. The chief of Spanish humanists, Juan Luis Vives, son of a persecuted Valencian Converso family, became one of the most profound disciples of Erasmus in Europe. At one point Cisneros had offered Erasmus a chair at Alcalá, and whereas the Sorbonne combatted Erasmian tenets, a Castilian theological conference at Valladolid upheld them. At that time Spain was probably the center of European Erasmianism, particularly between 1527 and 1532, when Erasmian humanists were the chief religious advisers of the crown and the Spanish ruler Carlos V hoped to encourage Catholic and papal reform in a moderate humanist direction. The failure to accomplish this, along with the radicalization and polarization of religious positions in Europe during the 1530s, led to a reaction in Castile and an erosion of the influence of such Erasmian counsellors as Juan and Alfonso Valdés.

The development of small circles of "Alumbrados" (Illuminists) was a separate phenomenon. Almost without exception Conversos in origin, Alumbrados espoused a somewhat intellectualized form of interior religion that stressed personal illumination and the love of God. They had little or nothing to do with Protestant or north European religiosity, but were prosecuted by the Inquisition in 1525 and largely suppressed.

The first half of the sixteenth century was nevertheless characterized by a sense of originality and of new development of thought and culture, in which the discovery and conquest of America played a major role. The terms *moderno* and *progreso* apparently first began to be used in Castilian in the 1520s. A sense of cultural continuity with the ancients persisted, but there was also a new feeling of having surpassed them in both the arts and practical affairs.

Spanish theologians and philosophers recognized the partial breakup of the medieval cultural and philosophical unity but maintained the primacy of religious thought, to be based not merely on authority but also on further conceptual and philosophical development that could be attuned to free will and the personal conscience. While the imperfections of Rome were recognized, the religious values and authority of Catholicism were affirmed. The idea of the overarching imperial unity of the Middle Ages was abandoned for new norms of natural law, and in the political sphere, of international law. Spanish theorists and moralists of international relations, led by Francisco de Vitoria, have thus frequently been given credit for initiating modern concepts of international law.

By the 1550s the Dominican theologian Melchor Cano was introducing a new methodology that emphasized study of the full range of historical sources, from the works of Christ and the Holy Scriptures through the apostles, Church fathers and councils, subsequent theologians and canonists, to serious secular historical narratives. Though deferring always to Church authority, this appeal to a broad range of historical sources went beyond the earlier humanism and helped to point the way for future theological study down to the twentieth century.

The main thrust of sixteenth-century Spanish theology lay in the elaboration of neoscholastic thought, culminating in the work of Francisco Suárez, one of the two or three greatest figures in the history of Spanish philosophy and the outstanding European neoscholastic of the age. While endeavoring to reconcile freedom and law, modernity and tradition, Spanish neoscholasticism recognized that the modern principle lay in a stress on the will and the conscience as well as on authority. Emphases varied: the Dominican Domingo Báñez recognized physical predestination combined with individual moral freedom, while Luis de Molina in his *Concordia* defined human freedom of the will acting in concert with divine volition. Biblical scholarship reached its high point in the Polyglot Bible of Antwerp (1568–72), which surpassed the earlier work at Alcalá but was choked off soon afterward by Catholic Reformation policy.

The political attitudes of sixteenth-century Spanish religious thinkers were patriotic and generally conservative, except in the areas of international law and conquest. Since Spanish tradition was founded on a complex network of laws, rights, and even representative functions, however, religious thinkers strongly upheld principles of legal rights and also, to some degree, of the limitations of power. Suárez's key work,

Defensa de la fe (1613), was explicitly antiabsolutist, emphasizing the authority of the laws of the kingdom and the function of delegation of power. It was held in theory that power and legitimacy lay only in the community, though the ideal of full and direct community representation as such was not advanced. Suárez did not go beyond advocating greater participation in the royal government, under which the civil power could be altered and mediated by the administration of laws and juridical institutions.

In the doctrines of natural law that formed much of the basis of social theory, private property per se was not held to be an inherent part of natural law but to be a logical consequence of it. The most radical of the civil theorists in the Church, Juan de Mariana, who advocated tyrannicide in dealing with extreme cases of oppression, suggested that property holdings should be redistributed if they became exessively concentrated.

This period was also one in which clerical historians laid the foundations of modern Spanish historiography, particularly in the use of original documents, as in Jerónimo de Zurita's *Anales de Aragón*, and in the scope of study, as in Mariana's *Historia general de España* (1601).

It should not be forgotten that within this full panoply of Catholic culture, Spain created and initially dominated an entire new range of secular literary genres and subgenres as well. "The tragi-comedy in prose . . . ; the purely national drama which . . . only the English came to match; the picaresque novel; the pastoral novel . . . ; the modern critical novel that sets forth the gist of human experience; and others of minor interest, such as the epistolary novel"[1] were all Spanish inventions. Some of the major new Spanish forms, especially the picaresque and critical novels, were unique for introducing new standards of prose realism that reflected both the critical temper of the sixteenth-century Spanish mind and the relation of that realism to moral and theological orthodoxy. A major difference between the other outstanding national literary culture of the period, the English, and that of Spain is the philosophical orthodoxy and moral restraint of the latter.

The Catholic Expansion Overseas and the Missionary Movement

One of the greatest enterprises of sixteenth-century Spanish Catholicism was the beginning of its massive missionary endeavor in the Americas. Christian missions in European history were not exactly a Spanish invention but very nearly so. Their origins lay in missions to the Muslims in the fourteenth and fifteenth centuries, when several score missionary

---

1. Otis H. Green, *Spain and the Western Tradition*, 4 vols. (Madison, 1964–68), 3:53–54.

monks and friars (not all Spanish) had met martyrdom preaching the faith in the emirate of Granada. Thousands of monks and priests left Spain in the sixteenth century to establish a new Catholic culture among the colonists and Indians of the new world. Much smaller numbers later journeyed through the Portuguese empire to East Asia in the broadest world missionary endeavor before the nineteenth century. The development of a Catholic culture in Spanish America was uneven at best, in some areas strong, in others weak. As in almost every case where Christianity was transplanted to an alien culture, it adopted syncretistic forms. Whatever judgment is ultimately placed on trans-European Hispano-Catholicism, it represented the greatest expansion of the Christian world in hundreds of years.

That expansion was destructive of native religions and cultures, yet the Spanish clergy provided whatever scholarly observation was available for the recording of this clash of cultures and of the native civilizations. They produced the first treatises on Amerindian languages, the first preanthropological and cross-cultural description of native societies, and the first serious studies and scholarly expeditions dealing with extra-European flora and fauna. They also produced the first examples among Europeans of a sense of the comparative history of civilizations, as this developed among Church writers and thinkers in Spain and Mexico. Theirs was the first suggestion of the early modern myth of the "noble savage," as applied to some American Indians.

Church missionaries and theorists also led the struggle for social justice for the American Indians. Some Spanish jurists sustained a doctrine of the "right of conquest" over the Indian population, but this was not accepted by the best minds in Spain. Francisco de Vitoria carried out an independent and penetrating analysis of the moral and legal problems of empire and of dominion over alien, non-Christian peoples. For Vitoria and his followers, Spanish dominion in the Indies could not be founded on mere conquest or assumption of superiority or divine right but required a complex of historical, religious, and legal factors. Legitimate empire carried with it major moral and spiritual responsibilities, which were in fact its prime justification, and had to be restricted and mediated by the tutelage of both natural and civil law.

Missionaries of the regular clergy carried on intensive struggles to protect the Indians from exploitation. The most famous of them, Bartolomé de las Casas, the Apostle to the Indies, was so outspoken in his denunciation of Spanish treatment of the Indians that he has even been accused of having founded the "Black Legend." Church advocates of the Indians' rights had a mitigating effect on conditions in Spanish America, but they were unable to dominate the mores of colonial society.

The Catholic Reformation

There is no doubt that the late fifteenth and sixteenth centuries were a time of significant deepening and intensification of religious spirit in Spain. The growth in religious culture and activism, as just described, was paralleled by expansion of religious involvement among part of the population as a whole. Religious confraternities increased rapidly in number during this period, and extended their functions in the towns to a broad range of religious and social activities. As many as one hundred different confraternities might be found in certain cities of no more than ten thousand population, an average of one confraternity for every hundred inhabitants. Though many of the functions of the confraternities were at least as much social as spiritual, there was a heightened sense of personal devotion as well. The increase in literacy, limited though it ultimately was, may have helped to produce the intensified awareness of the personal and interior dimensions of religion which became more common than in the Middle Ages.

The heightened religiosity of later-sixteenth-century Spain cannot be ascribed merely to imperial, social, or ceremonial form, for it projected a new model of Catholic holiness for human lives. Bartolomé Bennassar has termed it "an explosion of the divine," in which perhaps for the first time in western history the style of sainthood became a social model sought after by a significant cross-section of society, almost in the way that members of later societies would seek economic success, athletic prowess, or stardom as entertainers. Only in Italy was the Counter-Reformation Catholic model felt with equal intensity. Altogether, of thirty-one sixteenth- and seventeenth-century saints canonized after the conclusion of the Council of Trent, eleven were Spanish and fourteen Italian.

Serious personal standards of religiosity were transmitted to the literate upper and middle strata of society through a large number of new devotional books in the vernacular, ranging from the highly popular *Tercer abecedario espiritual* (Third spiritual primer) of Francisco de Osuna (1527) to the later *Subida del monte Sión* of Bernardino de Laredo and the *Retablo de la vida de Cristo* of Juan de Padilla. In the universities, where legal studies had predominated over theology, the situation was reversed in the later sixteenth century and theology received predominant attention. During the final decades of the century this much more conscious and pedagogical religious orientation reached the most humble members of society. Inquiries by the Inquisition revealed a steady rise in the proportion of peasants and laborers able to recite the Ten Commandments, the Ave Maria, and the Lord's Prayer, until by the 1580s and 90s such knowledge seemed generally diffused through Spanish society.

The intensification of religious consciousness also had important political consequences, for religion provided the most important bond between the several peninsular principalities of the Spanish dynasty. Through a century and more of struggles against Muslims in the Mediterranean and North Africa and against Protestants and their allies in Europe, intense and increasingly exclusive Catholicism more than ever provided the basis for a common Hispanic identity.

This was accompanied by a pronounced vein of messianism, first given voice during the conquest of Granada (1482–92) and then in the expansion overseas. When Isabel la Católica died in 1504, her testament bequeathed to Castile the continuation of the crusade against the Islamic world in North Africa, an enterprise that absorbed much Spanish money and blood during the first half of the sixteenth century. After the new king Carlos V succeeded to the throne of the central European Holy Roman Empire in 1519, Spanish monarchy seemed to become almost universal, and Spain was clearly positioned to play the leading role in Christendom.

This resulted, during the sixteenth and early seventeenth centuries, in the development of a strong sense of mission, and even an explicit "chosen people" complex, among Spanish leaders and spokesmen and apparently many of the common people as well. Salvador de Madariaga has termed it "autolatry" or a kind of self-worship, but the term is probably unfair. Spanish religion was disciplined by a different and higher set of norms than merely those of Spanish culture or national self-assertion, even though national politics and culture increasingly conditioned its nature and expression.

Development of Spanish religion was strongly influenced by the general historical and international milieu, and particularly by the effects of the Protestant Reformation. Confrontation with Islam and Judaism had already led the Spanish to take an uncompromising stand for absolute Catholic orthodoxy, so that the split developing in European Christendom soon became absolutely inacceptable to them. The fact that Protestantism was adopted by societies and states that were enemies of the Spanish crown and sometimes rivals of Spanish interests accentuated the categorical rejection of alternative religiosity. The only non-Catholics whom peninsular people had known were Muslims and Jews, perceived either as mortal enemies or exploiters and subversives. The same attitude was transferred to Protestants. Few of the religious, cultural, social, economic, or political features that encouraged Protestantism in northern Europe were present in Spain. Before 1558 the Inquisition could discover only 105 potential believers in Lutheranism in Spain, and two-thirds of these were foreigners.

By the late 1550s, however, two small groups of Protestants were discovered, one in Valladolid and the other in Seville. This news, together with many other rumors from at home and abroad, came after three or four generations of constant struggle against Muslims, crypto-Judaizers, and most recently, Protestant forces in central Europe. It induced a sort of collective paranoia, at least among state leaders and a portion of the clergy. A royal decree of 1559 forbade Spaniards to study in foreign universities, even Catholic ones, for foreign Catholicism was now considered flaccid and unreliable. The process of turning the Hispanic peninsula into a kind of cultural Tibet was under way. During the next year or so, the Inquisition prosecuted some 800 persons suspected of Protestantism, including many "Old Christians" of high social standing and no taint of Jewish background. The Holy Office went so far as to purge one archbishop of Toledo, holding the primate of the Spanish Church in jail for seven years before he was finally cleared and released.[2]

From this time on the cloak of orthodoxy became increasingly heavy. Religion for Spaniards had always been a matter of distinguishing themselves from menacing foreign cultures, and that sense of difference and of menace would lead to increasing exaggeration in the Spanish expression of orthodoxy. During the reign of Felipe II, which was just beginning, Spain would stand more strongly than ever as the champion of the Counter-Reformation and the sword of international Catholicism. As a result, Spanish policy during this era is often interpreted as having been dictated mainly by religious motives, sacrificing practical interest to crusading fervor. This impression is only strengthened by the central role of the Spanish crown and Church representatives at the Council of Trent in reforming Catholicism and maintaining the authority of the papacy.

---

2. The case of the archbishop of Toledo, Bartolomé de Carranza, was a significant one not only because of the rank of the person involved but also because of the way in which it illustrated the interweaving of personal malice and rivalry with economic interest and jurisdictional conflict. The Inquisition had only recently successfully petitioned for jurisdiction, albeit limited, over bishops, an authority here employed by the chief inquisitor to strike at a hated personal rival, the archbishop, who had been promoted over him to the primacy of the Church. Carranza was a Dominican friar and theologian who had written somewhat liberal and ambiguous *Commentaries* on the catechism and had served as personal confessor to Felipe in England during the latter's marriage to Mary Tudor. He was accused of heresy in his writings and in his conduct toward English Protestants. The papacy grasped that Carranza would not receive a fair hearing in Spain and insisted on the transfer of the case of Rome. The Spanish crown resisted for years, to avoid any reduction in jurisdiction of the royal Inquisition and to enable it to dispose of the income from this rich archbishopric as long as possible.

Such an interpretation is, however, quite wide of the mark in a number of respects. The coincidence of royal policy with Catholic objectives is in most cases also explainable by political motivations, because the religious split during the sixteenth century coincided with political and military antagonisms that found most enemies of the crown identified with Protestantism, or in the case of France, with the anti-Christian Turk. Carlos V did not at first move to crush Protestantism when it emerged in the German lands of his Holy Roman Empire, taking military action only after political and military tensions had built up over a quarter-century. Felipe II was rigorous against Dutch and Flemish Protestants in his Habsburg crown territories of the Low Countries, but would not have acted so severely had they not been political rebels against the state. The Protestant Elizabeth was left unmolested for nearly three decades, and the great Armada of 1588 was attempted only after severe military and political rivalry had developed. Both Carlos and Felipe let operations against the Turk slip in order to prosecute their intra-Catholic rivalry with the crown of France.

Relations between the papacy and the crown of Spain were often bad throughout the century and sometimes violent. Rebel non-Spanish mercenaries of Carlos's army sacked Rome in 1527. Several times popes joined or even led anti-Spanish coalitions. Paul IV (1555–59) was the bitterest foe of the Spanish crown, whose subjects he called "those dregs of the earth, that breed of Moors and Jews." During his reign the crown found itself for a short time in the embarrassing position of operating a royal army in Italy against the forces of the papacy itself, though the piety of Felipe II was ultimately expressed in his orders to the Duke of Alba to kneel before the Spanish-hating pope to ask forgiveness.

Felipe II followed what might be termed, not inaccurately, a dynastic policy of orthodox Catholic nationalism. Locked in a military struggle for the hegemony of western Europe, he saw religious orthodoxy as a mainstay of Spain and the empire, and the Spanish crown as mainstay of orthodoxy within its realms. Foreign prelates, even the pope himself, were not to be trusted in political, administrative, and financial matters, where they might be representing other interests. Even more than Fernando and Isabel, he tried to Hispanize fully the Church in Spain. Foreign appointees became even rarer, and he asked that Aragonese Franciscans and Cistercians be freed from French control, because of the suspected heterodoxy and divided loyalties of the foreign leaders of those orders. Later he endeavored to establish a completely separate Spanish section of the Jesuits. He delayed publishing the Tridentine decisions in Spain for fear that they might endanger the royal control of Church appointments. Ecclesiastical affairs were more fully dominated by the crown in Spain than in any other contemporary Catholic kingdom. In turn, there were times when the papacy looked upon the Spanish crown's frequent expressions of concern about Church affairs and the repression of heresy as pretexts for the extension of Spanish royal power.

Though there was little reason to doubt the sincerity of the Spanish desire to avoid or eliminate heresy, the papacy was rarely able to identify its political interests with those of the Spanish crown. Spain was simply too powerful; having won hegemony in Italy, it was sometimes in a position to coerce the papacy politically, and the papacy was not always disappointed when Protestant or other Catholic interests managed to check the might of the Spanish crown. Clement VII, for example, might have been able to head off the English schism had he not been under the coercion of Hispanic dynastic interests. This purely political tension between the papacy and the Spanish crown lasted throughout the century, and resulted in another breakdown of relations in the early 1590s over the question of the French royal succession.

More important than any political conflict with the papacy was Spanish initiative in the reform and reorganization of the Church. Spanish influence in the long, often interrupted deliberations of the Council of Trent (1545–63) was of fundamental significance and perhaps decisive. From Trent there flowed the new legislation on the Church and religious practice that provided much of the base for the Catholic Reformation of the second half of the sixteenth century.

The reformation of the Catholic Church in Spain carried out under Felipe II was in general more effective than any of the medieval reform movements. The problem of clerical education was given more attention than ever before. Trent decreed the establishment of a seminary in each diocese, and twenty were in operation in Spain by the end of the reign.

Local religion in Spain exhibited broad variation based on centuries of development of local cults, shrines, regional saints, and special liturgical features. The Catholic Reformation may have made less effort to control and reshape local religion in Spain than in some other countries. Despite minor variation in practice, there was little danger that distinctions in local religion would lead to schism or heresy in Spain. There, the Church already possessed a stronger organization than in some other Catholic areas, and in conjunction with the state, had formidable mechanisms of leadership and ultimate control.

There was, however, a major effort to standardize the performance of the liturgy throughout Spain. Equally important, parish priests were henceforth given the formal responsibility of preaching regularly at least once a week—an absolute innovation in some areas—and they were given a modicum of instruction in how to accomplish that task. Hymns, which were uncommon in the smaller churches, were also introduced widely with the intention of making them a regular feature of services throughout Spain.

Another aim was to establish firmly the sense of the sacred, not only in services and sacraments but in the physical environment of churches themselves. A major effort was made to eliminate secular activities and wanton behavior within and around church buildings. The secular plays performed in churches were thenceforth replaced by the new religious dramas, the *autos sacramentales*.

In ecclesiastical organization, the Catholic Reformation had several major goals. One was to establish a uniform system of parish organization throughout the country. The existing parish network was a crazy-quilt of historical evolution, and as noted earlier, some sparsely inhabited rural districts were virtually left out altogether. Reorganization was the more difficult because medieval endowments had placed nearly two-thirds of Spanish parishes under the control of secular lords or monasteries rather than of the direct Church organization itself. At any rate, the beginning of systematic modern parish organization dated from this time.

For the higher levels of organization, the goal was regular residency of bishops and serious attention to leadership. The Church had been under royal pressure for a century to eliminate absenteeism, and further progress was made in the late sixteenth and early seventeenth centuries. Spanish bishops would subsequently be known for their exemplary personal qualities if not for their wisdom, and this was one achievement of the sixteenth-century reformation.

All these reforms were not necessarily instituted as soon as the Council of Trent ended in 1563. Though some had already been underway in Spain, others were not begun until the 1580s and did not produce results until some time afterward. Though it is impossible to measure quantitatively, there is little doubt that the Catholic Reformation was ecclesiastically successful in Spain, despite the decline in vigor and creativity that set in two or three generations later. It reorganized much of the Church and produced a more serious and attentive clergy than before.

At the same time, it is important to point out the difficulty of separating some of the influences of the Counter-Reformation from the intensification of religion that had already begun in Spain during the late fifteenth and early sixteenth centuries. In many ways the latter had produced the former, so that new accents in Counter-Reformation religiosity were merely the continuation of trends that had started two generations or more earlier. One of the most pronounced new expressions was the greatly increased emphasis on Christ, the crucifix, and the

Passion in general. Though this had begun perhaps a hundred years earlier, there was a major upsurge in new devotions to Christ and the Passion as the Counter-Reformation reforms advanced in the last years of the sixteenth century. This was assiduously propagated by the Franciscans, by far the most numerous monastic order in the Spanish countryside. Mariolatry remained strong, but now much more frequently stressed representations of Mary's role in the Passion of Christ. Moreover, new brotherhoods of flagellants, who scourged themselves in imitation of the sufferings of Christ, grew in number during the 1570s and 80s, after having begun to expand in Spain earlier in the century. Thus the intensified religiosity of the Counter-Reformation and Baroque periods became increasingly vivid and dramatic, as common people acted out the sufferings of Christ and Mary in frequent processions.

This took the form of corporate and communal expressions of religious and social concern, as entire occupation groups and neighborhoods, or sometimes whole villages and towns, participated together in spiritual and religio-social activities. There seems little doubt that the many thousands of local confraternities and other religious groups served as an important bond of unity and cohesion for Spanish society in the severe trials that began to afflict it from the 1590s on.

Incredulity of a fundamental sort did occasionally exist in Spain, as Inquisition records reveal, but was even more uncommon than in other Christian countries. Much more frequent was a certain skepticism about miracles and visions, so that by the late sixteenth century it had become necessary to document carefully any new religious happening presented as an article of reverence. Some fundamental moral precepts proved difficult to establish, as well. Records indicate, for example, that fornication between unmarried consenting adults was widely accepted and even considered unsinful during the sixteenth century, though possibly less so by the succeeding period.

One secular cult that survived the reproof of the Catholic Reformation was the popular devotion to the spectacle of bullfighting. Even in this period, the activity seemed barbarous and un-Christian to other Europeans. The papacy attempted to prohibit Spanish bullfights in 1567, but after vigorous protests combined with defiance, including strong representations from the crown, relented in 1575, withdrawing the ban except for holy days.

The Catholic Reformation, like all major reforms in the Church, engendered significant religious orders to undertake or assist with its tasks. The most important was the Society of Jesus. The religious thought of its founder, the ex-soldier San Ignacio de Loyola, was rooted not in Hispanic orthodoxy alone but also in the introspective trends of sixteenth-century Basque religiosity, which differed somewhat from that of most of Spain. He was also influenced by the methodic, systematized spirituality of the *Devotio moderna* as practiced in the peninsula especially by the monks of Montserrat in Catalonia. The Jesuit order became, as is well known, the sword arm of allegiance to the papacy, emphasizing religious teaching, the struggle against Protestantism, and proselytizing among non-Christians. Its organizational form was original, for Jesuits were neither tied to monasteries (as were monks) nor required to live in communities (as were friars). They became the prototype for the modern activist order, for their fourth vow to the pope placed them in papal service for missions anywhere, and the spiritual discipline of Loyola's famous *Exercises* was intended to enable them to carry the discipline of the community with them as individuals. Others of the new orders stressed practical religious work and charitable activity. The most notable in this regard was the Hospitalarios de San Juan de Dios, but some of the older orders also moved in the same direction.

Another important new feature of the Catholic Reformation was the growth of the "Discalced" movement among a number of the major orders. The term means literally "shoeless" and referred to special sandal-clad groups of monks and nuns who emphasized a reformation of piety, austerity, prayer, and asceticism. The Discalced orders were intimately associated with the growth of the mystical movement in Spanish religion and culture between 1570 and 1630. Medieval mysticism had awakened comparatively few echoes in the ruder spiritual life of the Spanish kingdoms, but the great mystics of late sixteenth-century Spain took their place in the very front ranks. Such poets and spiritual leaders as San Juan de la Cruz and the altogether remarkable Santa Teresa de Jesús stand among the greatest figures of Spanish culture.

The repression of outside ideas that reigned in the 1560s and 1570s was eventually eased after the more moderate Cardinal Quiroga became inquisitor general in 1577. During the last two decades of the century there was greater liberty for a more critical vein of scholarship, and many of the new foreign scientific concepts were accepted and taught in the Spanish schools. Copernican doctrine, for example, was well established at Salamanca, the queen of Spanish universities, by the 1590s.

At that point the neoscholastic revival was at its height at Salamanca and other schools. The general expansion of education, both religious and secular, reached a peak that would not be equaled until some time in the nineteenth century. The Golden Age of Spanish literature and the arts was also nearing its height. It is doubtless true that the preponderance of religious themes and motifs in the art of the Golden Age was due in part to the wealth of sectors of the Church and of lay religious organizations able to commission much of the work done, yet the influence of secular patrons often differed only in degree. The masterpieces of Spanish secular culture clearly revealed in nearly all cases their association with the Catholic Reformation, reflecting a sense of human sin, themes of moral psychology, and frequent expressions of mysticism. Approximately one-third of all theatrical works of sixteenth- and seventeenth-century Spain, for example, can be classified as religious in content. This offers an interesting comparison with the exiguous religious drama of Elizabethan and Jacobean, not to speak of Restoration, England. Never in the history of the West has the culture and art of a people been so thoroughly identified with its religion.

THE SEVENTEENTH-CENTURY DECLINE

The whole problem of the seventeenth-century Spanish decline, or decadence, has become quite controversial in twentieth-century scholarship. Patriotic Spanish commentators insist that there was no decline except for the demographic debacle induced by plague. What happened, they say, was that Spain simply failed to change and develop as rapidly as the northwest European powers, leaving her extremely vulnerable by mid-century. One noted foreign scholar has argued, conversely, that the general concept of decline is exaggerated because domestic Spain had never really risen or developed to the heights claimed.

There has been a definite tendency to exaggerate the extent of the decline and in some cases to misdefine its character. The domestic economy of sixteenth-century Castile was never especially well-developed, even by comparative standards, but it nonetheless began to shrivel in the 1580s and 90s and declined further after 1600. The demographic drop commenced about the same time, and in fact the two are closely related. Whereas Spain as a whole may have had a population of nearly 10 million in the mid-sixteenth century, this had shrunk by at least one-third by the late 1650s. A devastating series of epidemics in the larger cities caused much of this, exacerbated by almost constant warfare, emigration to the colonies, and declining economic opportunity that encouraged celibacy and fewer families.

The sense of *desengaño*—disillusionment or disenchantment—became increasingly common in Spanish society by the second quarter of the seventeenth century. As late as 1619 one patriotic commentator could write that the events of modern times made clearly manifest that the role and identity of Spaniards was as that of the Hebrews of old, the chosen of God, but this was no longer generally believed by the 1640s. Probably the first major jolt had been the disaster which befell the Armada in 1588, and the series of plagues and foreign disasters that followed in the next fifty years shook the foundations of the messianic Spanish ideology. The cultural symbol for this malaise was of the course the venerable figure of Don Quijote, who, finally disabused of his grandiose illusions based on cultural romanticism and excessive ambition, reconciled himself with reality and died a repentant Christian death.

Spanish Catholicism also declined in the sense that it lost not so much its dedication as its energy and creative capacity. Related to this was the opposite development of a marked growth in the numbers of the clergy, of whom more apparently became less with regard to achievement. There was no precise census of the clergy during the seventeenth century, but in 1591 in Castile there were approximately 75,000 (20,697 monks, 20,369 nuns, and 33,087 secular clergy, of whom only about 13,000 were parish priests). Assuming the same percentage of clergy (about 1.2 percent) in the population of the rest of Spain, this would make a grand total of approximately 91,000. When the next complete national census was taken in 1747, it revealed a clergy much more numerous (140,000) in a smaller population. Presumably most of this proportionate increase came in the seventeenth century, yet it is doubtful that even at the low point of the demographic debacle in the 1660s and 70s the clergy quite made up the 3 percent of the population often cited in general histories.

The reason for this relative population explosion in the ranks of the clergy lay in the predominant Spanish social mentality in the face of drastically declining economic opportunity. The concern with status and honor common to all the aristocratic societies of the European old regime became even more obsessive in Spain than elsewhere. A history of conquest and expansion deflected common ambition from work and economic application into the pursuit of rank and status. It also led to the extremes of pride and touchiness for which the Spanish of that period were infamous both at home and abroad,—a pride that had led the more severe Spanish moralists to warn that a society so thoroughly wedded to pride and honor was in fact the very opposite of a truly Christian society. The seventeenth-century aristocrat who admonished his son to be "more honorable and less Christian" was not atypical. Emphasis on status and lineage rather than virtue was not a uniquely Spanish trait, but nowhere was it more widespread.

This situation was only exacerbated by the great expansion of formal education. The dynamics of the system certainly belied the notion that extensive nominal education is the main precondition to societal progress. That of Spain became ever more oriented toward the mere attainment and maintenance of status. Diplomas were basically licenses in law or theology and philosophy. They gave entrée to the bureaucracy, whose ranks in both Church and state were swelled with diplomates. Such an educational system did nothing to encourage keen, inquiring minds, productive new approaches, or a more efficient elite. Curricula sank into a routine that soon became backward by contemporary European standards. At the same time, leading universities maintained a placement service for clerical and bureaucratic positions that, in terms of sustained pressure on behalf of graduates, probably outdid the efforts of later twentieth-century American institutions. The educated were increasingly unconcerned with practical problems or creative service. On their professional level, they aped the nonproductive status-security fixation of the nobility. This involution of Spanish society, general resistance to the analytic dimension, stress on the medieval intellectual disciplines in opposition to change, and prizing of personalism rather than objective achievement converged to slow the society's cultural development and for a period in the second half of the century to block it altogether.

The swollen clergy thus became an institution of middle-class bureaucracy. The new emphasis on education coming out of the Catholic Reformation made diplomates desirable to the Church, while in a declining economy only the Church could offer "honorable" careers bearing status and security. Such padding of the ranks of the clergy diluted spiritual zeal, moral tone, and intellectual quality. There remained a saving remnant of truly devout and dedicated priests, and impressive overseas missionary work was still done by several orders, but this compared poorly with the achievements of the preceding century. Bloating of the ranks of the clergy was accompanied by a marked increase in religious festival days, depending on locality. If Sundays are included, the number of religious festival days for the calendar passed one hundred and in some areas reached nearly one hundred fifty.

With the clergy as greatly afflicted by the mania for honor and status as the rest of society, the obsession with *limpieza de sangre* (purity of blood) had soon entered their ranks. This concern to exclude descendants of Muslims and Jews from membership in all manner of societies, corporations, guilds, and other organizations had grown in Spanish society through the sixteenth century and reached its peak in the seventeenth. Around the year 1500 many of the most distinguished figures in Castilian church leadership were sons of Conversos and in a few cases Conversos themselves. By the 1540s they were being excluded from the universities, and later from parts of the clergy as well. The Church as a whole did not recognize the issue of *limpieza de sangre* as valid, since it was manifestly contrary to Christian principle, but many individual units of the Church took a different attitude. By the begining of the seventeenth century about half the cathedral churches of Spain had adopted such statutes regarding their resident clergy, as had many of the orders.

Nominal Catholic unity was finally made fully complete in the years 1609–12, with the expulsion of the last large blocs of Morisco population who had never genuinely been converted to Christianity. Since 1499, a whole series of short-lived evangelistic enterprises had been launched to convert the Moriscos. The Inquisition treated them relatively gently, and in 1571 accepted a general fine for the Valencian Moriscos rather than subjecting them to regular prosecution. In turn, however, the Islamic principle of *taqiyya* (precaution) permitted them to feign public acceptance, even though the crypto-Islamic identity of the Moriscos was known to all. Generally poor peasants and artisans, they nonetheless maintained clandestine schools, religious teaching, and services as best they could, and eventually even operated several clandestine printing presses. The great revolt of the Granadan Moriscos in 1568–71 brought dispersal of one of the largest communities, but several large ones remained in the east. Relations were maintained by some with Turkish spies and North African pirates. When the first, for long the only major, respite in the dynastic wars of empire finally came in 1609, the state seized the opportunity to deport approximately 300,000 remaining nonassimilated Moriscos.

Thus complete outward unity was achieved; yet internal conflict within the clergy probably became more intense during much of the century. Rivalries between orders, struggles for preferment, appointment, and jurisdiction, the administration or use of Church properties and income—all provoked considerable dispute. Wealthier orders like the Benedictines tended to identify with the aristocrats, whereas Franciscans were closer to the common people. The growth of the Jesuit order provoked considerable hostility. Animosity toward hierarchs was keenly felt, and clerics in university appointments engaged in bitter contests for chairs, conflicts which sometimes involved extremes of slander and distortion. There were even vendettas over the style of clerical clothing.

The ultimate authority continued to be neither the archbishop of Toledo nor the pope, but the crown. It retained the *regium exequator*, dating from the fourteenth century, that enabled it to control all papal communications. The majority of church spokesmen in Spain sided with the crown's authority even in disputes with the papacy, and during the first half of the seventeenth century a considerable number of regalist treatises were written by both lay and clerical Spanish jurists. In 1617 Felipe III protested the fact that the papacy had placed several of these on the Index. Disputes with the papacy over international politics that had been so common in the previous century continued, and the controversies over money increased. In addition, there were extended conflicts between leading Spanish prelates and papal nuncios, though at the same time, an ultramontane party existed within the Spanish Church. When, after the accession of Felipe IV, a special Junta de Reformación was established, it made an effort to renew the post-Tridentine reforms of the 1580s and 90s, which had never been fully consummated.

As the general decline deepened, it reenforced an increasingly morbid strain in Spanish religiosity which dwelt ever more on the *via crucis*. What foreigners used sometimes to perceive as the Spanish "cult of death" first grew to importance during the seventeenth century. In a work called *Libro de las cinco excelencias del español*, published by a Navarrese friar in 1629, the Spanish ideology was reaffirmed once more in terms of martyrdom. Its author repeated the frequent assertion that Spain inherited the mantle of the ancient Hebrews as a Chosen People, and indeed surpassed them because Spain had been given the mission of unifying mankind and converting distant continents. If the high cost of such a universal mission meant poverty and depopulation for Spain, the greater wealth and denser population of other European countries should not be envied; rather, "let them envy our depopulation, which we suffer in imitation of the work of the Apostles and the disciples of Christ."[3]

Somewhat paradoxically, the arts in general continued to flourish, enjoying the momentum of the previous century and supported by the patronage of a society directed toward court, aristocracy, and Church. The last great figures of Baroque literature, Baltasar Gracián and Pedro Calderón la Barca, active especially in the middle years of the century, reveal a different attitude from some of their predecessors. Gracián was the most enigmatic of Catholic moralists. His major works deal with the problems of achievement and self-realization in a world of shrinking opportunities, where true heroism is difficult to find. Similarly, Calderón's attitude is more critical and realistic and somewhat more ambiguous than that of earlier Spanish playwrights. After taking orders in 1651, he devoted himself primarily to religious *autos sacramentales*.

After reaching its high-point around the beginning of the seventeenth century, Spanish education went into decline. Neoscholasticism hardened into a dry, formalistic mold. There was no further theological or philosophical growth among Spanish thinkers, who instead gained renown abroad for the casuistry of "probabilist" ethics. This doctrine held that, in judging the licitude of an act, it is permitted to follow the opinion

---

3. Quoted in Albert A. Sicroff, *Les controverses des statuts de "pureté de sang" en Espagne du XVe au XVIe siècle* (Paris, 1960), 291–94.

favoring freedom of action, provided that it is seriously probable according to religious truth, even though a contrary opinion is even more probable. Such ethical casuistry was developed in the 1570s and flourished during the first half of the seventeenth century, particularly in the voluminous writing of the monk Antonio de Escobar y Mendoza, chief theorist of "laxism." By the 1650s, however, casuistic ethics were under attack and began to fall into disfavor.

The most popular religious writer of the entire period was probably the Madrid Jesuit Juan Eusebio Nieremberg. His general spiritual treatises and monographs, especially the *Diferencia entre lo temporal y lo eterno y crisol de desengaños* (1640), sold widely. Though his work possessed neither the literary quality nor the spiritual depth of such leading devotional writers of the Golden Age as Luis de Granada (who was widely read even in several Protestant countries), most devout and literate Spaniards read at least one "Eusebio," as his works were informally referred to.

In the history of ideas, the most notable Spanish religious figure of the late seventeenth century was Miguel Molinos, the principal exponent of what was called Quietism. In 1675 Molinos, who lived and worked in Rome, published a *Guía espiritual* that recommended, for those able to achieve it, a spiritual life of almost total contemplation, one that would eliminate the senses and achieve perfect internal peace. This was a possible development of Spanish Illuminism and certain aspects of mysticism and was denounced by the Papal Inquisition in 1685 as a subjectivist heresy. Molinos's work and following were suppressed.

There were new theological accents in popular religiosity during the seventeenth century, in line with post-Tridentine doctrine, that placed greater stress than before on purgatory and the function of penance. This was nonetheless secondary to further intensification of Mariolatry, which reached a new peak. The doctrine of the Immaculate Conception was in fact taken up as a national cause and successfully argued by the crown's representatives in Rome, though it would not be raised to absolute dogma for two centuries more. The proliferation of new confraternities, brotherhoods, and local congregations named for some aspect or function of the Virgin ("Nuestra Señora de . . .", "María Purísima de . . .") became a common feature of this century and the one following.

It wrought a striking change in girls' names, as Bennassar has noted:

> In the sixteenth century, women's given names in Spain were like those in other Christian countries. By the eighteenth century, however, a mutation had taken place: now the names almost always referred to some sanctuary of the Virgin. They have become

(María *del*, or *de la*, or *de los*) Incarnación, Visitación, Concep-
ción, Esperanza, Angustias, Dolores, Amparo, Rocío, Natividad,
Soledad, Maravillas, Nieves, Candelas, Estrella, Pilar, Montserrat,
and so on, given names that are obviously untranslatable. Again we
have a specifically Spanish characteristic: no other country of western Europe could produce such a list of given names.[4]

The grim years of the 1640s and 50s, a time of military and demographic disaster, accentuated key modes of religious expression. A multitude of new shrines and chapels were established in Castile during these
decades, and considerable effort seems to have been made to restore
older churches and monasteries in order to renew popular devotion and
seek divine assistance. The sufferings of Spain only intensified the common emphasis on the *via crucis* as the dominant motif in popular
theology.

Such times accentuated the hypertrophy of the religious vocation, and
the leading social historian of this period stresses the relative popularity
of the clergy in Spanish society. There does seem to have been, if
anything, less anticlerical feeling than in earlier times. Though the reforms of the fifteenth and sixteenth centuries had been at best only
partially successful and avarice, ignorance, and concubinage were still
fairly endemic, the clergy were recognized for their role in education and
especially in charity. As the number of destitute and vagabonds increased, the Church provided the main source of relief, primarily of the
sopa boba, simple soup kitchen, variety. In addition to schools and
simple charity, however, the Church also maintained a good share of the
hospitals, asylums, and special care centers of the land. In the devastating
plagues that struck down hundreds of thousands of Spaniards during the
first half of the century, the clergy almost alone, save for family members,
was responsible for caring for the stricken. While some of the more
serious orders of the previous century, such as Jeronymites and Reformed Carmelites, did not prosper, others in the newer orders added
their numbers to those of the parish priests who ministered to the
parochially disadvantaged south.

Charity was not merely a necessary feature of a society functioning
within a shrinking economy that generated hordes of beggars; it was
positively encouraged by Spanish theology. During the preceding century, the new west European tendency toward a "modern" system of
state-organized charity and poor relief, combined with work, was categorically resisted by prominent Spanish religious spokesmen. Private

---

4. Bartolomé Bennassar, *The Spanish Character* (Berkeley, 1979), 89.

charity was deemed indispensable and was liberally practiced without thought of more productive alternatives.

The mass charity-and-begging contrasted with the extreme ostentation and conspicuous consumption that were also characteristic of classical Spanish society. The amount spent on dress and display by the wealthy was generally reckoned to be proportionately the highest in Europe. The common denominator for ostentatious and impoverished alike was probably an inordinate love of spectacle, which was cultivated to a greater degree in Spain than anywhere else. Secular spectacle was led by court, theater, and bullfight; religious spectacle centered on processions and major festivals, particularly of Holy Week and Corpus Christi, and the now increasingly infrequent autos-de-fe.

The common picture of seventeenth-century Spain is of a flight from life or at least serious work, accompanied by morbid fixations and an increase in superstition, wrapped in exaggerated formalism, ritualism, and gross hypocrisy. All these tendencies certainly existed, though they were hardly confined to the seventeenth century. Part of what was seen by foreigners as unparalled social hypocrisy was simply the standard contradictions of the culture. Spanish sexual mores in certain respects had always been rather relaxed. Francis Willughby, an English traveler in 1664, complained of "the multitude of whores" and concluded of Spaniards that "for fornication and impurity they are the worst of all nations, at least in Europe."[5] This was a frequent reaction of foreign travelers.

Moreover, there probably was more indulgence in vice on the part of both the upper and lower classes in the seventeenth-century cities, high aristocrats living in self-indulgence, a large lower-class underworld battening off crime and prostitution. The rate of violence in a place like Madrid was very high, and there is some documentation for a more cynical attitude toward common morality. As Henry Kamen has shown, certain clerical guidelines on abortion were remarkably tolerant. Marriage was more often mocked than in the sixteenth century, while the *galán de monjas* (wooer of nuns) became a standard figure in the erotic typology of the period. *Ensalmadores* (casters of spells) and paganistic *saludadores* or *curanderos* (healers) had always existed in Spanish Christian society. Whether they really increased in number during the seventeenth century or were simply more frequently noticed by a more literate society is difficult to say.

For several centuries, the most striking verbal contradiction in the highly sacralized Spanish culture was its exaggerated propensity for sac-

---

5. Quoted in Henry Kamen, *Spain in the Later Seventeenth Century, 1665–1700* (London, 1980), 296.

rilege and blasphemy, carried to a greater extreme in Castilian than in any other western language. This has probably been the natural human counterpart to the almost absolute degree of religious identity established.

If all these negative traits increased in tendency or proportion during the era of decline, this may have been the result of a certain cynicism or demoralization that accompanied the disillusionment with practical affairs. It should be recognized, however, that decadent attitudes most emphatically did not carry the day, win formal acceptance, or establish a new world view. New negative tonalities were introduced and certain vices probably became more pronounced, but the general social and religious culture was little altered thereby. In Spanish religious practice, deviation in some details had never meant basic defection.

Among the lower classes, religious sensibility seems to have been increased by the "popular mission" movement, particularly in the two Castiles and Andalusia. This movement was almost exclusively the work of the Jesuits, the Franciscans, and the Capuchins and consisted of local evangelistic campaigns in villages and small cities by small groups of religious. They preached an intense and graphic brand of hellfire-and-damnation revivalism, illustrated by vivid paintings and sketches of the nether regions. Apparently the effect of their visits was great, if somewhat temporary, and brought many into more direct confrontation with religious choice.

Whatever the reality of some social practices, the tone of public moralizing increased. Intermittent closing of the theaters in Madrid and other large cities led to a long period of prohibition in the latter part of the century, and there was a new movement to close up brothels altogether. The quality of Spanish religiosity may have stagnated and indeed deteriorated, but its formal expression tended to become even more intense.

Spanish Tradition and Western Culture

Those who hold to the Weber thesis concerning the relation between Protestantism and capitalism contend that a strongly Catholic country like Spain was inevitably incapable of carrying out drastic transformation of its economic structure and sociocultural framework in the seventeenth century. This is doubtless true, though not because of Spain's Catholicism alone. Catholic France, where probably more people were killed in the name of Catholicism than in Spain during the sixteenth century, was not similarly handicapped. It became one of the economic leaders of the world in the seventeenth century, placing Spain in a thoroughly dependent position. Catholic Belgium would later be the only country to industrialize as rapidly as England. The obstacles to new development in

Spain did not lie in the religion as such but in the Spanish culture in which that religion was embedded.

No other people except the Portuguese (who generally shared the Spanish experience) so thoroughly identified themselves with the medieval western culture. Spanish religiosity in turn was thoroughly enmeshed in the psychology, values, and social structure of that culture. Though the Spanish Golden Age did generate some new perspectives and opportunities, they were relinquished in favor of further elaboration and transmission of the main features of cultural tradition. The Spanish achievement in itself was to have carried that traditional medieval culture to its highest peak, introducing significant new features in the process.

For northwestern Europe, however, the seventeenth century marked the beginning of a drastic transformation of the traditional western culture. Only those societies which had already started to transform part of that culture with other ideas and values were in a position to achieve rapid new social and economic development. For Spain, this possibility was precluded not so much by Catholicism as by the option of the Spanish state and society to reject the partial opportunities opened to them in the sixteenth century and cling obsessively to tradition and the increasingly hollow formalism that it involved. When this attitude began to change, Spain was well over a hundred years behind northwest Europe, culturally as well as economically.

Well into the twentieth century, Spanish traditionalists would argue that from a spiritual and moral point of view the Spanish option had been correct, no matter how weak it left the state and the economy. Yet any serious analysis of the medieval tradition raises doubt on this score. Western culture had been constantly changing for hundreds of years, increasingly emphasizing rational and practical thought and restlessly generating new technologies. Some of these changes had made the Great Reconquest and the historical creation of Spain possible in the first place. Spanish traditionalism in fact tried to freeze a certain phase and national form of the culture, not quite the same thing as following the full western tradition. In the increasingly dynamic society and culture of early modern western Europe, such an enterprise was foredoomed.

TRADITION AND REFORM: THE EIGHTEENTH CENTURY

The eighteenth century, the final period of the Old Regime and of the traditional culture in Spain, is usually seen as an era of reform and of enlightened despotism. There is little reason to quarrel with this general appraisal, though religion and the Church underwent less change than did government administration and some other secular institutions. From the

Catholic point of view, the century was distinct and significant because it was the first era in Spanish history in which cultural change developed largely outside the framework of religious thought and the educated clergy. Enlightenment thought in Spain was almost never anti-Catholic, and reform policy was always religiously orthodox, but the new culture was critical, rationalist, and primarily secular. It marked the beginning of the transition to modern liberalism and capitalism in Spain, and ulti-mately, one of its goals was the transformation and reduction of the role of the clergy in national life. Traditional forms of government and social hierarchy remained largely intact, yet the attitudes of the elite and the content of the culture began to change significantly.

The introduction of new rationalist philosophy and a renewed interest in mathematics and natural science had begun in the 1680s. Early En-lightenment thought, imported primarily though not exclusively from France, slowly expanded during the first half of the new century. Diffu-sion of science and critical culture was led by the Galician Benedictine, Benito Jerónimo Feijóo, known to all students of Spanish didactic litera-ture, who played a major role in the transmission of critical attitudes during the first half of the century. Only in the last third of the century did Enlightenment culture broadly penetrate the educated classes of Spain, and then primarily in its more practical and philosophically neutral aspects. Freethinking and anti-Christian attitudes were scarcely voiced until the very end of the century. The critical Enlightenment of the eighteenth-century in Spain, therefore, took place nominally within the framework of Catholic culture, and attempted to reform administration without introducing any new religious or ideological alternatives per se.

Bourbon Regalism in Spain

The primary goal of the new Bourbon dynasty in Church affairs was to implement a policy of "regalism" or extension of royal authority. This was scarcely novel in theory, since such ambitions on the part of the Spanish government went all the way back to the Visigothic monarchy. Ever since the establishment of papal organization and jurisdiction in the eleventh century, Spanish rulers had sought to reduce Rome's authority in everything but theological matters and to increase their own once more. The Habsburg crown of the sixteenth and seventeenth centuries had pursued a regalist program of coresponsibility, working strenuously for internal reform of the Church while striving to defend and expand the faith throughout the world. By contrast, eighteenth-century regalism was partly of French inspiration and was both narrower and in some respects more radical. It was not primarily interested in religious reform, but concentrated on political and financial domination of Church activities and the replacement of papal by royal authority as much as possible.

After the decadent Carlos II (1665–1700), last of the Habsburg rulers, had died without issue, the new century began with a disastrous Succession War between rival candidates from the French Bourbon and Austrian Habsburg dynasties. At the end, the victorious new French Bourbon prince who became Felipe V of Spain (1700–1746) had to preside over the loss of nearly all the remaining empire in Europe. Typically, both sides in the contest invoked the cause of religion. The papacy was eventually pressured by rival powers into recognizing the Habsburg claimant in 1709, leading to the crown's expulsion of the papal nuncio from Madrid and a break in diplomatic relations. All the while the clergy played an intensely active role in the struggle within Spain. Both the new king and the Austrian pretender were anathematized, the former by a minority, the latter by a majority, of the Church leadership. Diocesan funds were used to raise entire regiments of troops for the depleted Spanish forces, while the clergy literally took up arms on both sides, one Carmelite rising to the rank of temporary army general. To that extent, it seemed as though little had changed since the reconquest.

The Bourbon dynasty was able to establish a centralized monarchy over nearly all of Spain for the first time since the Visigoths. It also strove for equivalent jurisdiction over church appointments and finance. Full relations with the papacy were restored with the end of the Succession War but were interrupted again by political conflict in 1718–20 and again in 1736–37. A formal Concordat was negotiated in 1737 to try to resolve these issues but amounted to little more than a vague agreement to support the status quo. The main regalist breakthrough came with the conclusion of a second Concordat sixteen years later, in 1753, during an era of papal weakness. While the papacy reaffirmed its universal patronate over Church appointments, it granted to the Spanish crown the right of nomination, or de facto patronage, to nearly all the appointments and benefices of the Church in Spain and not merely to the high offices already under royal jurisdiction. The system that had existed only in the empire and in the kingdom of Granada was now established throughout the peninsula, and altogether about 50,000 ecclesiastical benefices came under royal control. In addition, financial contributions from Church income to the crown, which had been made in varying degrees for centuries, were now regularized. The papacy would in turn continue to receive regular income from the Spanish Church, and for the new concessions it was compensated at the cost of well over a million Roman escudos, capitalized at an annual rate of 3 percent.

The 1753 Concordat was hailed with jubilation by the crown, its ministers, and some Church leaders as marking a veritable revolution. Papal political influence and financial extractions were greatly reduced, leading the Marqués de la Enseñada, one of the chief ministers, to remark with considerable exaggeration but evident relish that it was a greater triumph to expel the Romans than the Moors. The papacy allowed itself to be convinced in part by arguments from the Spanish hierarchy that regalism would provide more attentive leadership and raise standards among the clergy, and in part by the expenditure of 174,000 escudos in bribes to various churchmen in Rome.

The reign of Carlos III (1759–88) marked the high point of regalism and reform. This ruler has a well-deserved reputation as a Spanish examplar of "enlightened despotism," yet it is important to understand what is meant by such a phrase when it refers to Spain. The enlightenment of Spanish reformers referred to technical, administrative, and economic plans primarily. None of the crown's ministers were freethinkers, and all considered themselves good Catholics. They did not challenge religious values or even central philosophical precepts save as they applied to certain practical matters.

Relations with the papacy in fact improved somewhat during this climactic reign of Spain's eighteenth-century development. The most drastic single step undertaken in religious policy was the expulsion of the Jesuit order from Spain and the empire in 1767, following similar measures undertaken by the crowns of France and Portugal. Hostility toward the Jesuits on the part of the state stemmed from their identity with the papacy and from their position of influence in education and society. In general, royal policy favored the diocesan clergy, because the latter staffed basic Church activities and was directly under royal control through terms of the Concordat. The orders were viewed much more critically as more independent of state authority and possibly tending toward ultramontanism, while the Jesuits were clearly the most independent and ultramontane of all. They were charged with defending obscurantism and obstructing the reform measures of the government, and with being a destructive moral influence because of their use of casuistry and laxism in moral teaching. The Jesuits had long been the elite order within the Church, and had excited envy and jealousy among other portions of the clergy for generations.

In 1771, four years after the expulsion of the Jesuits, the regalist autonomy of the Spanish Church was further expanded by papal authorization of the Tribunal de la Rota Española, an enlargement of the special ecclesiastical appeals court that had existed since 1529. Its judges would henceforth be appointed by the crown, and its jurisdiction was increased, giving the Spanish Church the greatest internal juridical autonomy in the Catholic world.[6]

Jansenism was the name given to the reformist party in both state and clergy, yet the term had very little to do with the actual religious orientation of seventeenth-century French Jansenists. What the Spanish Jansenists had in common with the earlier French religious movement was a critical and reformist attitude, insistence on rigor and sobriety, and hostility toward certain dominant established groups such as the Jesuits.

Carlos III was generally able to count on the support of reforming prelates during his reign, even though an opposition party of varying strength usually existed among part of the hierarchy. The most significant changes that took place within the Church itself had to do with the improvement and modernization of the seminaries. Seventeen new ones were founded during the century, and their curriculum was expanded beyond the rote memorizing of neoscholastic principles. A study of history, sciences, mathematics, and new standards of hermeneutics was added to the training of priests in some of the seminaries, just as the regular university system was being expanded and transformed.

The internal reform of the Church and clergy was not a major goal of government, so much as further administrative and economic change. Church wealth lay primarily in its large endowment of land, permanently "amortized" under mortmain, just as were most aristocratic estates. Though the Church held only a little more than 15 percent of the land of Spain, one census indicated that its holdings were responsible for nearly 25 percent of national agrarian production and income. This indicated that Church lands were normally more productive than the average. During the reign of Carlos III, the state eventually forbade major new endowments and amortization of land to the Church without government approval. Royal ministers regularly devised further plans for opening more sections of Church income to taxation, and even for permanent "disamortization"—that is, indemnified confiscation—of some of the smaller categories of Church wealth.

In this respect, the policies of the final phase of the Old Regime foreshadowed major aspects of liberal anticlericalism and the assault on Church properties during the century that was to follow. Compared with the rather significant expropriations that took place in certain parts of Catholic Europe during the later eighteenth century, no major confiscations were carried out in Spain until the time of the French Revolutionary

---

6. The Rota Española continued to function until 1932, when it was closed by the papacy after the separation of Church and state, which eliminated the binding effect of some of its decisions. It was subsequently restored under the Franco regime in 1947.

and Napoleonic wars at the very close of the period. Yet amid the full institutional norms and religious culture of the Old Regime, the first plans were made for a systematic use of central government power to effect economic change and reduce the economic basis of ecclesiastical institutions.

Popular Religiosity

Eighteenth-century Spain looks rather different from the point of view of popular religiosity. In this area there was general continuity with the Catholic reformation piety of the preceding age. The emphasis on popular evangelism and the religious conversion of nominal Catholics had already borne fruit in the increasing frequency and intensity of religious observance, to the extent that the seventeenth and eighteenth centuries together can be said to represent the apex of popular Spanish religiosity. Moreover, it may be that the eighteenth century represented the higher level of religious practice of the two. Norms of conduct were better observed by the clergy, and the intensity of devotion shown by the common people in general was equally great. Though works of charity were still important, the primary emphasis of popular religiosity in early modern Spain, in keeping with Tridentine precepts, lay on individual salvation. In early ages, Spanish people may have prayed for community protection or military victory, but seventeenth- and eighteenth-century piety was devoted to the saving of one's soul. Formal religious observance was probably near an all-time high, as was the practice of individual prayer. All the formal and external practices that made up Baroque Hispanic religiosity—the processions, religious festivals, and public ritual—continued. In this regard the eighteenth century was the last major period of traditional Spanish popular religiosity.

Yet by the very end of the century there were signs of change. In some cities, processions seemed to generate rather less enthusiasm than they had in earlier generations, and the full Baroque began to wane. The emphasis on the *via crucis* in popular theology declined, and religious expression tended to become more Marian in orientation and less Christ-centered. This more benign direction in religious devotion did not, however, become firmly established until the nineteenth century.

The Clergy in the Eighteenth Century

The eighteenth century is the first period for which we have reasonably reliable census data on the size of the clergy. Confusion has nonetheless arisen from the practice of including servants and assistants in the counting, as well as lay brothers and sisters in monasteries and other

TABLE 2.1
Numbers of Spanish Clergy in the Late Seventeenth Century

Year	Secular Clergy	Regular Clergy	Nuns	Total
1769	65,287	55,463	26,665	147,415
1787	59,396	52,300	25,365	137,061
1797	57,490	53,178	24,007	134,675

Source: Guía del estado eclesiástico seglar y regular de Espāna e Indias. . . . 1806, *cited in M. Revuelta González, S.J., Política religiosa de los liberales en el siglo XIX (Madrid, 1973), 36.*

personnel who had not taken full ecclesiastical vows. During succeeding generations, liberal publicists often used such misleading global statistics to exaggerate the number of actual clergy in traditional society. The most precise totals are presented in the accompanying table.

An early census of 1747 is more difficult to interpret, but indicated a total clergy in the neighborhood of 140,000. Ecclesiastical population appears to have grown slightly in mid-century and then declined rather steadily during the three concluding decades. During the last part of the century, the only growth registered occurred among the more active, less secluded male orders. Since the Spanish population grew rapidly during this period (especially during the middle years of the century), the clerical proportion was diminishing, from not quite 2 percent in 1747 to only 1.28 percent in 1797. Compared with other Catholic countries, a few of which had slightly higher proportions of clergy, this was not excessive. The notion of Spain as a particularly priest-ridden land, statistically correct in the mid-seventeenth century, no longer conformed to reality.

Major administrative and structural imbalances within the Church, stemming from the Middle Ages, far outlived the Counter-Reformation. Disparities of size and wealth between various dioceses, on the top level, and individual parishes, on the bottom, remained extreme. For centuries there had been a tendency for the more self-indulgent of the clergy, whether diocesan or in orders, to crowd into urban centers and cathedral chapters, leaving distant and poor rural parishes to look after themselves. The 1768 census revealed that there were approximately 2,500 more parishes than parish priests in Spain, even though more than a third of the entire diocesan clergy, or about 20,000 priests, were without benefices. Both the crown's ministers and reformers within the Church proposed to reduce the number of supernumerary urban priests and inactive monks and nuns, while increasing the number of parish priests and missionaries. They were pleased to find that the 1787 census revealed an increase of approximately 6 percent in parish priests, leaving less than 1,400 parishes without their own curate. (In fact, of course, some priests served more than one parish.)

The main animus of government reformers was directed against the orders, criticized by the spirit of the new age as unproductive and parasitical, monopolizers of landed endowments that should be opened to broader use. Membership in the orders in Spain, which had for a long time been disproportionately Franciscan, apparently declined more than 20 percent during the second half of the century. There seems little doubt that slow cultural change, and even more the growth of economic opportunity, were reducing the number of new candidates, and in proportion to the total population, shrinking them perhaps by half. The tendency toward atrophy in the regular clergy is further indicated by the fact that no new orders were introduced into Spain during this entire century, in contrast to their frequency in the preceding age. Perhaps the most positive achievement was somewhat greater consistency after mid-century in observing the rules of monastic life.

The reawakening of critical standards also provided some evidence that Erasmian approaches had never entirely died out within the Spanish clergy, however submerged. During the second half of the century the quality of Spanish prelates tended to improve, and they became increasingly vigorous in attempting to correct the kind of idiosyncratic belief and dubious ceremonialism among Spanish believers that was now generally agreed to be mere superstition. There is also evidence that greater attention was once more paid to preaching and that its quality improved somewhat.

One sign of new vitality was the renewal of missionary activity in Spanish America during the second half of the century. The Franciscans led the way in opening new territory in northern Mexico and the western stretches of North America, while the Jesuits continued major efforts in Paraguay and elsewhere until their expulsion.

Another notable achievement of the age was the most lengthy compilation of national Church history to be found anywhere in the world. In 1737 the Augustinian Enrique Flórez began publication of his *España sagrada*, which with the aid of collaborators and many decades of work eventually became a forty-nine volume compendium of Church history. The extent of materials was most impressive, though the presentation was uncritical in the extreme.

Yet when all is said and done, eighteenth-century change was rather more significant in terms of government attitude and policy than in the transformation of the Church and clergy. The quality and emphases of Spanish religious life, both clerical and lay, were altered only moderately, and the general character of Spanish religiosity changed comparatively little.

The main vehicle of popular evangelism, the mission movement, weakened significantly during the course of the century, and the general emphasis on externalism and ceremonialism was scarcely altered. Some effort was made on a regional basis to reduce the inordinate number of religious festivals, but no general reform was carried out. Despite an impressive formal reorganization of the curricula of universities and seminaries, there was no new religious thought of any consequence. To that extent, the eighteenth century was a sterile age, producing not a single theologian worth mentioning. Toward its close, even the benefits of the educational reform were placed in doubt as a new stagnation set in, accompanied by increasing indifference or indiscipline on the part of seminary students.

A reform movement of "enlightened" clergy began to crystallize in the higher and middle ecclesiastical ranks in the 1780s and 90s to seek correction of the perceived decadence of religious institutions and the inauthenticity of much of popular religiosity. Its goals were to improve the quality of Church appointments and ecclesiastical performance, reform education, discipline many of the orders, and introduce greater simplicity, directness, and doctrinal purity in common religious practice. The enlightened clergy were sometimes supported by reformist ministers in Madrid during the 1790s, though the latter were much more interested in administrative and economic domination than in spiritual reform.

More numerous than the enlightened reformers were the conservative critics among the clergy. They had become painfully aware of the lessened influence of the Church, and of increasing domination by the state that also weakened the Church's financial base through direct confiscation of properties. Though a minority of prelates and educated middle-rank clergy still pressed for enlightened reform, the majority grew more and more pessimistic about the Church's relation to the emerging culture and society of the liberal age. The persecution unleashed in the 1790s by the revolution in France raised their alarm to a peak of intensity.

The traditional Spanish ideology had gone into decline, discouraged by rationalist cultural and political criticism. It was nevertheless far from dead. All of Spain's wars during the century, fortunately mostly minor, had been preached from the pulpit as veritable crusades against the enemies of God. The sufferings of the Church during the revolutionary era abroad, together with its new problems in Spain, were seen as punishments for the sin of society as a whole. Just as in earlier times

Spanish Catholics had likened themselves to the original Chosen People or their decline to the sufferings of Christ, so by the 1790s did many Church spokesmen compare their situation to that of the ancient Jews during the age of the prophets. Amid the French revolutionary wars, they held that only through the return to traditional religious principles could Spain regain God's favor and its own national health.

3

The Challenge of Liberalism

THE INTRODUCTION of modern liberalism early in the nineteenth century produced the first major break in the history and institutional relationships of Spanish Catholicism since the eighth century, more than a mllennium before. Though that break was by no means a complete one, it altered fundamentally the character of Church-state relations, the economic basis of the Church, the relation between religion and society, and even certain aspects of religiosity in general.

LIBERALISM AND REACTION, 1810–33

The political term *liberal* is of Spanish origin, and of course traditionally referred to qualities of personal largesse and generosity before the Spanish initiated its application to politics early in the nineteenth century. Liberalism filled a long period of Spanish history, an entire century and more stretching to the 1930s, thus giving Spain one of the earliest and longest eras of classical liberal politics of any country in the world. At first, it would have seemed a dubious candidate for such a role. The French *Encyclopédie méthodique* had earlier dismissed the country as having made no contribution to modern progress whatever and as therefore presumably being poorly situated to participate in major modern movements for change.

The precocity of Spanish liberalism was the result first of all of historical accident in the form of French military invasion in 1808, which swept aside the regular Spanish government. Yet there is nothing anomalous in that, for a great many of the fundamental political changes all around the world in modern times have been provoked by war, invasion, defeat, or some combination thereof. In the Spanish case, however, there would have been no possibility of any immediate revolutionary change in the form of government had it not been for the Napoleonic overthrow of the Spanish ancien regime.

Spanish liberalism emerged in three stages. The early stage of preparation, involving the introduction and adoption of modern critical and reformist ideas from abroad, slowly developed during the course of the eighteenth century. By the 1770s and 1780s this involved the discovery of Spanish history and the definition of a kind of liberal tradition, resting on the role of medieval parliaments and earlier efforts to limit royal power. Such concepts paralleled certain reform policies of royal administration, and did not assume the goal of a direct change in regime until several small clandestine political circles were formed under the impact of the French Revolution in the 1790s. From that point on, liberal ideas based on an amalgam of French moderate or Girondist liberalism and Anglo-American constitutionalism spread rapidly among the middle- and upper-class elite. The third stage, involving the creation of a liberal regime, began with the French invasion and the first modern parliamentary elections in unoccupied Spain in 1810.

It is important to understand that the convening of a liberal parliament in Cádiz in that year was but one event in the great patriotic drama of the War of Independence (1808–14) against the Napoleonic empire. For long in the English-speaking world, this was referred to parochially as the Peninsular War, an appendage to a continental drama more than twenty years in duration. For Spaniards, it was by far the most important and traumatic event in all their history between the Succession War of 1700 and the great Civil War of 1936.

The War of Independence was the second great modern war of national liberation (after that of the United States), and in many ways the first modern guerrilla or people's war. It involved all strata of Spanish society in a great uprising against a foreign conqueror who not only proposed to implant a radical new French ruler (Napoleon's brother Joseph) but also attempted to introduce revolutionary institutional changes derived from the French upheaval. It immediately became a veritable holy war in the fullest sense of the term. After the succession struggle, the minor wars of the eighteenth century had merely been preached from pulpits by some of the clergy as holy wars; the independence struggle was waged by priests and monks in person with every possible means at their disposal. Religious leaders throughout the country revived the traditional Spanish ideology, calling upon the faithful to reaffirm Spain's divine calling and resist the French at whatever cost. Monks, increasingly spurned during the preceding century as parasitic and useless, played an especially prominent role, becoming prototypical leaders of a popular resistance militarily as well as spiritually. There was apparently not a single province in all of Spain that did not produce at least one guerrilla band led by a priest or monk. Nothing like this had ever happened before in any country occupied by Napoleonic forces.

The Cádiz Constitution

With Spain's legitimate ruler in French exile, the Regency Council nominally in charge of the resistance succumbed to pressure from patriotic and progressive opinion in the upper classes to convene elections as broadly as conditions permitted for a new modern parliamentary assembly that would convene in Cádiz. Though nominal terms of household suffrage were broad, the elections were not very representative because of the prevailing illiteracy and disturbed wartime conditions. Since much of Spain was under French occupation, about one-sixth of the deputies were *suplentes* or substitutes selected mainly from among exiled liberals in the unoccupied south. Spain's first modern parliament thus represented a sort of self-selected elite of middle- and upper-class liberals.

At the inception of formal Spanish liberalism, there were four different positions, broadly speaking, among the clergy. At the extreme left stood a very small minority of *afrancesado*, or pro-French, clergy. Some of them were extreme reformists and others mere opportunists. They supported the French Napoleonic regime in Spain in the interest of a modernized and rationalized Church system, and their numbers were exaggerated by the fact that part of the clergy in the main occupied areas had to render formal obedience to the new Bonapartist system. In most cases, this seems to have been much more a matter of political necessity than philosophical or spiritual conviction.

Considerably more numerous were the patriotic liberal clergy, fruit of the reform movement of the 1780s and 90s mentioned at the close of the preceding chapter. Altogether, approximately 90 of the 300 deputies at Cádiz—nearly one-third of the total—were ecclesiastics, most of them liberal, drawn mainly from the better-educated middle and upper ranks of the clergy. In most cases, their primary interest lay in the internal reform and purification of the Church, but they gave direct support to constitutional liberalism to achieve a freer, more enlightened and independent Spain. They judged that this would also provide the best opportunity for an orthodox but nonetheless reformed Catholic Church.

At the very same time, a strong majoritarian counter-tendency was forming through all ranks of the clergy. Since the 1790s many Catholic spokesmen had insisted ever more loudly that the integrity of the faith and of Spanish culture itself could be defended only by wholesale rejection of all the impious modern doctrines of pseudo-enlightenment that exalted human reason and rejected God. As the disasters of war, plague, and economic decline were followed by full-scale invasion, prophetic voices called on Spaniards to repent, unite, and return to the ways of their fathers. This conservative majority, weakly represented at Cádiz, would accept constitutional liberalism only insofar as it could be made fully compatible with traditional ecclesiastical structure and practice, a compromise not easily achieved.

To their right stood a new reactionary minority whose position was steadily becoming more intransigent. The ultrarightists, growing in number since the 1790s, insisted on radical re-Catholicization and total rejection of every aspect of liberalism, even at the risk of requiring an extension of traditional monarchist power, which theoretically was to be made fully congruent with Church authority.

The constitution produced by the Cádiz Cortes in 1812 reflected the views of the first full generation of Spanish liberals, lay and clerical. It proclaimed the principle of national sovereignty rather than monarchical right, abolished the special legal status and landed seigneurial rights of the nobility, established formal civil equality, placed legislative power in the hands of a broadly elected parliament, and limited the power of the crown.

The new constitution and the legislation that accompanied it were considerably more conservative in the sphere of religion. Though nearly all the liberals, including clerics, wanted to pursue properly enlightened reform of religious institutions, nearly all the lay liberals also considered themselves good Catholics. The constitution therefore began with the invocation of the Holy Trinity. It stipulated that "the religion of the Spanish nation is and will be perpetually the apostolic Roman Catholic, the only true faith. The nation protects it through wise and just laws and prohibits the exercise of any other." Toleration was thereby categorically excluded.

A series of ecclesiastical reform measures were legislated the same year. The most important was abolition of the Inquisition, followed by the reestablishment and reform of monasteries, which had been totally abolished in the French zone. A more distant goal was the increasingly coveted disamortization of Church properties. The real beginning in that regard had been made not so much by the reformers of Carlos III as by the war governments of his son, Carlos IV (1788–1808), who had gained papal approval for a whole series of fiscal and landed expropriations needed to help pay for the long series of wars beginning in 1793. It has been estimated that as much as one-sixth of Church lands had already been confiscated by the time that the War of Independence began. The Cádiz liberals hesitated to go much farther, specifying only a few minor categories, such as landed endowments of ruined and deserted monasteries, whose property would be auctioned by a special government agency created for that purpose.

While the Cortes met in Cádiz, the new political institutions which it was creating were not at first contested by the traditionalist clergy. What drew the ire of much of the hierarchy and of the conservative clergy was the abolition of the Holy Office and the consequent freedom of expression that followed. A new Spanish genre of radical journalism came quickly to the fore, producing demands for thoroughgoing reform and a certain amount of categorically anti-Christian writing. The spiritual unity of Spain had obviously vanished, and by 1813 most of the Church leadership was demanding that it be restored through the return of the Inquisition.

The journalism of nascent Spanish radicalism was met by a new formulation of traditionalist ideology. In the next few years a series of pamphlets and books restated the position of most of the Church leadership, invoking the historic Spanish ideology, the structure of ecclesiastical institutions, and the historically close association of the Church and a strong, traditional monarchy. This literature reached a climax in the frankly entitled *Apología del altar y el trono* (1818) by Rafael Vélez, subsequently archbishop of Santiago. The *Apología* created the basis of a new, now reactionary political theory that sacralized the powers of traditional monarchy in the interest of religion. Such an approach was not at all unprecedented, but it shifted the emphasis in the Church's relation to royal power, which Church leaders in the past had not striven to expand in such an unambiguous manner.

The First Fernandine Reaction, 1814–20

The "alliance of throne and altar" was common to much of post-Napoleonic Europe, but outside Spain it was usually accompanied by accommodation to technical aspects of the reform of the clergy and ecclesiastical administration initiated in the Napoleonic era. When Fernando VII returned from exile and overturned the new Spanish constitution in 1814, he rejected all reform and exercised a more absolute form of monarchy than his father had ever attempted before the invasion. The Inquisition was restored, all changes canceled, and the Jesuits brought back to Spain after nearly half a century. Scores, perhaps hundreds, of liberal clerics fled into exile, and the Holy Office busied itself not so much with morals and religion as with the prosecution of Masonry and the other secret societies that had become the organizational mainstay of liberalism. The clergy provided the strongest base of support for this reactionary neo-absolutism, which proved much more despotic than eighteenth-century Spanish monarchy, and totally unenlightened.

The full pomp and tone of traditional religiosity were restored, and the crown appointed a total of sixty new bishops, giving the hierarchy of the Church a particularly reactionary quality it had not possessed for about a hundred years. Neoabsolutism did not, however, bring theocracy, but rather the manipulation of the Church in the political interests of the cynical but wily Fernando. One of the most bizarre aspects of the reaction was the royal order for the reincorporation of exclaustrated monks secularized by the French administration, which had temporarily abolished the monasteries altogether. In the interim, many monks and friars had lost their sense of vocation. The reincorporation edict produced extreme internal conflict in many monasteries and was often simply impossible to carry out. Within twelve years (1808 to 1820), the population of the orders in Spain declined from about 46,500 to 33,500, losing by a fourth. In addition, the impact of the war and liberalism produced new social attitudes, at least in the cities. Church leaders decried the "relaxed" moral conditions, the many marital irregularities, and an apparent decline in the number of vocations for the secular clergy, as well.

The reaction lasted scarcely six years, because it was unable to govern on the narrow basis defined for itself. The wartime economic depression continued, intensified by the revolt of the American empire and the cost of futile attempts to subdue it. As usual, the crown relied on the Church as a major source of income, but ecclesiastical income had suffered equally, in some cases declining by more than 50 percent within twenty years. Inept neoabsolutism was suddenly brought to a halt by the first successful military pronunciamiento in Spanish history, one which restored the constitution in 1820.

The Constitutional Triennium, 1820–23

Fernando's reluctant but official acceptance of the new regime, together with the formation of a moderate new government, disarmed Church opposition. The papal nuncio announced the Church's indifference to questions of political regime and the hierarchy urged the faithful to respect the new government. Hundreds of liberal priests returned from prison or exile. Though not so numerous as at Cádiz, they nonetheless made up nearly 25 percent of the deputies of the new liberal parliament (54 of a total of 247) elected in 1820. The second abolition of the Inquisition was received by religious spokesmen with relative equanimity, and the new parliament named an ecclesiastical reform commission, composed primarily of Churchmen, to rationalize and reorganize the diocesan and parish structure of Spain.

Freedom of the press in 1820 brought an outpouring of radical literature pent up for six years, and also the beginning for the first time of a kind of radical anticlerical agitation which had not attended the original phase of liberalism. The Jesuits were expelled for the second time and their properties confiscated once more. Even more severe was the parliament's new *ley de monacales*, which abolished outright the strictly monastic orders and eliminated all convents with less than a minimum of residents, laying down new rules for the remainder. Within two years this resulted in the shutting down of more than half of all the convents of the male orders in Spain and the secularization of approximately 7,300 more regular clergy (over 20 percent of those remaining).

By 1821 a basic split between moderate and radical liberals had occurred, with the *exaltados*, as the latter were called, taking over parliament the following year. The truce with the Church began to break down, and as early as 1821 traditionalist priests were helping to organize small guerilla bands in the mountains of the northeast. Meanwhile, new financial legislation reduced by half the tithe payable to the Church, so that the liberal state would be able to collect, directly, more taxes of its own. This soon had the effect of reducing curates in some parishes to absolute penury. In 1822 the Cortes of the *exaltados* forbade further ordinations to the priesthood until a new ecclesiastical reform plan could be worked out by parliament itself. Presented early the following year, this provided for limiting the papacy to a merely advisory role in Church appointments, redrawing diocesan boundaries to coincide with the new provincial borders, abolishing the tithe altogether, and substituting for the tithe a special Church tax to pay the salaries of the clergy.

By that time a state of armed civil war existed in the northeast between the liberal state and traditionalist insurgents. A neoabsolutist Regency Council set up in the Catalan Pyrenees received strong support from disaffected clergy, especially monks and friars, who joined guerrilla bands in impressive numbers.

> Over 100 [clerics] perished in the royalist assault on the city of Cervera, while an ex-Trappist lay brother, Antonio Marañón, terrorized rural districts with a band of unruly troops exhorted into battle with the cry: "Long live the King and Religion. Death to the Constitution!" For every friar who took up arms, many more gave the royalist cause their support through preaching and propaganda. The Franciscans of Catalonia later boasted that they had pro-nounced "constant invectives against triumphant impiety" in the churches where they preached. . . .[1]

Even so, the Spanish civil war of 1822–23 was not one between Catholics and anticlericals, but technically between liberal and reactionary Catholics. Though the more radical *exaltados* rejected Christian

---

1. William Callahan, "The Origins of the Conservative Church in Spain, 1793–1823," *European Studies Review* 10:2 (April, 1979), 217.

identity altogether, the great majority of Spanish liberals were formal, and in many cases practicing, Catholics. At least one cardinal and four bishops, as well as hundreds of priests, directly supported the liberal cause. None of this prevented the liberal government from adopting a harsh policy toward opposition clerics. Eleven bishops were exiled and two imprisoned, along with numerous lesser clergy. The bishop of Vich was murdered along a roadside, and fifty-four other ecclesiastics were executed or simply murdered in the province of Barcelona alone, where all convents and monasteries were closed.

The Second Fernandine Reaction, 1823–33

The liberal triennium and the civil war were abruptly brought to an end by the invasion of a French army—the "hundred thousand sons of St. Louis"—in support of the royalists. Once Fernando VII was restored to full power, a repression much more extreme than that of 1814 was launched against the liberals. Its harshness shocked even the crown's ultraconservative French allies. In ecclesiastical affairs, almost all measures of the triennium were simply reversed: the full tithe was restored and old boundaries and jurisdictions were reestablished, monasteries reopened, and properties returned.

The liberal clergy were thoroughly suppressed, and from 1823, the reactionary traditionalist character of the Spanish Church was fully established, almost without internal opposition. Authoritarian royalism received the complete political and pastoral support of the clergy, who exhibited little in the way of Christian charity to the defeated liberals. For the next decade Spanish Catholicism was characterized by a narrow triumphalism of the most uncritical sort. Whereas some parts of Christian Europe, both Catholic and Protestant, were undergoing a partial renascence of Christian thought and culture and developing new pastoral activities or institutional models, the Spanish Church clung to an obscurantist traditionalism.

To some extent it went even beyond that, for the mid-1820s also gave birth to a new form of nineteenth-century radical right. The trauma of conflict with liberalism led the most extreme groups of clergy and Catholic laity, known as *apostólicos*, to demand an authoritarian theocracy— something which *sensu strictu* had never existed in Spanish history—in the name of purified tradition. For them, the alliance of throne and altar, customarily manipulated in the interest of D. Fernando's throne, was not necessarily enough. By 1825 the king had made clear that however much political use he might make of the Church, and that was most extensive, he had no intention of allowing the Church leadership or radical theocrats to intervene in state affairs, or even to administer those aspects of Church administration that had come under state purview since the mid-eighteenth century. Nor would he reestablish the Inquisition. In its place the crown permitted the Church to organize "Juntas de Fe" (Committees of Faith) in each province to safeguard religious purity. Their function was much more limited, but they did earn the distinction of prosecuting the Valencian Deist Cayetano Ripoll, whose execution in 1826 is often reported erroneously as that of the last victim of the Inquisition.

Though it has often been said of Fernando VII that he learned nothing about contemporary statecraft, he had in fact imbibed some knowledge of it. The experience of 1814–20 had shown that monarchy required more than complete executive power to govern effectively and endure. It had to have the support and service of capable elites and had to develop a minimal efficiency. Within a few years the crown was collaborating with moderates who could help it with economic policy and state administration. The crown preferred a more efficient state police to an Inquisition.

Consequently the government of Fernando VII was steadily outflanked to the right and in 1825 had to suppress a minor revolt by a strongly absolutist general. As the crown's semipragmatic drift toward the right-center increased, the extreme traditionalist faction registered growing disillusion. By 1827 it had begun to look primarily to the childless king's younger brother and heir, D. Carlos María Isidro, a narrow-minded, pious, and bigoted traditionalist. Thus the political following of Carlism started to form some six years before the political situation itself erupted into a new civil war.

This final decade of restored traditionalism was disillusioning for conservative Catholics in more than one respect. The impact of cultural change on the middle and upper classes and on the urban population in general was becoming painfully apparent. Though the faith was not and could not be formally challenged, the most important sectors of society no longer exhibited the unquestioning formal religiosity of the preceding century. The Church was experiencing a genuine crisis of new vocations, even though the mid-1820s registered the first increase in more than a quarter-century. Among the educated classes skepticism and extreme anticlericalism often lay just beneath the surface. In addition, the superficiality of the religious identity of many among the urban lower classes and the neglected areas of the south was becoming increasingly difficult to ignore.

No political response alone could remedy this emerging religious crisis. Some effort was made to revive the popular missions movement that had petered out during the preceding century, and some of the more serious secular clergy placed new emphasis on pastoral work. For approximately a decade, apologetic literature of diverse genres flourished. At the same time, among much of the clergy, there appeared to be a lack of genuine vitality that precluded creative endeavor. Reports from the papal nuncio complained of standard deficiencies: ignorance, sloth, avarice, and a lack of attentiveness.

The great reform of clerical morals attempted by reform movements for a millennium or more had never been completed, and yet a change in attitudes and behavior among a significant part of the clergy seems to have been underway by the second quarter of the century. Drunken and ill-behaved priests might sometimes still be the scandal of rural districts, but a challenged clergy threatened in its very existence did become more serious, prim, and circumspect in its behavior. The extent of concubinage seems to have declined enormously, at least by mid-century and probably earlier. The sensual, self-indulgent clergy of Spanish tradition was being transformed into the somber, puritanical clergy so familiar to later-nineteenth- and twentieth-century Spain.

RADICAL ANTICLERCIALISM
AND THE MODERATE COMPROMISE, 1833–74

Three attempts were necessary before liberal institutions finally replaced traditional monarchy in Spain. After the abortive experiences of 1810–14 and 1820–23, the third and decisive round began late in 1833 with the death of Fernando VII. This crafty, dissembling monarch had dismayed the ultratraditionalist followers of his younger brother by successfully fathering a healthy daughter, Isabel, three years earlier. The Salic law of succession in the Bourbon dynasty (never a traditional Spanish principle) was then abrogated to permit a female to inherit the throne, something that had not happened in Spain for almost 350 years. The succession was received with hostility by the supporters of Don Carlos, and the widowed queen mother and regent, María Cristina, seeking support elsewhere, appointed a new government of moderate liberals on behalf of the child Isabel II in 1834.

Carlism

A few traditionalist bands had formed in the hills right after the death of Fernando, and Don Carlos soon raised the banner of revolt. This initiated the First Carlist War (1833–40), longest and most destructive of the three major liberal/traditionalist civil wars of nineteenth-century Spain.

The papacy remained neutral, refusing to recognize either contender though continuing normal diplomatic relations with Madrid, while nearly all the Church hierarchy rendered obedience to the new government. In some regions, however, especially the non-Castilian and particularistic northeast, most of the local clergy came out on behalf of Don Carlos. The familiar figure of the priest or friar bearing arms against the "enemies of God" emerged once more.

Though Carlism received significant support in the conservative rural regions of Aragon and Catalonia, its principal base lay in the Basque provinces and Navarre. The sources of its appeal were multiple and complex and were not merely derived from a greater degree of religiosity. First of all, the Basque provinces and Navarre were the only parts of Spain to preserve a significant share of their medieval regional rights after the eighteenth-century centralization. Nonetheless, their exemptions and privileges had been under attack by regalists and centralizers for several generations just as those of the Church had been. Basques and Navarrese easily combined both sets of interests, conveniently identifying their regional rights with those of true religion. Since their local laws and institutions were more directly threatened by liberalism than were those of any other part of Spain, the defense of what they interpreted as legitimacy and tradition in the royal succession was all the more important. Even the liberal assault on traditional privilege might be perceived as a general threat, for it meant the leveling of institutions and rights and a change in economic values, the more menacing to a region where property was less ill-distributed than in other parts of Spain.

Paradoxically, the Basque region had been for nearly a thousand years the least Christianized part of the peninsula; its conversion had not been completed until the eleventh and twelfth centuries. Conversely, it may have been the part of Spain most deeply affected by the post-Tridentine Catholic Reformation, whose outstanding single figure was the Basque Loyola, founder of the Jesuit order. Though the lack of research in Basque religious history prohibits very firm conclusions, there is some evidence that reformed Catholicism was more effectively and fully integrated with the local way of life than in other parts of Spain. All Spanish peasants were Catholic; some accepted religion as a necessary form, but for Basques it was more deeply involved in their social and regional identity. A more conservative kind of anticlericalism not associated with liberal centralization would probably have aroused much less opposition.

For about five years, the small Carlist zone preserved the preexisting structure and norms of Catholic life. The pretender himself lent careful obedience to religious precepts, and was so attentive to religious counselors that his ambulatory government approached the norm of theocracy. The revivalist spirit was enhanced by the resumption of popular missions among Basque and Navarrese villages. Carlist territory became the haven of hundreds of Spanish monks and friars fleeing persecution and exclaustration in the central and southern provinces. For Carlists, the civil war was as much a *guerra divinal* as the struggle against Muslims or French agnostics, and the traditional bull of crusade, with its promise of indulgence, was preached to the faithful.

Violent Anticlericalism and Disamortization

Even though most of the clergy did not support Carlism directly, the new liberal regime was determined to move against what it interpreted as the reactionary structure and economic monopoly of the Church. Though moderate on most issues, the new Martínez de la Rosa government of 1834, like the preceding liberal regime of 1820–23, extended state power far beyond that of eighteenth-century regalism, proposing to introduce sweeping changes in religious institutions by fiat of the secular power. It first expropriated the income of certain vacant Church positions—with the careful exception of parish curates—and forbade the hierarchy to fill them, so that the revenue could be applied to the public debt. Any monastery from which a monk had deserted to join the Carlist ranks was ipso facto suppressed, while all novitiates for the remaining orders in Spain were immediately drafted as recruits for the *cristino* army (as the forces of the queen-regent were termed). A new Junta Eclesiástica, composed primarily of the most moderate bishops, was then established to study the reorganization of Church districts and ecclesiastical administration that had been debated off and on for a quarter-century.

Much more sinister was the outbreak of popular anticlerical violence in Madrid in July 1834, to a degree unprecedented in Spanish history. Anticlerical propagandists, apparently from the radical secret societies of Madrid (not necessarily Masonic) spread the rumor that the Jesuits and groups of friars had caused a recent cholera epidemic among the people by poisoning the public water supplies to punish the liberal capital for its impiety. Similar inventions were to become the stock-in-trade of vulgar anticlerical propaganda in modern Spain, which was similar in tone and psychology to the crude anti-Semitism elsewhere that routinely concocted ritual murders of children by Jews. The radical mob was becoming a standard feature of the larger cities of nineteenth-century Spain, and rioters attacked the Jesuit college in Madrid, killing a number of its inhabitants (including Juan Artigas, Spain's leading Arabist scholar), before going on to even more numerous murders at the monasteries of Franciscans, Carmelites, and Dominicans. Altogether somewhere between fifty and one hundred were slaughtered. The violent anticlericalism of modern Spain was born.

A process of radicalization undermined successive liberal administrations and produced severe factionalism that led to sharper conflict and ever more extreme policies. The new Toreno government of 1835 suppressed the Juntas de Fe that had replaced the Inquisition, again abolished the Jesuit order in Spain, and decreed the liquidation of all convents and monasteries housing fewer than twelve regular monks or nuns. During the months of July and August new anticlerical riots broke out in six cities. Two monasteries were burned at Zaragoza and twenty-nine friars murdered. In Barcelona, approximately twenty-five monasteries were attacked, some completely destroyed. Scores of monks—according to some accounts between one and two hundred—were killed in the Catalan capital.

A few days after the papal nuncio was withdrawn from Madrid in September 1835, a more radical government was formed under Juan Alvarez Mendizábal. The principal challange facing it was to organize resources for the struggle against Carlism, with war finance a key problem. The Mendizábal government decided to gain new revenue by seizing and selling the property of the religious orders. It soon proceeded to complete the process initiated under Carlos IV and then accelerated by the Bonaparte regime and the liberal triennium of 1820–23 by almost completely suppressing the male orders in Spain, opening the way to thoroughgoing *desamortización*—government confiscation and sale—of their properties. This virtually ended the life of these orders in Spain for the next fifteen years. Only a small number of regular clergy devoted to missionary or charity work were exempted. The female orders were less affected, though convents devoted exclusively to contemplation or housing fewer than twenty nuns were also suppressed.

As indicated in table 3.1, the number of monks and friars in Spain had been dropping rapidly, the main decline resulting from the dissolution of monasteries in the occupied zone during the War of Independence. In 1835 approximately 31,000 remained in holy orders. Of these, it is calculated that about 7,000 were placed among the secular clergy in diocesan

TABLE 3.1
Membership in Spanish
Monastic Orders, 1787–1835

1787	48,067
1797	49,365
1808	46,568
1820	33,546
1835	30,906

Source: *Manuel Revuelta González, La ex-claustración 1833–1840 (Madrid, 1976), 14–17.*

and parish roles in the years that followed; the great majority lived on as secularized state pensioners, receiving a pittance from the central government. Nuns were treated more leniently. Only convents not engaged in charity or teaching were suppressed, together with all those housing less than 20 nuns. There are no reliable statistics from which we can know how many of the approximately 15,000 nuns and 700 convents in Spain were affected by these measures.

The general disamortization of Church lands, followed by that of common lands, has long been recognized as the key single socioeconomic event of nineteenth-century Spain. When the process was finally completed—the last church lands were were not sold until the 1870s—nearly the entire landed endowment had been confiscated and about 15 percent of the surface area of the country had changed hands. The government's object was threefold: to raise funds to wage the war against the Carlists; to weaken the Church as a bastion of traditionalism and make it subject to and financially dependent on the state; and to further strengthen the liberal regime by creating a new society of middle-class landowners who would be loyal to the new regime.

The disamortization was carried out with general inefficiency. Lands were often sold at bargain prices and the state eventually realized less income than expected. Objectives two and three were, however, largely realized: the financial basis of the Church was gravely weakened, and the foundations of the liberal middle and upper classes were strengthened. Some effort was made to preserve a considerable portion of the artistic patrimony contained in the convents, chapels, and other properties of the orders, but nonetheless much priceless art was lost, destroyed, or allowed to deteriorate.

Disamortization was of course a process common in one form or another to all Europe. It occurred in Protestant countries at the time of the Reformation and in Catholic regions in the eighteenth and nineteenth centuries. The Spanish disamortization came relatively late, and its economic consequences were stimulating only in the short run, though that is not merely the fault of the disamortization itself. In the twentieth century, the disamortization has had the reputation of a sort of evil genie responsible for the socioeconomic ills of modern agrarian Spain, an agrarian reform in reverse that placed much of the country's best farmland in the hands of a new moneyed secular oligarchy while multiplying the difficulties of the ordinary landless peasant.

It seems more likely that the economic effects of the disamortization have been exaggerated. It is true that much of the best land was purchased by members of the upper middle class, but this varied from region to region. Ownership or control of land had already been heavily concentrated in few hands in some areas, and the process was merely intensified by the disamortization. In other regions where there were proportionately more peasant landowners or holders of usufruct—that is, where the peasantry was already more independent and slightly better off—more of the land went directly to peasants. The results of the disamortization in terms of land ownership thus generally reflected existing conditions and tendencies rather than creating them *ab ovo*. Nor was the disamortization itself responsible for the lack of agricultural development in Spain later in the nineteenth century. In England, where productivity increased much more, land ownership was also heavily concentrated. The sources of developmental lag were much too complex to be imputed to one single land transfer process.

In fact, the terms of the disamortization process, clumsy though it was, accurately reflected the doctrines and program of early nineteenth-century liberalism. Even the radicals, who were becoming known as Progressives, were not democrats, but espoused a broader form of censitary liberalism based on property and education. They believed that the independence and property of the Church had to be reduced as an obstacle to the reform of institutions and to economic prosperity, just as they considered monks and nuns a parasitical drain on society unless engaged in teaching or some other practical activity. And yet the majority of Spanish liberals remained generally Catholic and attached considerable importance to the role of the Church and of religion in society, properly channeled.

The whirligig of liberal politics soon produced a more moderate government than that of Mendizábal, which fell in May 1836, but this in turn was succeeded three months later by a new radical cabinet headed by José María Calatrava. With it was restored the original liberal constitution of 1812, and this, coming on the heels of the recent torrent of anticlerical legislation, provoked the papacy to break formal relations with the Spanish government. By that point, anticlerical politics had momentarily exhausted itself, and no significant new measures were forthcoming during the remainder of the Carlist War.

In 1837 the Cádiz constitution was replaced (for eight years, as it turned out) by a more radical new constitution that nonetheless preserved the privileged place of Catholicism as the official religion and was not accompanied by further legislative attacks. The new consitution did guarantee limited toleration for other faiths, however, arousing fears among Catholic leaders that it might soon lead to full religious freedom. Any such danger was nullified by the return to power of the right-wing liberals, now known as Moderates, in the last year of the Carlist War. Their ecclesiastical program aimed at conciliation with the Church. By

1839, the new regulations were moderated somewhat in practice, and the Spanish government endeavored to restore full diplomatic relations with Rome.

The final victory over Carlism in 1840 assured the triumph of the liberal revolution in Spain, but it also opened the way for the complete unfolding of the liberal-radical dialectic in Spanish politics. A broad popular revolt in Barcelona started a process that brought down the regency of the queen-mother, María Cristina, in mid-1840. The Progressives seized power under General Baldomero Espartero, their military champion, who was elected regent by a new parliament the following year, thus becoming the only Spanish general before Franco to act as chief of state. The new Progressive regime was also predicated on a radicalization of the Church-state struggle. The papal nunciatura, which had remained open in Madrid despite the earlier recall of the nuncio, was closed by the Spanish government in October 1840 and its vice-director expelled from Spain.

The attitude of the Spanish hierarchy was expressed in a collective letter of twenty-five bishops to the pope, dated October 1, 1839. They detailed the persecution inflicted by the liberal regime since 1834: the suppression of the monastic orders, confiscation of the lands and other properties of the orders, elimination of the traditional legal immunities of ecclesiastics, complete abolition of tithes and *primicias* (first fruits), exile and even imprisonment of clergy who spoke out, interference in internal administration and recruitment, reduction of personnel, all compounded by further plans to expand the disamortization to include all the landed endowment of the Church. Of the twenty-five signatories, eighteen had been driven from their dioceses by the government, while those remaining had seen their internal authority and civil rights severely restricted. By this time many other sees had fallen vacant and could not be properly filled because of the Church-state conflict. Of the fifteen remaining prelates who did not sign the collective letter, apparently only six can be clearly identified as proliberal or compromisers, the others not participating because of illness or poor communications.

Only two liberals spoke out in opposition, the bishops of Astorga (in León) and Barcelona. The more intelligent and forceful of the two was Torres Amat, of Astorga, who informed the pope that he had always been well treated by the liberal regime and blamed the recent problems on the fanaticism, superstition, and ignorance of the Spanish, both traditionalist and radical. These had impeded a just and orderly solution.

Gregory XVI, who held papal authority in this period, needed little encouragement in his rigid antiliberal stance. His secular dominion in the papal states was threatened by Italian liberals, and papal security was dependent on the Austrian empire, which vigorously supported the Carlist cause in Spain.

The Espartero regime in turn announced extension of the disamortization to the remaining properties of the Church. There was some talk in 1841 of forming a French-style "civil constitution of the clergy" for Spain, or even, more extravagantly, of a schismatic national Spanish Catholic Church, somewhat on the Anglican model. This was possibly encouraged by the strong British influence behind the Espartero regime, but it was so unrealistic that it was soon forgotten.

The common perception abroad was of a Spanish society divided into mutually exclusive bands of fanatics. In his *Handbook to Spain*, published in 1845, the British traveler Richard Ford wrote that "the whole nation is divided into two classes—bigoted Romanists or infidels; there is no via media." Like many foreign notions of Spain, this seemed outwardly plausible but was in fact altogether untrue. Despite their militant anticlerical policy, most of the Progressivist leaders, even, were aware that some sort of modus vivendi would have to be worked out with Rome.

The Moderate Compromise

The opportunity, however, came only after the overthrow of the Espartero regime in 1843, followed by the installation of a Moderate government in Madrid the following year. The Moderates, in fact, represented the new liberal establishment of the landed upper and upper middle classes. Taking the place of the aristocratic stratum of the Old Regime, with whom they merged financially and politically, they incarnated the new Spanish conservatism of the nineteenth and early twentieth centuries. Rapprochement with the Church was high on the Moderate list of priorities, for religion was seen as a necessary bulwark for moderate and practical institutions, and a shield against dangerous radicalization of the kind so recently overcome with the ouster of Espartero.

In July 1844, the Moderate administration of González Bravo therefore announced the suspension of further sales of the property of the secular clergy and the feminine orders. Further sales of property of the male orders were subsequently terminated as well, bringing to a conclusion a process that within a period of eight years had confiscated 73,308 units of property of the orders and 54,753 units belonging to the secular clergy, together with 14,292 titles of mortgages and bonds.

Relations were further improved by ratification of the new moderate Spanish constitution of 1845, which replaced the more radical document of 1837. The new constitution, which save for two interludes would remain, with certain changes, the charter of Spanish government for nearly eighty years, recognized that "the Catholic, apostolic and Roman religion is that of Spain" and pledged the state "to maintain the religion and its ministers." It granted a number of prelates ex officio seats in the Spanish senate, while supplementary legislation set an annual budget for the maintenance of the clergy and other Church expenses. This obligated the state to make up the entire difference between the Church's remaining major sources of income and the stipulated budget. The papacy then negotiated a new agreement in April 1845 that restored normal relations with Madrid, formally recognized the young queen, Isabel II, and renewed all agreements in force as of the time of the death of her father. Though division within the government prevented official Spanish ratification, the rupture between the Church and the liberal state was clearly being repaired.

Six more years of negotiation followed, leading to the Concordat of 1851, which became the cornerstone of Church-state relations in Spain for the next eighty years. The new relationship was built through a series of political and diplomatic negotiations, assisted first of all by the accession of Pius IX in 1846. Given his subsequent role in Church history, it is sometimes forgotten that this pontiff began his reign as the first liberal pope, the pope who encouraged efforts toward a new modus vivendi with the liberal state. After a momentary setback in 1847, when a more rigorous *puritano* ministry proposed to complete the disamortization of remaining Church properties, relations were smoothed once more by a new government under the Moderate strong man, General Ramón María Narváez. His administration acquired momentary reknown by maintaining complete order in turbulent Spain amid the European revolutions of 1848. Moreover, though the new constitution said nothing about the prohibition of non-Catholic religions, a new penal code was introduced providing for the punishment of "crimes against religion." During the summer of that dramatic year relations between Madrid and Rome were completely normalized for the first time in nearly a decade. Finally, after revolutionaries caused the pope to flee from Rome late in the year (initiating his conversion to conservativism), the Spanish government took the lead among European powers in organizing military assistance to restore papal rule, dispatching 4,000 troops to the papal states some six months later.

The new Concordat, culminating this rapprochement, proclaimed the Catholic unity of Spain and obligatory religious instruction at all levels of schools. The Spanish state guaranteed its protection to the Church and promised the ecclesiastical hierarchy full freedom in the exercise of their jurisdiction. Diocesan boundaries were partially reorganized under the nine archdioceses of Spain, and the authority of bishops throughout their districts was expanded. The two charitable orders of St. Vincent de Paul and San Filippo Neri were authorized in Spain, plus "one other order of those approved by the Holy See"—an ambiguous definition that led to much controversy later. Orders of nuns devoted to education and charity were also officially approved.

The two principal concessions made by the papacy were to continue the broad terms of the *patronato regio* first conceded a century earlier—allowing the government in effect to intervene in Church nominations and administration down to the parish level—and to accept the basic disamortization of Church lands as an irreversible fact. As a corollary, the papacy removed the previous condemnation of those who had bought Church properties, a great relief for thousands of nominal Spanish Catholics who had done so, and this helped to open the way for the general financial settlement, the most important single aspect of the 1851 Concordat.

The Concordat recognized the full right of the Church to own property and to acquire, through normal means, more property in the future, though this right was not specifically recognized in the case of the three orders. The Spanish state recognized the Church's title to all those properties then under the state's administration but not yet sold, title to which was transferred back to the state, to amortize the national debt in return for state bonds bearing 3 percent annual interest. Several articles detailed the levels of income for the principal ranks of Church personnel, down to parish curates. It was stipulated that whenever the income from the remaining properties and endowments of the Church failed to reach the assigned levels of income for clerical personnel, the difference would be made up by the state, though the volume of state support was not specifically defined.

During the next two years a series of further laws and administrative directives supplemented the Concordat in detail. The effort of these was to regularize, systematize, and centralize aspects of Church administration under Spanish law. They enhanced the central authority of the bishops in each diocese with respect to cathedral chapters and all lower levels of the clergy. Under the Old Regime the tendency of state policy had been almost the opposite, seeking for centuries to avoid too strong and independent an hierarchical structure. The elimination of particularism and local autonomies in ecclesiastical administration reflected the liberal state's drive for centralization in the political sphere and its desire to recreate the Church in its own image.

Renewal of Anticlericalism in the Progressivist Biennium, 1854–56

The initial honeymoon between the Church and moderate liberalism lasted only three years, until the Progressives regained power through armed revolt in 1854. The new biennium of Progressivist government, which lasted until 1856, brought immediate resumption of anticlerical measures. Some of the more notable included limitation of the hierarchy's right to internal censorship, restriction of residence of clergy in the capital, prohibition of secondary instruction and of lay students in Church seminaries, censorship of the political content of sermons, suspension of the entry of novitiates into legally recognized orders, abolition of further formal conferral of holy orders, and a purge of ex-Carlist military volunteers among the clergy.

These measures were climaxed in February 1855 by sweeping extension of the process of disamortization to all remaining state and municipal lands and all those properties still in possession of the Church. When it was protested that this directly violated the recent Concordat, the minister of finance replied that the papacy had already agreed to large transfers under that agreement. Even if this did violate the Concordat, it was further argued, the state had every right to do so, since it was superior to the Church in all secular matters. Altogether, in 1855–56 the state seized nearly 13,000 more properties of the orders that had somehow escaped earlier confiscation, and approximately 130,000 units of property of the secular clergy, most of which had not been subject to the earlier disamortization.

This move brought another rupture of relations with Rome. Protests were all the more vigorous because of the growing strength of the Catholic revival which had begun in recent years, and the usual exile of dissenting prelates ensued. A further administrative directive of the Progressivist government in October 1855 converted the clergy into direct employees of the state, stipulating that at the beginning of the new year they would all be paid monthly through the provincial administration of the Spanish state treasury.

Despite the ferocity of their attack on Church interests, even the Progressivists of 1855 remained within the boundaries of a kind of Catholic, as distinct from antireligious, anticlericalism. Their new constitution (which typically survived only one year) reaffirmed the Catholic unity of Spain and made no provision for religious liberty. Another generation would be required to transform the anticlericalism of economic ambition and administrative control into the anticlericalism of ideological principle.

The Moderate Compromise Resumed, 1856–68

When the Moderates rallied to overthrow the Progressivists in 1856, they canceled all the new anticlerical legislation but did not return confiscated Church properties. These were too important to the new social and political elite of Spain, and the papacy finally reconciled itself to that fact. A new agreement was worked out in 1859 as a codicil to the Concordat, reaffirming the Church's right to all the property that it had possessed. Becaue of the "inconvenience" of administering such possessions, the Church agreed, it in turn would hand over to the state all the units confiscated in 1855–56 in return for 3 percent bonds, the rate of capitalization of the properties to be determined by Church leaders in each district. Thus the great landed endowments of the Catholic Church in Spain disappeared finally and definitively before the onslaught of liberal capitalism.

The final decade of the Isabeline regime (1858–68) was at first dominated by the Liberal Union, led by General Leopoldo O'Donnell, who attempted a coalition of the more liberal Moderates and some of the more reasonable Progressives. His goal was to transcend the recurrent cycles of one-party government and restricted access followed by riot and revolt. Though only temporarily successful, the O'Donnell "long government" of 1858–63 negotiated the new agreement with Rome and followed a circumspect policy in Church relations. It benefited from a sudden and dramatic apotheosis of Church-state rapprochement during the brief Spanish-Moroccan war of 1859–60. This minor conflict, pressed to a victorious conclusion by the O'Donnell government, was preached by the Church throughout Spain as a veritable crusade against the infidel, reviving the old terms of Spanish ideology once more.

Yet foreign policy almost as quickly proved a liability for the government, for the Liberal Union was closely associated with the French Second Empire of Louis Napoleon, which in turn championed the new national state of Italy that had united most Italian territory in 1859–60 and threatened the papal domains themselves. This led to a cooling of ties between the Spanish government and Church leadership in the early 1860s.

The new situation encourgaged the clergy to withdraw from involvement in political issues and concentrate on ecclesiastical and pastoral duties, yet the extent of state power inevitably led to renewed conflict on other levels. There were now problems arising from the state budget, the government's approval of even minor appointments or administrative changes, the organization of Catholic teaching in the schools, multiple issues of censorship and libel, and the extent of freedom for Protestant missionaries and churches, which had grown in number.

After the fall of O'Donnell in 1863 the government turned sharply to the right. The last years of the reign of Isabel II were a time of reaction that steadily narrowed the regime's base of support. In this twilight, neo-Catholicism became the order of the day, and the new orientation was led by the queen herself. Doña Isabel was poorly educated and politically irresponsible, but she was also pious to the point of superstition and was heavily influenced by a small court circle of ultraconservative and Catholic advisors. These peculiar political circumstances of the mid-1860s led Church leaders to hope for a further rollback of anticlerical legislation, such as reapproval for all the orders to return to Spain and the full employment of monks and friars in pastoral and evangelical activities.

The outstanding ecclesiastical figure of these years was Antonio María Claret, probably the major single figure in Spanish evangelism during the nineteenth century. Earlier the archbishop of Havana, he became the personal confessor of the queen and her principal advisor on religious policy. He was a quasi-mystical ascetic, and an enormously successful popular religious writer and promoter of internal missionary activity who was subsequently canonized by the Church. In state policy, he provided such guidance in the selection of new names for the episcopacy that Madrid's choices in these years were approved almost automatically by the papacy. The new generation of Spanish church hierarchs of the 1850 and 60s were noteworthy for their backing of the conservative liberal monarchy in Madrid, and even more for their total devotion to the papacy, whose new dogma of infallibility they staunchly supported at the international Church council of 1870.

Even a right-wing liberal such as Narváez, governing once more in Madrid, was embarrassed by the publication of Pius IX's encyclical *Quanta cura* and the *Syllabus of Errors* in December 1864, for they condemned the basic principles of nineteenth-century liberalism and affirmed the temporal sovereignty of the papacy. After due deliberation, the government finally authorized full publication of these documents in Spain in a royal order that specified this was being done "without prejudice to the regalian rights of the crown or the rights and prerogatives of the nation." The positions of the encyclical and the terms of the royal authorization were in fact antithetical, but this verbal compromise was acceptable to both sides.

When Narváez's last government had finally to ratify official recognition of the new secular Italian state in 1866, it was showered with protest from Spanish Catholic opinion and received literally thousands of letters of censure. The pope himself proved more understanding, realizing that it was politically impossible for Madrid to delay recognition longer. He was well aware that by comparison with its neighbors Isabeline Spain had once more regained its country's old position as the most Catholic of nations. Despite recent traumas, the character of Catholicism in Spain probably more fully reflected the principles of *Quanta cura* than in any other land.

The Democratic Interregnum:
Toward Separation of Church and State, 1868–74

This brief era of security and support for the Church lasted no longer than had its predecessor, the first Moderate decade of 1844–54. The regime, together with the Bourbon dynasty itself, was overthrown in 1868 by the most broadly based military revolt of the nineteenth century. The new rebellion was backed by active bands of civilian radicals, who set up "revolutionary juntas" in many parts of Spain, particulary the east, center, and south. This revolt was directed primarily against the restrictive right-wing liberalism of the Isabeline monarchy, and secondarily against the latter's close association with the now reactionary papacy of Pius IX, whose categorical condemnation of liberalism and stress on Church independence had, as we have seen, been too strong even for the conservative government of Narváez. Spanish radicalism at this point was more advanced ideologically as well as stronger in social support than in earlier decades. In its extreme advocates, anticlericalism was giving way to antireligiosity. Half a century earlier religion had been viewed as a bulwark of an outmoded institutional order whose structure needed to be brought up to date. The new generation of radicals, no mere liberals but mainly democratic federal republicans of a rationalist utopian persuasion, viewed religion as a fundamental evil that must be repressed and possibly extirpated altogether. Thus in many towns the new revolutionary juntas initiated vigorous persecution late in 1868, restricting the freedom of action of bishops and clergy, sometimes closing or looting churches and attacking priests physically.

The new government in Madrid, led by the Progressivist General Juan Prim, had more limited goals. Its aim was to complete the work of early nineteenth-century liberalism by introducing political democracy with complete economic and cultural freedom. It endeavored to assure Church leaders of its moderation, yet encountered considerable difficulty at first in restraining the anticlerical republican mobs in many cities.

The Society of Jesus was officially expelled from Spain for the fourth time in October 1868. A recent decree of the Isabeline regime permitting those orders recognized by the state to hold property was annulled, and all houses and landed property acquired by religious orders in Spain after July 1837 were confiscated. The inhabitants of these buildings were given the choice of finding some other religious home in which to settle or of secularizing themselves. The orders recognized by the Concordat of 1851 were suppressed, and only a few feminine congregations devoted to teaching and charity were allowed to remain. Further state support of seminaries was canceled, and the theological faculties in universities were definitively suppressed. Despite its pledge of moderation, the new democratic regime had no intention of recognizing a free Church in a free state. All these anticlerical measures were carried out in the first weeks of the new regime, however, before the government was able to get the local revolutionary juntas under control. Its policy became progressively more moderate, and some cabinet members began to wonder if they had not already gone too far. Instructions were even sent to provincial administrators not to be too rigorous in enforcing the new regulations.

Catholic laymen were quick to take advantage of the new freedom of association introduced by the democratic monarchy. This somewhat paradoxically made it possible to implement the new Catholic policy, encouraged by the Vatican of Pius IX, of organizing independent Catholic associations to act exclusively on behalf of religious interests in helping create a "perfect society" of the Church and its members. The aims were in theory spiritual, not political, but amid this drastic change in Church-state relations political issues came to the fore. The Marqués de Viluma, a conservative activist, began to form the first of a series of new "Asociaciones de Católicos" in November 1868, only weeks after the initial anticlerical decrees of the new regime.

These were the forerunners of the subsequent Catholic Action in Spain, and one of their first goals was to organize a mass signature campaign in opposition to the government's announced intention of introducing religious liberty. Three million signatures, the authenticity of many of them contested, were collected on mass petitions in favor of Catholic unity. The campaign was weakest in the southern half of Spain and strongest in Navarre, the Basque provinces, and the northwest. In addition, the Associations promoted the mass distribution of devotional literature and of propaganda in support of the Catholic political position. They formed other units, called Catholic Studies, to improve and support teaching in Catholic schools, and were active in fund-raising on behalf of both the Church in Spain and the papacy. By 1869 a beginning was also made in the organization of Catholic lay women's and youth groups.

All this had little influence on the new democratic constitution introduced that year. Four clerics—two bishops and two priests—were elected to the constituent assembly, but one of the priests, from the Alcalá Zamora family (subsequently very prominent in liberal politics), even voted in favor of religious freedom. The new constitution was the first to introduce universal male suffrage, but it rejected the republicanism of the new radical generation in favor of a reformed democratic constitutional monarchy. It reaffirmed the Catholic identity of the state, yet also guaranteed religious freedom. Article 21 of the new document declared:

> The nation obligates itself to maintain the services and minis-
> ters of the Catholic religion. The public or private exercise of any
> other cult is guaranteed to all foreigners resident in Spain, with no
> limitations other than the universal rules of morality and law. If
> some Spaniards profess a religion other than the Catholic, the dis-
> positions of the preceding paragraph are also applicable to them.

This immediately raised the problem of whether the clergy, their
salaries now a part of the state budget, would be willing to swear allegiance to the new constitution. In other Catholic countries such as France
and Belgium, the clergy had already accepted national constitutions at
least as liberal and tolerant as the new Spanish charter. After some
months and considerable pressure from the new Spanish regime, the
Vatican informed the Nunciatura in Madrid that there was no necessary
reason why the clergy could not swear allegiance. The Spanish Church
hierarchy almost unanimously concluded otherwise, however, thus proving truly "more Catholic than the pope." By that point the government
lived in fear of the effects of a new Carlist uprising in Navarre and the
Basque provinces, which was repressed only with some difficulty. Clerical
opposition was seen as the main source of support for the new insurgency.
In mid-1869 the ministry of justice ordered bishops throughout Spain to
have their clergy preach obedience to the new government and do nothing to aid the Carlists, requiring them to withdraw the ecclesiastical
license of any priest who failed to comply. Even though the military
situation was under control, in March 1870 the ministry of justice issued a
decree requiring all ecclesiastics to swear allegiance. This was at first
generally ignored. Under further government duress, the bishop of
Almería alone among Spanish hierarchs authorized the staff of his diocese to swear, but only 11 of 38 canons and 24 of 189 parish priests did so.
This issue was never satisfactorily settled during the three remaining
years of the democratic monarchy.

At the beginning of 1870, Don Amadeo of Savoy, a younger son of the
new king of Italy, ascended the Spanish throne to preside over three
troubled years of increasingly bitter and difficult factional politics. From
the beginning, this scion of the dynasty that had terminated the temporal
domain of the pope was viewed with hostility by Catholic opinion. The
only point of temporary reconciliation during his brief reign was probably
the series of celebrations held throughout Spain the following year in
honor of the twenty-fifth anniversary of the reign of Pius IX. Even some
republicans joined in the festivities.

New violations of Catholic tradition continued to embroil Church-
state relations. Civil marriage was instituted in 1870 for the first time in

Spanish history, and the cemeteries were secularized in the following year. The new regime, like its anticlerical predecessors, vigorously imposed its own nominees on Church administration, making its new selections from the most liberal clerics, who were regarded as undesirable both by the Spanish hierarchy and the Holy See. Poor economic conditions, which had been partly responsible for the downfall of the Isabeline regime, placed severe limitations on the new government. The Church budget suffered especially; it was progressively reduced year after year until it was only a fraction of the 1868 level. During the early 1870s the Church was largely thrown back on its own resources and the contributions of the faithful. It faced great economic stringency that forced a reduction in most of its activities and even the closing of some churches.

Don Amadeo abruptly renounced the throne in February 1873, declaring Spain to be impossible to govern, and then asked forgiveness from the Vatican for having sworn to uphold a non-Catholic constitution and for other offenses against the Church. The king's departure left the moderate liberals defenseless. They immediately collapsed before the new offensive of the federal republican movement, which inaugurated Spain's First Republic that same month.

The grand novelty of the First Republic in Church relations would have been the first separation of Church and state in Spanish history, had this newest regime lasted long enough to ratify its own constitution. New parallel legislation was also prepared to establish the principle of a free Church in a free state. This would have renounced state patronage and other formerly regalian rights, while recognizing the Church's complete right to property and freedom of organization, association, and teaching. Yet the Republic never fully completed its own constitution, because it had to face two different revolts, one internal and the other external. Its own federalism undermined it, for provincial federalists throughout southern and eastern Spain began to set up "cantons" that declared de facto independence of Madrid. In Navarre and the Basque provinces, revolt had already begun to smolder four years earlier. Advent of a new anticlerical Republic fanned these sparks into a full-scale new Carlist insurrection. The Federal Republicans could not even govern their own political movement, much less Spain as a whole. They were overthrown by a military revolt at the beginning of 1874 after less than a year in power. By that point the cycle of radical politics had finally exhausted itself, and the way was open for a new conservative compromise that would prove somewhat more lasting than that of the Isabeline regime.

4

The Catholic Revival

LIBERALISM'S assault on the Catholic Church reflected the cultural changes in the elite wrought by modern critical thought and the new economic values stimulated by the introduction of modern capitalism. The philosophical and political doctrines of liberalism helped to stimulate the takeover of public institutions but did not suffice to complete the transformation of society and culture. The consequence was that nineteenth-century liberalism represented a kind of halfway house in modern development: it displaced the old regime but stopped far short of democratization or a complete and radical reorganization of society. The first liberals soon became the new conservatives and sought the same institutional supports that had sustained their predecessors in the old regime. Moreover, beneath the level of national politics and the discourse of the elite, the traditional culture was still ingrained in much of ordinary Spanish society.

The substance remained for a strong reaffirmation of the traditional religion as soon as formal political circumstances permitted. This revival based itself on the traditional culture of much of the population and the revised attitudes of the political elites. It was expressed through a new work of evangelism and the expansion of religious devotion, but its regrowth proved highly uneven, differentiated by social class and geographical region. Moreover, the revival was limited by its increasingly close dependence upon the newly dominant political and social sectors, and failed to recapture the complete popular dimension of the traditional religion.

As in the case of many spiritual and cultural movements, there is no comprehensive date for the beginning of the Catholic revival in later nineteenth-century Spain. Major turning points can be traced from pivotal developments affecting Church-state relations, such as the Concordat of 1851 and the restoration of the conservative monarchy in 1875, but the expansion of Church activities and the intensification of religiosity among certain social groups was a cumulative process that approached a high plateau in the 1880s and 90s.

The potential for Catholic renewal existed as soon as Spanish liberalism first began to stabilize in moderate form during the 1840s. Modern Spanish conservatism in the guise of conservative liberalism emerged during that decade and established most of the terms on which Spain would be governed all the way down to the overthrow of parliamentary monarchy in 1931. Yet the establishment of modern conservatism, like so much of nineteenth-century Spanish politics, was spasmodic and convulsive. The regime of the Moderate party was interrupted in 1854 for a biennium and then eliminated altogether for six years by the first democratic interregnum in 1868. These convulsions were due in large measure to the political division, incompetence, and narrowness of the conservatives themselves, though the strength of the progressivist and radical sectors of liberalism would not have been so weak as they were after 1874 had they not had such full opportunity to thoroughly discredit themselves through excess and ineptitude in power.

The main phase of Catholic revival did not begin until after the conservative restoration, but it built on the foundations of the 1840s and 50s. The architect of the restoration system, Antonio Cánovas del Castillo, charted a clear course of compromise in the new constitution of 1876, modeled on the original Moderate charter of 1845. The Catholic identity of the Spanish state was fully restored, along with the complete authority of the Concordat, whose terms were moreover interpreted quite broadly in the Church's interests. The rapprochement between Catholicism and conservative liberalism, sought by political conservatives ever since the formation of the original Moderate party in the late 1830s, was thus brought much nearer consummation.

Yet Cánovas had become perhaps the wisest and most experienced politician in Spain, and he therefore strove to avoid the exclusive narrowness and intolerance that had brought the downfall of the preceding Isabeline regime. His successor to the Moderates was officially entitled the Liberal-Conservative party, and he sought to provide greater access and accommodation than had his predecessors. In reestablishing the identity of Church and state in Spain, the new constitution also provided for the toleration of non-Catholic groups, though they were denied full freedom of publicity and proselytism.[1]

---

1. The inroads of Protestantism, so alarming to Catholic leaders, remained modest in the extreme. By 1875 there were only 33 Protestant congregations in all Spain with no more than 2,000 members altogether, located mainly in Madrid, Barcelona, Seville, and the island of Menorca (under British occupation in the late eighteenth century). The largest denomination was the Evangelical Church, of Calvinist origins, with less than 500 members, followed by the Baptists, of North American inspiration, with about 250.

Thus the conservative restoration did not lead to a full alliance with the Church, at least in formal political terms. The assaults suffered during the preceding half-century had resulted in the stiffening of Spanish Catholic policy, which for long refused to accept fully even a conservative brand of liberalism. Cánovas himself remained suspect to ultra-Catholic opinion.

The degree of compromise already accepted by most Catholics in such countries as France and Belgium was rejected by Catholic leadership in Spain. One major reason for this was that moderate Catholicism continued to be outflanked by the most vigorous and enduring counterrevolutionary and traditionalist movement in Europe. On two occasions (1833–40 and 1872–76), Spanish Carlism had not merely risen in full-scale revolt but had created a state and a set of administrative institutions in "liberated" Basque and Navarrese territory. Portuguese Miguelism alone among other European traditionalist movements could equal this achievement. During the second major Carlist war against the anticlerical regimes of the democratic interregnum, Carlism had not received such broad support among the clergy as during the 1830s, but that was partly because of the military success of the Spanish government in containing the Carlist insurrection geographically. One encouraging feature of the last war had been the lesser degree of fanaticism and ferocity shown by both sides, but Carlism remained as an organized political force still firmly entrenched in its home territories. It constituted an extreme right whose very existence threatened and pressured the more moderate sections of Catholic opinion, and thus encouraged a more intransigent attitude among Spanish Catholics in general than would have been found in some other Catholic lands by the 1870s and 80s.

Although there was no complete political *ralliement* to the restored conservative regime, relations were relatively peaceful and positive throughout the quarter-century of the restoration era (1875–1900). The Spanish situation paralleled the general tendency toward de facto rapprochement between the Church and conservative liberal regimes in Portugal and parts of Latin America during that period. A number of prelates accepted seats in the only partially elective Spanish senate under the new system, though the system was never endorsed as such. More important, the Church took advantage of the restoration of its privileges to initiate a major renewal of religious activities that fully accepted the new social context of liberal capitalism by that point established in Spain.

At the same time, all this was carried out in an attitude of the most pronounced papalism or ultramontane Romanism probably ever seen in Spanish Catholic history. The trauma of the nineteenth century had convinced the Spanish episcopacy that their only security lay in the almost exclusive leadership of Rome. The struggle with liberalism created a closer identity with and reliance on the papacy than had the Protestant Reformation. The figure of Pius IX as martyr of the Vatican was greatly mythified and the same extremes of veneration shown his successors. In the fund-raising drives to support papal expenses that had begun in the Catholic world during the 1860s, the faithful of Spain proved the most generous of all in generating financial support. In 1895, thirty-three bishops issued pastorals emphasizing that the temporal dominion of the papacy was consubstantial with its spiritual authority, and it has been suggested that the real leader of the Spanish Church between 1868 and 1936 was not the primate in Toledo but the papal nuncio.

CULTURE AND PHILOSOPHY

A renewed effort was made in Spain during the second half of the nineteenth century to define and create a modern Catholic culture, ideologically exclusive of the inroads of liberalism. This produced no major new theorists or original concepts but did stimulate extensive new educational and cultural activity.

The two major figures in nineteenth-century Catholic thought, Jaime Balmes and Juan Donoso Cortés, both produced their major work during the earlier years of the Isabeline regime. Balmes, a young Catalan priest who died in 1848 at the age of thirty-eight, was the leading Spanish Catholic apologist of the century. His most famous work, *El protestantismo comparado con el catolicismo* (1844), emphasized the creative role of Catholicism throughout western history and its freedom from the individualistic excesses of Protestantism. Balmes strove to preserve as much as possible of traditional Catholicism while coming to grips with modern challenges, and strongly insisted on the Christian roots of modern liberties. Like certain other prominent Catholic theorists and activists who followed, he hoped to bring political unity to Spanish Catholicism and stability to Spanish institutions through a marriage alliance between the two branches of the dynasty. Balmes's *Reflexiones sobre el celibato del clero* (1839) and *Observaciones . . . sobre los bienes del clero* (1840) present ideal role models for clergy. The *Cartas a un escéptico* (1843–44), his second major apologetic work, defends the Tridentine definitions of Christian faith and institutions. Balmes denied any contradiction between faith and liberty, for only spiritual enlightenment could bring genuine freedom, all of which he found compatible with a responsible form of modern liberal institutions. At the climax of his brief but meteoric career, he began to attempt the reorientation of the stagnant field of Catholic philosophy in Spain through his *El criterio* (1845) and *La filosofía fundamental* (1846).

Juan Donoso Cortés, who also died young in 1853, was the most influential political philosopher of modern Spain, in terms of the degree of theoretical interest that he sparked in various parts of Europe during and after his lifetime. An Extremaduran hidalgo who became a high-level diplomat at mid-century, Donoso's approach was grounded in what he perceived as the inevitable breakdown of modern liberalism and capitalism. His chief work, the *Ensayo sobre el catolicismo, el liberalismo y el socialismo* (1851), stressed the destructive and degenerative tendencies of liberalism together with the social and cultural failures of capitalist materialism, which he believed would end in massive alienation and class struggle. Donoso saw liberalism resulting in atheistic socialism, whose chief incarnation he identified with remarkable prescience as most likely to be Russia because of its great strength, despotic institutions, cultural backwardness, and aberrant spirituality. His ultimate prognosis was apocalyptic, for Donoso saw salvation only in a purified Catholic system that would fully transcend a fallen liberalism. Before the challenge of the revolutions of 1848 he called for temporary dictatorship, yet he had no illusion that mere authoritarianism could contain the problems of modern society. Donoso himself supported the most conservative wing of the Moderates and did not favor political dictatorship under a general or bureaucrat as an enduring solution to what he saw ultimately as cultural and spiritual problems.

The outstanding Catholic writer of the restoration period proper was Marcelino Menéndez y Pelayo, greatest Spanish scholar of the nineteenth century. Before winning a chair in the history of literature at the University of Madrid at the age of twenty-one, he participated in a notable polemic against secular liberals in 1876 over the history and contributions of Spanish culture and science. These he ardently defended. Menéndez y Pelayo recognized that the principal Spanish achievements lay in the realms of religion and esthetics, but he also pointed out the accomplishments of Spanish science in the sixteenth and early seventeenth centuries, as well as those of secondary figures in other periods. To him, Spanish culture would always be distinguished by its particular religious identity: "Spain, evangelizer of half the world, Spain, hammer of heretics, light of Trent, sword of Rome, cradle of San Ignacio. . . . This is our greatness and our glory: we have no other."[2]

In his later years, Menéndez y Pelayo went on to become director of

---

2. Marcelino Menéndez y Pelayo, *Historia de los heterodoxos españoles* (Madrid, 1955), 6:508.

the National Library, member of parliament, briefly, senator, and chief celebrity and strong man of Catholic culture. His main works, all mammoth multivolume affairs, were *La ciencia española* (1876), *Historia de los heterodoxos españoles* (1880–82), *Historia de las ideas estéticas en España* (1883–91), and *Orígenes de la novela* (1905–10). His *Obras completas* fill sixty-two volumes, nearly two for every year of his adult career. Menéndez y Pelayo was obviously not without bias, yet he also had a strong sense of scholarship and was quick to rectify errors. He possessed a keen feeling of responsibility and friendship toward his colleagues, even toward such anti-Catholics as the great novelist Benito Pérez Galdós, and his approach became increasingly moderate in his later years.

Though the attempt to create a fully articulated new Catholic culture failed, some effort was made to revive traditional Spanish neoscholasticism. The leader here, and one of the outstanding figures of the Church in the restoration period, was the Asturian Dominican Ceferino González, later cardinal (1884) and briefly primate of Spain (1886–89). In 1864 he published his three-volume *Estudio sobre la filosofía de Santo Tomás*. González, who was relatively tolerant and broad-minded for a Spanish prelate of the time, made a genuine contribution to the revival of Thomism, though it was not of the intellectual depth or originality of subsequent French and Italian neo-Thomist scholars.

The main lines of Spanish culture reflected the chief intellectual and literary trends of nineteenth-century European liberalism. Nonetheless, there was considerable representation of conservative Catholicism among the late-nineteenth-century Spanish intelligentsia. A significant minority of university professors remained traditionally Catholic, and Catholic writers still held places of prestige in the literary world. The most important were the Romantic poet and playwright José Zorrilla (d. 1893), the novelist Pedro Antonio de Alarcón (d. 1891), "Fernán Caballero" (Cecilia Böhl de Faber) (d. 1877), who initiated realist and *costumbrista* novels, the Catalan priest and epic poet Jacint Verdaguer (d. 1902), and Manuel Tamayo y Baus (d. 1898), formally the most polished Spanish dramatist of the century. Much more important in his own way was the Catalan architect Antonio Gaudí (d. 1926), whom some have called the greatest creative genius of modern Spain. His highly unusual and original architecture, which made him the outstanding European artist working with reinforced concrete at the beginning of the twentieth century, was philosophically and conceptually grounded in his religious mysticism and cannot be understood apart from the culture and attitudes of the Catholic revival.

Yet the most influential new school of thought among the university intelligentsia was the philosophy of Krausism, introduced in the 1850s and 60s by the philosophy professor Julián Sanz del Río. Derived from an obscure Austrian Idealist philosopher, Krausism was a vague, nebulous sort of pantheism or rationalist panentheism, adjusted to the liberal and progressive principles generally fashionable in the western world. In practice, it was strongly oriented toward education, stressing individualized instruction and practical learning methods involving student experimentation and initiative. In politics, it favored liberal democracy, in opposition to the established institutions of conservative liberalism. Krausism exerted considerable sway among educators and professors into the early twentieth century and came to inform much of the philosophical atmosphere of several of the main universities of Spain. It has sometimes been suggested that Krausism, with its imprecise but hopeful emphases and definitions, was particularly attractive to certain intellectuals in a country like Spain, intellectually liberal but still not by any means fully secularized culturally.

EDUCATION

Expansion and renewal of Catholic education was central to the revival. New educational facilities were concentrated especially at the secondary and higher levels. The universities had been taken over by the state in 1835, and after some confusion, the theological faculties associated with them had been definitively suppressed in 1868. Diocesan seminaries therefore became proportionately more important than before. Reorganization and expansion of the seminary system began with a new "Plan de estudios eclesiásticos" approved in 1852; enrollment had climbed from about 16,000 to 24,376 by the following decade. Four seminaries were raised to the rank of "pontifical universities" by terms of the Concordat of 1851, and six more were given that rank in 1896–97, followed by Comillas (Santander) in 1904. Meanwhile a new university college for lay students was opened at El Escorial by the Augustinians. The organization of pontifical universities did not, however, turn out to be fully satisfactory, and in a subsequent rearrangement of 1931 only Comillas and Salamanca retained that status.

The outstanding educators among the Spanish clergy, and the greatest of the teaching orders, were the Jesuits, for whom the late nineteenth-century revival was an Indian summer of activity. They had left behind 112 colleges when first expelled from Spain in 1767. During the half-century from 1880 to their last expulsion in 1932 the scope of their activities increased greatly at both the higher and secondary levels. They opened the first university in the Basque provinces at Deusto (Bilbao) in 1886, a school that played a leading role in the formation of the Basque elite during the first half of the twentieth century. The Jesuits also devoted special attention to the establishment of a number of small scientific centers. Their major review, *Razón y Fe*, founded in 1901, was perhaps the best intellectual journal published by the Church in Spain.

Quantitatively, the chief expansion of education took place on the secondary level. Given the extreme shortage of state schools, the Catholic Church was able to reestablish its position as the principal educator of secondary students and especially of girls, who were the particular province of the rapidly expanding communities of nuns. During the nineteenth century, primarily after 1851, 74 new congregations of nuns were established in Spain, and of these, 58 were devoted to the education and other training of girls. By 1900, of the 597 communities of monks in Spain, 294 were devoted to teaching, as were 910 of the 2,656 communities of nuns.

The burgeoning of Catholic secondary schools reestablished the Church's position in the education of most of the middle and upper classes, but the higher ambitions of Catholic education and culture were not realized. A significant intellectual renascence, as distinct from the expansion of pedagogy, never occurred. The scholarly and intellectual activity of Spanish Catholicism remained essentially mediocre, and new ideas had to be imported primarily from France, particularly during the first years of the restoration era, to be supplemented more and more by translations from Italian after about 1885. Catholicism continued to lose ground among the intellectual and literary elite of Spain.

The Catholic educational revival was a central factor in stimulating the new wave of anticlericalism after the turn of the century. There were two dimensions to the animus of liberals and radicals toward the expansion of Catholic secondary schools. One was opposition to the basic domination of secondary education itself. The other was a cultural reaction on the part of intellectuals and educated middle-class people in somewhat broader numbers against the inadequacies of the style and content of the Catholic curricula. Thousands of former students among the middle classes reacted against the form of education they had received, once they reached their maturity. Whether or not it was the result of this kind of personal experience, revulsion against a perceived pedagogical backwardness later became central to the thinking of the intellectual leaders of the new anticlericalism.

THE REELABORATION OF RELIGIOSITY

As important as educational expansion was the reelaboration of religiosity that took place in later-nineteenth-century Spain. A renewed emphasis on preaching and popular evangelism, begun, in fact, in the era of Claret in the 1850s and 60s, brought with it new attention to the role of singing and church music. Popular missions expanded in scope, led principally by the Jesuits and certain other key orders such as the Capuchins, Redemptionists, Passionists, and Paulists.

This revival was accompanied by considerable growth in popular religious publications and the establishment of a series of new popular or parish libraries. The earliest and largest was the Librería Religiosa founded by Claret in Barcelona in 1847. The distribution of catechisms was central; those most widely used were the bilingual Catalan-Castilian catechism of José Costa y Borrás, sometime archibishop of Tarragona, and one published in 1848 by Claret. There was also a steady increase throughout the century in the number of volumes of sermons published. Devotional writings circulated in ever-increasing quantities. The all-time bestseller (indeed, probably of all books published in modern Spain) was Claret's *Camino recto y seguro para llegar al cielo* (first Catalan edition, 1843; first Castilian edition, 1846), of which several million copies had been distributed by the early twentieth century. Translations of foreign religious works, especially French, increased considerably, as did the number of religious journals; perhaps the most influential of the journals was *La Cruz* (Seville-Madrid, 1852–1915), which enjoyed semi-official status. Also important was the development of the diocesan bulletins as a regular means of communication in each district from about the 1850s on.

The approach of Spanish devotional literature was highly moralistic and full of traditional piety (stress on the vanity of the world, the brevity of temporal things, the inescapable consequences of sin), with much more emphasis on legalism than on the doctrine of love. Until the latter part of the century, the style was emotional and somewhat Romantic, aimed at touching the heart. Doctrinal content was often slighted in favor of repetitive words and affective phrases. Above all, there was strong encouragement to obedience and to constant participation in the sacraments, and in the formal ritual of worship. Bible study was largely discouraged despite two new Spanish translations of the Scriptures during the century. The personal and existential aspects of religion were emphasized little, though after 1875 there was some change in temper toward the more practical in devotional literature. The cultural or esthetic quality of most such publication was not distinguished, and there was a continuous tendency to follow certain contemporary French models of new religiosity and devotional literature.

Religious associations of lay people flourished in late-nineteenth-century Spain. Many of the traditional confraternities still existed and began to take on a more active life, while new ones were founded. Confraternities themselves were often organized on the basis of profession or neighborhood, but the new tendency was to form devotional associations for the purpose of religious exercises themselves. New eucharistic associations spread rapidly, and one female group was said to have more than two million members by the early twentieth century. Marian associations burgeoned and rosarian devotions expanded, while other associations which venerated the Holy Family and St. Joseph grew also.

In this regard probably the most important new emphasis was the formation of associations to worship the Sacred Heart of Jesus, a special center of devotion from the mid-nineteenth to the mid-twentieth century. Major monuments to the Sacred Heart were erected, outstanding among them the one in Bilbao, a city which had the distinction of being perhaps the most religious industrial city in Europe. This trend was climaxed by Alfonso XIII's inauguration of a great monument on the Cerro de los Angeles west of Madrid in 1919, when the crown officially dedicated Spain to the Sacred Heart.

The revival of the broad encouragement of formal spiritual exercises dates from about 1880. Conversely, the modern Catholic liturgical movement was slow to penetrate Spain. It began to make headway only after 1900, and then particularly at the abbey of Montserrat outside Barcelona.

This intensification of formal religiosity largely reiterated the traditional styles and motifs of Spanish worship. Though there were more publications encouraging mental prayer and meditation, the emphasis remained on formal practice rather than internal conviction. There was a general increase in the use of the sacraments, and expansion of the number of large public processions. Pilgrimages greatly increased both in frequency and size. National religious congresses became ever more frequent, and special new services based on elaborate liturgies or particular objects of devotion were more and more common.

Critical commentary by progressive Spanish ecclesiastics in the 1970s and 80s has made the formalistic emphases of the nineteenth-century revival seem like a typical Spanish religious idiosyncracy. In fact, the earlier French revival, on which much of Spanish activity was patterned, also relied strongly on the administration of sacraments, the insistence on regular practice and attendance at Mass, and mass pilgrimages. The French also introduced more elaborate decoration in churches, more use of music, incense, banners, and large processions. They also used large numbers of beads, scapulars, and medallions and encouraged an emotional brand of piety. This was general and common, not merely Spanish, Catholic practice.

It is nonetheless true that the Spanish revival of traditional forms with newer stylistic accretions made little effort to involve religion with the new problems of the day. Many of the social and cultural dilemmas posed by Spanish development after the turn of the century found no response in the typical patterns of Catholic religiosity or in the formal doctrines of the new Catholic schools.

THE CLERGY

The Catholic revival did not succeed in countering the general decline in numbers of secular clergy. The latter numbered 38,563 in 1859 but only 33,403 at the close of the century, despite considerable growth in the general population. Whereas in 1859 there was one priest for every 401 Spaniards, by 1900 the figure was only one to every 531, a proportionate decline of 28 percent. Galicia, since the ninth century the region of heaviest church endowment, remained proportionately the best supplied with priests, having in 1900 one for every 412 inhabitants, a figure superior even to the Basque provinces' one for every 458. The Spanish Levant, like the south always underendowed at the parish level, had only one diocesan priest for every 862 inhabitants. A slight statistical increase in secular clergy was beginning to register at the turn of the century, but in general the number of seminarians was declining (from 17,800 in 1889 to 15,789 in 1902).

The normal pattern was to form religious vocations early, at around ten or twelve years of age. Candidates were drawn disproportionately from the small town and peasant society of the Catholic north, and in the vast majority of cases came from families of modest means. Despite the effort to expand and reform the seminaries, funds were limited, and the renovation that occurred was less than profound. Some students held scholarships, but most were required to pay tuition fees, and this was difficult for many. On the other hand, some nominal seminarians had little intention of entering the priesthood, and in certain seminaries it was said to be not uncommon to threaten to withhold examinations unless fees were paid.

The great growth in the clergy came not in the secular clergy, which remained routinized and relatively sclerotic, but in the orders, which experienced a veritable renascence, as in France during the late nineteenth century. Of the seventy-four new female orders introduced into Spain during the nineteenth century, sixty-three were established after the 1851 Concordat. The door was opened fully to male orders only after the restoration of 1875, and in the last quarter of the century thirty-four new ones were established, and these opened a total of 115 new monasteries. By 1902 the number of monks and friars, exiguous in 1850, had grown to 10,630, and that of nuns to 40,030. (In France, which then had a population nearly double that of Spain, the number of religious had similarly grown, from 37,000 in 1851 to 162,000 in 1901).

The regular clergy generally excelled in quality and energy as well as in numbers. The orders seem to have attracted the best of those following a vocation in the late nineteenth and twentieth centuries. Their expansion created a generally youthful regular clergy which approached its task with zeal and sometimes an imagination not found in the diocesan ranks. It was the regular clergy that began to respond, also, to the new challenges of teaching, social work, and a more popular form of evangelism. They set better examples (even though concubinage among the seculars was in decline throughout the century) and generally provided much of the tone of Spanish religious life. Without the new contributions of an expanded regular clergy, the revival could not have taken place as it did.

The twelve provinces with the greatest density of regular clergy consisted of a Basque-Navarrese belt (Alava, Guipúzcoa, and Navarre), which notably did not include the industrialized province of Vizcaya; an agrarian zone of Catalonia and Aragón (Gerona, Lérida, and Huesca); a section of Old Castile (Santander, Burgos, and Logroño); and the provinces of Valladolid, Castellón, and Cádiz. The most sophisticated and original of the new feminine orders tended to be concentrated in Catalonia. Conversely, in Galicia there was an inverse correlation between density of secular and regular clergy. This is sometimes explained by the interest of Galician peasant families in having a son in the priesthood to advance family interests, something that could not be readily achieved from a monastery. In Cádiz the new communities of regular clergy supplemented the secular clergy, locally weak in numbers, though monks and friars did not take over regular parish tasks.

Recruitment to the clergy in general remained relatively democratic. This had always been somewhat characteristic of Spanish Catholicism, though in the heyday of the traditional aristocracy (late medieval and early modern periods) high positions in the episcopacy were disproportionately reserved for ecclesiastics of upper-class origin. (On a lower level, similar differentiations were found in categories of feminine convents.) By the nineteenth century, however, the reliance of the Church on the modest strata of north Spanish society was reflected in the nomination of prelates, many of whom came from the lower middle classes of the north. Conversely, appointment of new prelates from the upper classes was most common in areas in which lower-class religious participation was weaker, as in the south. There a significant number of new prelates of upper-middle- and upper-class origin were appointed to the episcopacy during the restoration era, probably also in large measure because the

government and politics of that period were disproportionately dominated by upper-class southern conservatives.

Clerical incomes as usual varied greatly. The primate received the
same stipend as the prime minister (45,000 pesetas a year—$9,000 in the
currency of the day), while ordinary parish priests received anywhere
from 850 pesetas (about the same as a Civil Guard or some of the more
fortunate among country schoolteachers) to 2,500 pesetas per year.
Bishops and their canons, who represented scarcely 3 percent of the
clerical population, absorbed about 15 percent of the state clerical
budget. Little or no provision was made for the retirement of elderly
priests (or for most other members of society, for that matter), so that
they frequently became the objects of charity for lack of alternate support. Moreover, in years of stringency, the regular stipend was reduced
by varying amounts (by 25 percent in 1882, for example, and 10 percent in
1883) to help balance the national budget. Arrears or reductions for state
schoolteachers in local government budgets were sometimes even more
severe. Some sections of the clergy thus continued to live in relative
poverty, and certain aspects of Church activities continued to be poorly
financed. It was not unheard of to hold sales of irreplaceable art objects in
order to raise money.

The situation of the monastic orders might be either better or worse,
depending on individual circumstances. Older orders that had once possessed large endowments did receive some compensation from the disamortization, either in state bonds or in payments that were sometimes
invested in industry. New orders, particularly those less associated with
the new expressions of upper-class religiosity, had no such support and
were often hard put to maintain themselves. This led various of them to
undertake small-scale industrial and mercantile ventures, producing and
selling specialty foods, religious articles, minor luxury items, textiles, and
other materials. Grievances about price-cutting by monastic producers,
some imagined and others justified, became a factor in the renewed
anticlericalism that developed after the turn of the century.

The nineteenth-century clergy continued to maintain the missionary
tradition of the Spanish Church. Though the Spanish completely failed to
equal the worldwide expansion of French and Italian Catholic missions
during this period, they remained very active in Latin America and in the
chief remaining colonies—Cuba, Puerto Rico, and the Philippines. This
was, once more, especially the work of the regular clergy, for Spanish
seculars did not become seriously involved in missions until about the
middle of the twentieth century. Outside the Hispanic world, Spanish
missionaries were most active in Indo-China, and also expanded into

Africa. It might further be remembered that the first archbishop of San Francisco, José Sadoc Alemany, was a Spanish Dominican.

REGIONALISM AND REGIONALIZATION

During the second half of the nineteenth century, Catholicism was progressively reestablished within the structure of conservative liberal and capitalist society in Spain. Though it did not completely make peace with the political system in terms of full Catholic participation until after the turn of the century, the Church had established a de facto compromise with the new social structure by the time of the restoration. New evangelism and expanded religiosity were aimed especially at the middle and upper class, and they were generally successful. By the late nineteenth century the new social and economic elite, which had never been religiously anti-Catholic during the earlier years of anticlerical tension, had become very broadly identified with the religion once more.

For the first time in Spanish history, religious identity and observance were becoming rather sharply divided by region and by social class. The north, broadly speaking, was both nominally Catholic and generally devout and observant. The poor and backward agrarian southern half of the country remained nominally Catholic, but it was neither devout nor observant, and the landless peasant masses were becoming increasingly alienated from formal religion, which they now identified with the antagonistic new institutional structure of modern Spain. What was true of poor, frequently landless peasants in the south was also becoming much more true—at least by the beginning of the twentieth century—of the working classes in the growing industrial cities of the north and northeast. Parish organization had always been weak in the south. Disamortization and other restrictive state policies discouraged extension of Church facilities to meet the growth of urban population as well. Institutional leaders concentrated religious recruitment and educational facilities disproportionately in middle-class districts. Thus a large proportion of the middle classes, along with the upper classes, were held for Catholicism, but by the end of the nineteenth century, urban workers and poor southern peasants were being lost. In general the elite, the rural population of the north, and much of the middle classes remained rather strongly Catholic; poor southern peasants, urban workers, and a good portion of the lower middle classes were strongly anticlerical and becoming anti-Catholic.

Religion was closely associated with a new form of modern political dissidence, regional nationalism, that had emerged by the end of the nineteenth century. Regional nationalism was probably an inevitable development in Spain, given the lack of effective national integration and the weakness of central Spain nationalism. A Spanish state had emerged under Fernando and Isabel in the late fifteenth century when there was not the most remote possibility of a unified nation. Religion served subsequently as the main unifying agent under the Spanish monarchy. When modern nations were developed in other parts of western and central Europe during the nineteenth century, Spain was rent by civil war, internal discord, and lagging cultural and economic development. The particularism of the Middle Ages was thus never fully overcome. Once monarchy, empire, and religion had either weakened or disappeared as unifiers, the profound internal divisions and regional disequilibria made it almost impossible to avoid the expression of strong political regionalist movements.

This had been foreshadowed as early as the first civil war of 1821–23, when royalism and traditionalism had been disproportionately concentrated in the particularist areas of the northeast. The tendency had been accentuated with the two Carlist civil wars, which were also to some extent regionalist conflicts. In the last years of the nineteenth century, traditionalism began to give way to a kind of modern nationalism, first in Catalonia and then, more slowly, in the more conservative Basque provinces. Whereas traditionalism had rested on the old social order and on peasants and clergy in particular, modern regional nationalism would depend much more on the middle classes, and in Catalonia on the modern industrial bourgeoisie. Such a change was not consummated, however, until after the turn of the century and the evident failure of the Spanish system in the final colonial debacle of 1898.

Throughout most of the nineteenth century, in fact, the Catalan bourgeoisie endeavored to cooperate with the Spanish system, and in turn after 1875, the Spanish regime made a particular effort to cooperate with Catalonia. One counterpart sought by the Catalan elite was a native Catalan episcopate rather than a Church leadership of non-Catalan prelates. This the government by and large provided during the last quarter of the century.

The most learned of the new Catalan prelates, Josep Torras i Bages, bishop of Vich, made a significant contribution to the emerging theories of Catalan identity and particularity. His books *La Iglesia y el regionalismo* (1887) and *La tradició* (1892) delineated a superior Catalan culture, more Catholic than that of the rest of Spain, which it was the duty of pious Catalans to affirm. Torras i Bages speculated that "perhaps there was no other nation so completely and solidly Christian as was Catalonia" under its historically separate constitution.

The situation in the Basque provinces was different, for there a native episcopate would probably have produced a provincial Church leadership of hostile Carlists. Therefore a policy of appointing native Church leaders in this region was not fully adopted until after 1900. The Basque provices underwent two generations of transition in the late nineteenth and early twentieth centuries as Vizcaya and then Guipúzcoa began a major industrialization. This at first had relatively little effect on the indices of religiosity, and in fact well into the twentieth century the Basque provinces would remain one of the most religious industrialized regions in the world. It affected economic and then political attitudes very much, however, as a new Basque bourgeoisie adopted moderate and practical policies in cooperation with the Spanish government. The structure of full traditionalism, and hence Carlism, was progressively eroded in the industrialized regions. By the 1890s it was slowly being replaced by a new, more modern form of particularism in the Basque nationalism being created and elaborated by Sabino de Arana y Goiri, son of a Carlist shipbuilder.

Basque nationalism was more extreme than Catalanism. It was at first strongly separatist, and only grudgingly gave way to the goal of broad autonomy in association with Madrid. There was a left-wing variant of Catalanism from the start, but no leftist form of Basque nationalism really emerged until the development of ETA in the 1960s. Arana y Goiri based nationalism as much as possible on tradition, and to him Basque tradition was synonymous with extreme religiosity. The first statutes that he drew up for the movement in 1895 would have made a new Basque regime a virtual theocracy, since every aspect was to be subordinated to religion, even though governmental power was to rest exclusively in the hands of secular authorities.

Nationalism drew significant support from the local Basque clergy almost from the start. Without their backing the movement might have been hard pressed to win the support of the Vizcayan and Guipúzcoan lower middle classes that it had won by the early twentieth century. By that time, it was Basque nationalism more than an eroded Carlism that was seen by Madrid as the main danger among the Basque clergy. Eventually in the twentieth century, orthodox traditionalists would be favored in Church appointments there, with the ostracism from high Church positions previously applied by Madrid to Carlists then being employed against Basque nationalists.

THE INTERNAL CONFLICT OVER CATHOLIC POLITICS

The introduction of democratic political mobilization in Spain in 1868 had, as mentioned in the preceding chapter, led to the formation of the first general laymen's organization for the defense of Catholicism through political and propaganda activity. The resulting Association of Catholics functioned in most parts of Spain (twenty-eight provinces) during the democratic interregnum, but languished and died away after the restoration of political stability and Church privilege under Alfonso XII. Only the simultaneously formed Catholic Youth organization survived, continuing to expand during the restoration period, particularly in Catalonia.

A few lay leaders still felt the absence of any national Catholic lay organization or party, however, and a move was made by Alejandro Pidal y Mon, heir to two major families prominent in the Moderate party of the Isabeline period. He feared for the long-term stability of the new system and the protection of Catholic interests, since the Liberal Conservative party was never a Catholic party per se, and its main rival, soon to be known as the Liberal party *tout court*, threatened a revival of anticlerical legislation. Therefore in 1881 Pidal formed a Catholic Union having the same goals and many of the same leaders as the old Association of Catholics. Yet it received the direct support of only that fraction of Catholic opinion that was more flexible in tone, and it was strongly attacked from the Carlist right.

In 1884 Pidal journeyed to Rome to explain his position and seek papal support. The current pontiff, Leo XIII, was beginning to encourage what would later become an attempted *ralliement* to the new liberal and anticlerical Third Republic in France, but his policy toward Spain was always more cautious. The papacy did not actually discourage Catholic organization with a view to influencing the Spanish system, but it considered the existing compromise reasonably satisfactory and believed that no political concessions to the system were really necessary in Spain. The traditionalist extreme right was much stronger than in France. Its basic position was codified in a new book, entitled *El liberalismo es pecado*, published that year by the Catalan priest Félix Sardá y Salvany, the most popular and extreme apologetic writer of the period.

Pidal did not lose his authorization but simply left on his own, and he therefore chose direct collaboration with the Spanish Conservatives, accepting the offer of a ministry in the third Cánovas government of 1884–85. In November 1884 in the encyclical *Inmortale Dei*, the pope provided further encouragement for Catholics to collaborate discreetly in the politics of liberal regimes, but this was largely ignored in Spain. There a lecture by the Grand Master of Spanish Masonry, the Madrid university prefessor Miguel Morayta, in favor of total academic freedom could still cause a scandal. Protests by some of the more outspoken members of the episcopacy were not sufficient to provoke government action, however.

Though the new regime had fired a number of anticlerical academics in 1875, it drew the line at further censorship, and the pope advised the Spanish hierarchy to be less aggressive.

The most moderate and progressive attitudes in the Church were to be found among some of the Catalan clergy, where Casañas, the bishop of Urgel, had Sardá y Salvany's book submitted to a council of theologians for possible reproof. This the council refused to do, endorsing it instead, but certain other leaders encouraged a Catalan presbyter, Celestino Pazos, to publish an article in refutation of Sardá. A meeting of twenty-four prelates in Madrid on the occasion of the funeral of Alfonso XII in 1885 endorsed the suggestions of *Inmortale Dei*, and emphasized that so long as theology and morals were safeguarded, Catholics were free to participate in diverse political forms. Though an appeal to the Sacred Congregation of the Index in Rome brought theoretical endorsement of Sardá and reproof of Pazos, who was forced to move to Madrid, the tendency toward rapprochement with conservative liberalism grew.

It even affected Carlism, whose more moderate followers sensed the need to modernize their program. They proposed to renounce any ambition of restoring the Inquisition (still a *sine qua non* for diehards) and even accepted the principle of limited toleration. In 1887 D. Carlos "VII" even spoke of the need for having a properly constituted traditionalist parliament prepare a traditionalist "constitution." When Carlist ultras adopted a hypercritical position, the pretender insisted on his personal authority as an ultimate criterion of party leadership. The extremists, led by Cándido Nocedal, rejected mere "absolutism," and insisted on pure theocracy and "Christian monarchy," which led to their expulsion from Carlist ranks in 1888. Nocedal and his supporters then formed the Integrist party of intransigent traditionalists. Though at first a significant minority of Carlists joined them, their schism betrayed the weakness more than the strength of their position. The Integrist faction maintained an organized existence down to Nocedal's death in 1906 and even beyond, but steadily declined.

Catholic alienation from nineteenth-century institutions was being overcome even in Spain. The main body of opinion followed neither the Integrists nor the more moderate main-line Carlists, but the conservative collaborationism of Pidal y Mon. Though only a portion of the hierarchy would go so far as to support collaborationism directly, it gained much support among Catholics of the Army officer corps, always potentially influential; among the Catholic intelligentsia; and among the elite of the politically active faithful in the middle and upper classes. Throughout this period, as during the Isabeline era, most serious Catholics either did not participate in politics at all or did not participate as Catholics, with the exception of the traditionalists, so that support in this dimension was not easy to measure. The general tendency of Catholic opinion was more and more toward Catholic collaboration in the politics of the liberal state to further Catholic interests.

Leo XIII encouraged this with a series of carefully worded encyclicals that distinguished between the objectionable aspects of doctrinaire liberal ideology on the one hand and the pursuit of legitimate goals within the context of contemporary political institutions on the other. To participate in a liberal parliamentary system or even in the government thereof was no longer held to be the same as being "liberal" in the objectionable sense of *Quanta cura*.

In Spain, one of the main obstacles to further Catholic political participation was the political factionalism dividing the faithful. The traditionalists would not cooperate with moderates and had already split among themselves. Moderates could not agree, at various times, on whether to try to work with mainline Carlists, to form a new conservative Catholic party, or to try a cooperate with and reform the existing secular Liberal Conservative party. A series of six national Catholic Congresses were organized by the Church leadership between 1889 and 1902 to discuss these and other issues. They were never able to reach effective conclusions about a new policy. As during the reconquest, the papacy endeavored by means of encyclicals, direct messages, and interventions of the nuncio to impose some unity on conflicting Spanish Catholic factions, but without success. The Spanish Church was perhaps the most ultramontane in Europe, but Spanish Catholic activists could never agree to follow any single domestic leadership in internal affairs. This immobilism and division was ultimately grounded in the ultraconservative complacency that dominated Catholic attitudes after 1875. If the existing Spanish regime, even when governed by the regular Liberal party, was now the most respectful of Catholic privilege of any European government, what need was there for a further Catholic political party or program? Complacency and factionalism thus precluded any organized *ralliement* along French lines, for none appeared to be needed amid the conservative, de facto proclerical liberalism of late-nineteenth-century Spain.

One major new effort was, however, begun in 1891 by Bishop Antonio María de Cascajares of Calahorra, one year later named archbishop of Valladolid. A former army officer, Cascajares was one of the most dynamic and ambitious prelates in Spain. Impressed by Catholic political organization in Germany and Belgium and by new efforts in France, he was also aware that the kind of political compromise represented by Cánovas was slowly losing its effectiveness, and that the initiative in

Spanish affairs seemed to be passing to the Liberal party led by Sagasta. Support for Cascajares's effort was slow to develop but received a boost in 1894 when a major group of Spanish Catholics, in pilgrimage to Rome, were harassed by a somewhat violent anticlerical demonstration when leaving the port of Valencia. Speaking to the group in Rome, the pope stressed the importance of striving to protect Catholic rights and interests through unified action in the fullest possible use of legal institutions, acting always under the guidance and tutelage of the episcopacy. Cascajares judged this the further encouragement he had been seeking, and by early 1895 brought out a small booklet entitled *La organización política de los católicos españoles*, basing his argument in part on the encyclical *Inter innumeras sollicitudines* (1892), which had encouraged Catholic participation even under the existing republican and mildly anticlerical institutions of France. Yet though Cascajares attracted the support of a few other members of the hierarchy, and though the queen-regent, Da. María Cristina, thought highly enough of him to obtain his papal nomination to the cardinalate that year, his proposal generated scant interest. A possible major ally, the Catalan shipping magnate and most active Catholic layman in Spain the Marqués de Comillas, was also enlisted, but finally rejected the enterprise. What Comillas did do in 1894, following the example of an Italian initiative, was to take the lead in forming the Junta Central de Acción Católica, stimulating a lay association introduced six years earlier.

The Spanish government entered a new phase of conflict with the outbreak of the final Cuban revolt in the last months of 1895. As the situation degenerated, Cascajares returned to his theme in a pastoral letter of September 1896. In the following month he abandoned his archepiscopal residence to establish himself in Madrid, carefully positioned for intrigue. As pressure against the last Cánovas government mounted, Cascajares's plan seems to have been to help provoke a final crisis which would be followed by the introduction of a broad conservative coalition government. This was evidently to be composed of regular Conservatives, Carlists, military figures, apolitical Catholics, and even a few patriotic Liberals such as Cascajares's personal friend José Canalejas. The aims were political realignment, conservative and patriotic reform, and that ultimate goal of diverse Catholic politicians since the 1840s, a marriage alliance between the two branches of the dynasty.

Once more the cardinal encountered frustration, though a new star appeared on the horizon in the spring of 1897 with the return of the former captain-general of Manila, Camilio Polavieja. Known as the "Christian general," Polavieja was more closely identified with Catholic political interests than any major activist in the military hierarchy.

Moreover, since he had been largely successful in repressing rebellion in the Philippine archipelago, he could be presented as a victorious general as well. For the next two years, right-wing Catholic opinion saw in Polavieja a political leader and possible savior from the defeat of the Spanish system. He came to represent a vague Catholic populism, though the concept of a "Spanish Boulanger," applied by a few historians, seems exaggerated. Polavieja had the ambitions but neither the range of support nor the novelty of program of the French war minister of the preceding decade.

The assassination of Cánovas in August 1897 increased uncertainty, but his lieutenants soon reorganized the Conservative party, once more frustrating Cascajares's plans. The cardinal nonetheless continued his visits to Madrid and pressed his goals in a new pastoral letter of February 1898. As the full dimensions of national catastrophe developed during that disastrous year for Spain, support for Polavieja grew. He issued his first political manifesto in September, disavowing any intention of forming a new party but calling for a broad patriotic movement of reform: honest administration, national unity, tax reform, equal terms of military service, decentralization, and financial retrenchment. By the end of the year, the general had come to an agreement with Francisco Silvela, Cánovas's heir as head of the Conservative party. The result was co-optation into the political system that brought him a cabinet post but quickly dissipated his personal support. His resignation in 1899, two years before the death of Cascajares, was followed by political oblivion.

LAGGING RESPONSE TO SOCIAL PROBLEMS

Nineteenth-century urbanization and the changes in the social and economic structure of the countryside led to major new social problems and made certain old ones more visible. These were exacerbated by a rapid growth in population, a near doubling during the course of the nineteenth century, the greatest demographic increase in Spanish history. Disamortization and full capitalist market exploitation led to a signficant expansion in the area of land under cultivation at mid-century, but this declined considerably in later decades because of poor techniques and the marginal quality of most of the land. Nor did the Spanish peasantry take up emigration to quite the same extent as did those of some other south European countries, despite the evident opportunity in Latin America. The consequence by the end of the century was the expansion of a new urban and rural proletariat for whom a very slow-paced industrialization in northern cities could not produce enough jobs. Underemployment was endemic, and the standard of living in the south-

ern countryside probably declined in relative terms. Poverty and resentment were even more evident in the cities than elsewhere because of the
concentration of population.

Traditionally, the Church had been the chief provider of charity and
welfare. It was estimated that before the disamortization it had operated
over 7,300 shelters, more than 2,200 hospitals, 106 orphanages, and 67
foundling homes. The elimination of much of the Church's endowment
income made it impossible to continue many of these or required that
they function on a reduced scale. The Church thus found itself unusually
ill-equipped to deal with want and social distress at the very time that
their concentration and expression, if not their proportionate volume,
became more intense.

The principal response was made by the religious. Many of the new
congregations of nuns devoted themselves to charity and work among the
poor, means were found to open a certain number of new hospitals to
replace those that had been closed, and new orphanages and foundling
homes were established, though on a limited basis. As early as 1702, a
priest in Madrid had set up a special cooperative pawnshop and savings
and loan organization for the poor, and some soup kitchens for the
destitute were maintained in the larger cities, just as in earlier times. A
number of new savings and charity organizations for the poor were
created, and there were also free schools, lunch programs, and special
recreation programs operated by the orders in some cities. Yet all these
touched only a small fraction of the urban poor at century's end.

By the turn of the century the Church was being denounced by the
new Spanish revolutionary left for having endorsed capitalism and made
a close alliance with the bourgeoisie. It was true that the Church was not
hostile to the new capitalist order as such. The material advantages
produced by liberal capitalism in Spain, though not on the order of those
in northwest Europe, were nonetheless evidenced by the general increase
in production and wealth and the improved conditions that had spurred a
growth in population. The Church had always supported the principle of
private property, properly adjusted, along with freedom of the will and
the liberty of the individual juridical personality.

The Church leadership did not, however, endorse capitalism *tout
court*. While denouncing the atheism, materialism, violence, and collectivism of the new revolutionary left, pastoral letters and circulars also
occasionally condemned the luxury, injustice, and indifference of the
newly wealthy. A diocesan synod at Jáen in 1872, for example, had
denounced as "sins that cry to heaven" the exaction of usury, holding
back of wages, or using the effects of depression to lower pay scales
unduly. Such criticism was relatively infrequent, however.

What liberal capitalism did create was a new differentiation and competition between social groups, one that had never before existed in the same way. Thus in a country slow to complete the early stages of industrialization, the disparities of wealth and the limited opportunity for the workers were felt more keenly than in the traditional society or than in the more rapidly growing, more generally prosperous economies of other north Atlantic countries. "Class struggle," not an especially prominent feature of Spanish history, would in the early twentieth century become more severe in Spain than anywhere else in western Europe. Spain was beginning to provide a unique and explosive mixture—a high degree of freedom and representation on the one hand, combined with the maximum of frustration and contradiction in the development of a modern industrial system, begun in the 1830s but not completed until the 1960s and 70s.

To this, the Church responded in general with calls for patience, submission, discipline, Christian charity, and the religious conversion of all. In the sixteenth century, local Church leaders had helped to take the initiative in political and social revolt. After the experiences of the nineteenth century, the Spanish Church counted rebellion among the very gravest of sins. Though it affirmed the standard of social justice, in the short run it counseled all sectors of society to be content with their lot. The pronouncements of some Church figures occasionally even used such unfortunate terms as "masters" and "servants" in referring to social classes.

Probably the most common attitude of the clergy and upper-class Catholics to the socioeconomic problems of the industrial era was reflected in a report to Madrid priests by the Congregation of the Hospital of San Pedro in 1883:

> Religion is the bond that unites man with God. What will become of man if that bond is broken? If the connection is loosened, how can man resist the fierce assault of so many enemies? It is desired, and properly so, that the worker respect the authorities . . . ; therefore above all see to it that he fears and loves God. Obedient workers are sought who do not rebel or participate in strikes . . . ; therefore strive to have them love and imitate Jesus, the very model of patience and resignation in the workshop of his most chaste earthly father. Dedication and love of work are recognized as necessary in a worker . . . , therefore let him view work, rather than as a right to compulsory retribution in this world, as a religious duty, whose exact fulfillment will be rewarded with eternal recompense in Heaven.[3]

---

3. Quoted in Javier Tusell, *Historia de la democracia cristiana en España* (Madrid, 1974), 1:20.

Yet a few individual members of the regular clergy had taken the initiative earlier in trying to form special Catholic associations among urban workers. These first efforts revealed no ambition whatever to organize Catholic syndicates (trade unions)—a concept that did not really develop in Spain until the 1890s—but were normally called "workers' circles" and were meant for counselling, religious instruction, and social assistance. The first of these were organized by a Carmelite monk of Carlist background in Barcelona in 1851. He was expelled from the city by the authorities three years later because of his Carlist affiliations. Other workers' circles were organized between 1865 and 1872 in such diverse cities as Madrid, Manresa, and Alcoy, but seem to have died away.

New efforts were launched during the restoration. In 1877 Ceferino González, the Thomist scholar and later primate, took the initiative as bishop of Córdoba in encouraging new workers' circles. These flourished briefly, enrolling 3,000 workers and operating sixteen small schools for workers' children, but did not long survive the bishop's transfer to Seville in 1881. Similarly, in 1879 José María Urquinaona, the bishop of Barcelona, founded a "Friends of the Workers" association to provide social assistance among Barcelona workers, an association that had an equally brief life.

The only ecclesiastic who achieved any success at all in worker organization during the restoration was the Jesuit evangelist Antonio Vicent. He was a follower of the nineteenth-century theorists of Catholic corporatism in France and Austria, and hoped ultimately to organize harmonious corporations of employers and workers. The initial step was to form workers' circles on the local level that would bring together owners and employees and work for spiritual and social meliorism under the authority of the Church hierarchy. Vicent's first successful circle was organized in Tortosa in 1879, and his groups increased steadily in membership during the two decades that followed.

The beginning of modern social Catholicism is often dated from Leo XIII's famous 1891 encyclical *Rerum novarum*. This pontiff had already approached the social question in five earlier documents. In the new encyclical he refuted radical socialist theory but also rejected extreme doctrines of capitalism, emphasizing Catholic responsibility to deal with social problems. The authority for new Catholic social associations to resolve social issues was affirmed without specifying whether they should represent both workers and employers or only workers, or whether they should be formally confessional or not.

The pope's encyclical drew a significant response from the Spanish episcopate, which commented on it in more than twenty new pastoral letters, but this response was only feebly translated into practical initiatives. Social problems were the theme of several new books by Spanish Catholics, including one by Vicent, and of three new Catholic journals founded during the decade. The leading lay activist was the Marqués de Comillas, the Catholic millionaire businessman from Barcelona, who promoted the formation of a Consejo Nacional de las Corporaciones Católico-Obreras (National Council of Catholic Worker Corporations) in Madrid in 1896 to serve as an umbrella organization that would coordinate both the Vicent workers' circles and other religious, charitable, and mutual-assistance groups for Catholic workers that were being formed. Yet the workers' circles themselves were primarily religious and recreational associations, and even Vicent later admitted that they were not very effective in promoting the workers' material interests. Their most successful undertaking was the organization of a large workers' pilgrimage to Rome in 1894, subsidized by Comillas. The nominal membership by 1900 of 48,500 in the workers' circles and 27,500 in other diverse groups tended, if anything, to exaggerate their significance and achievements.

A workers' circle of Madrid typographers was apparently converted into a Catholic trade union in 1897, the first such in Spain, while the last in the series of six national Catholic Congresses, convening five years later, officially endorsed the idea of *sindicatos católicos* (Catholic trade unions as distinct from mixed workers' circles), but interest and initiative were wanting. Catholic opinion distrusted workers' organization and even found it difficult to support mixed Catholic workers' circles. After the turn of the century this situation would change, but only very slowly, and the social and regional cleavages between Catholics and non-Catholics of Spain would increase.

5

Clericalism and Anticlericalism in the Early Twentieth Century

THE EARLY twentieth century was the time of the last phase of the Catholic revival in Spain, and also the time in which the revival began to fade away in a society increasingly attuned to secular issues. The very success of the revival had aroused new opposition to Catholicism, yet by the time of World War I the old struggles over religion, politics, and culture seemed to have given way to social, economic, and military concerns. This is not to indicate that Catholicism generally lost influence or power during the long reign of Alfonso XIII from 1902 to 1931. Formally, the very opposite was the case. All the positions of privilege reestablished under the restoration, with only the most marginal exceptions, were retained, and the new king was fully respectful of the Church, which in fact he tended to favor. By the second decade of the century, however, Spanish society and culture were beginning to change more rapidly, while the Church was not, and the disjunction between Catholicism and a part of Spain's population continued to grow. The major spiritual and devotional emphases of the revival continued and some attention was given to popular missions and evangelism, but little appears to have been accomplished to halt the de-Christianization of large numbers of the southern peasantry and of urban workers. Memoirs of evangelists tell impressive tales of the hostility and alienation felt toward the Church in certain districts of the south.

The new pontificate of Pius X (1903–14) was generally well received in Spain, whereas the relatively more aristocratic and sophisticated leadership of Leo XIII had led Integrists to pray for the conversion of the pope. Though Pius X continued his predecessor's efforts to overcome the factionalism of Spanish Catholics and to encourage a more coherent and organized social and political response, his direction was perceived as more conservative and traditional and in general more reassuring to the faithful in Spain. Pius vigorously maintained the principles of authority and hierarchy and repressed the proponents of theological modernism in the Church. The Spanish clergy caused not the slightest difficulty in this regard, being truly "more Catholic than the pope." Despite their cultural reliance on the French for theological writing and new devotional and educational approaches, Spanish clergy and laymen rigorously eschewed anything tainted with novel or liberal ideas. The conservative course of Pius X's pontificate was in fact guided in considerable measure by two of the most influential Spanish prelates in Rome in the last two centuries or more: the Vatican's secretary of state, Cardinal Merry del Val, and the Catalan Capuchin, Cardinal Vives i Tutò, secretary of the Sacred Congregation of Religious Orders, who played a major role in the condemnation of modernism. His extensive influence led Roman wits to say of Vives i Tutò that "Vives è tutto" (Vives is everything).

The diocesan or secular clergy increased slightly in numbers during the early years of the century, then declined during the 1920s to number little more than 30,000 by 1930. Membership in the orders followed a roughly similar trajectory, totaling a little over 50,000 in 1930. Although it is as difficult to reach definitive conclusions about the overall financial condition of the Spanish Church in the early twentieth century as in any other period, it is clear that incomes of the regular clergy declined slightly. This was a period of general though not extremely rapid inflation, but the salaries paid the secular clergy by the state scarcely increased. The discounting done at various times by penurious governments was eventually done away with, though the 14 percent *donativo* ("gift," but really an income tax) on all but the smallest salaries remained. Liberal governments tried to reduce the stipends still further, while the hierarchy continually urged adjustments upward. During the years 1924–27 the Primo de Rivera dictatorship, generally quite favorable to the Church, increased state spending by 21 percent but the clerical stipend only 2.65 percent.

It is difficult to conclude that the Church itself benefitted directly from the modest Spanish economic expansion of the early twentieth century. Contributions are said to have flattened out and declined, proportionately, fairly steadily. Often the capital collected by the diocesan leadership was invested in state bonds that barely kept pace with inflation. Only a few of the wealthier orders, with capital invested in industry, may have actually improved their situation. Most had no significant sources of regular income. Though some were partially supported by state bonds held in compensation for earlier property confiscations, they lived in considerable measure from fees paid by individuals, and sometimes by municipal and provincial governments, for their work in education and social services. Most of the orders continued to face major problems, and several engaged in commercial activity on a modest scale (partly devoted to religious artifacts) to help earn a living. By the early years of the century, fees that subtracted from the funds available for other state employment, and the small businesses which were accused of competing with ordinary workers, had become major targets of the new anticlericalism.

THE ANTICLERICAL OFFENSIVE OF 1901–12

Anticlericalism has been a feature of Spanish and other west European societies in varying forms for about a thousand years. It was endemic at times during the Middle Ages and played a major role during the Reformation. Before the nineteenth century it was often exhibited by otherwise pious Catholics, and in its earlier and sometimes milder forms was not to be confused with antireligiosity. What may be called traditional anticlericalism involved criticism of the clergy for their failures and excesses and not for their religious role itself. The anticlericalism of the Catholic Enlightenment similarly fit into this category, as did, for that matter, the early if drastic reforms of Spanish liberalism.

Antireligious anticlericalism emerged in Spain in 1820–21 and assumed more violent form in the 1830s and again during the democratic interregnum, only to die away or be repressed in the more conservative atmosphere of the restoration. Unlike the earlier anticlericalism, which often stemmed from political or economic rivalry or from criticism of the personal and cultural shortcomings of individual clergy, antireligious anticlericalism was ideological in origin and categorical in nature. It was opposed to religious belief and influence in society, and proposed to reduce or eliminate it. This was to be accomplished, first, by eradicating all special perquisites and privileges of the Church, and second, by outlawing, or in extreme cases liquidating physically, the clergy. Antireligious anticlericalism was the consequence of the radical dimensions of modern liberalism and of materialist revolutionary philosophies, particularly in social and cultural atmospheres that had not undergone full modern secularization.

It is nonetheless too simple to pigeonhole anticlerical attitudes and policies in the dichotomous categories of Catholic and antireligious, for in late nineteenth- and early twentieth-century Spain, various strains of moderate liberal anticlericalism fell somewhat ambiguously between the two. Some moderately anticlerical Liberal party politicians were still practicing Catholics, as were a small number of republicans, even though both tended to be associated more and more with radical antireligious groups. Within the Liberal party and among diverse republicans, attitudes toward the Church and religious issues varied greatly, ranging from endorsement of the status quo by some Liberals to extreme incendiary violence on the part of some republicans.

However measured, anticlerical agitation increased considerably at the turn of the century. The decade that followed the disaster of 1898 was the heyday of "Regenerationism" in politics and public discussion, involving diverse strategies for reform and renewal of society, economics, and major institutions. Conservative regenerationists concentrated on political and economic issues that involved technical institutional reform. Liberal and radical regenerationists raised more fundamental issues, and one of the chief among these was the role of the Church and of religion in general in Spanish life.

The revival of anticlericalism has been variously traced to several major sources. Most commonly, it has been held to be a reaction against the Catholic revival itself, the reestablishment of Church privilege, the new alliance between Church and state, and the great influence of Catholicism in culture and education. These were all undoubtedly major factors. By the turn of the century the Church had once again become part of the social and political establishment, and it was more overtly identified with the new upper classes than with any other sector of society. Though excluded from most of higher education, it dominated secondary education and had considerable influence in Spain's lagging primary schools. At the same time, an extraordinary gulf was developing between the Church and the urban lower classes and landless peasants, among whom Catholic endeavors were either absent altogether or almost unintelligible in cultural terms, exposing a broad social base to new anti-Catholic agitation.

There occurred meanwhile a rather slow but progressive ideological radicalization of the Spanish left. Its major nineteenth-century form was democratic republicanism. Weak and divided for two generations after the total failure of 1873–74, republicanism nonetheless remained in the background as the alternate ideology if the conservative monarchy should falter. Rooted in the eighteenth and early nineteenth centuries and socially based on the secularized portions of the middle classes, republicanism stressed political and cultural change in which enmity against the Church was as central as opposition to the monarchy.

The second phase of radical ideology took the form of revolutionary collectivism and came to Spain rather later than to most European lands. The unique feature of the revolutionary left in Spain was, of course, the strength of anarchism (in the form of mass anarchosyndicalism) during the early twentieth century. Anticlericalism at first played a fundamentally different role in the anarchist movement than it played in the Spanish Socialist party, both qualitatively and quantitatively. The latter, primarily of Marxist bent, was based on "scientific" materialism and focused on political and economic issues. The anarchists were apostles of rationalism and a new morality, and stressed broadly cultural and social issues in a manner quite different from the Socialists. To the anarchists, traditional religion was at least as much a barrier as capitalism to the inauguration of a new morality and culture. They therefore made anti-clericalism a necessary frontispiece of revolution, while to the Socialists it was more of a natural concomitant, requiring less attention.

In the early twentieth century, the cultural elite and the Spanish intelligentsia in general were little attracted to either neo-Catholicism or revolutionary ideology. Spanish culture on the formal level was at that point more strongly oriented toward nineteenth-century liberalism in a rather archaic sense than was that of any other European country. The general attitudes of most writers and scholars could be best described as liberal in diverse shades, ranging from the conservatively and moderately liberal of a sort fashionable in other lands a century earlier to radical liberalism of the form dominant in early Third Republican France. Anti-clericalism was general and fashionable, but its virulence and intensity varied greatly from sector to sector.

Anticlerical propaganda was fed by a special subculture of journalism and republican or libertarian propaganda, at the head of which stood the radical publicist José Nakens, who founded the newspaper *El Motín* (The Riot) in Madrid in 1881, and for nearly thirty years made it the banner of anticlerical publication. Second only to Nakens were the writings of an alleged ex-priest who published under the name of Constancio Miralta, and churned out a series of book-length purported confessions and diatribes against the vices of the clergy, replete with detailed accounts of orgies in convents and so forth.[1] By the turn of the century, this propaganda was swelling in volume, encouraged by both anarchists and the more radical republicans, the latter finding it the most probable ploy to increase their fortunes among the lower-middle and lower classes of the larger cities.

THE LIBERAL PARTY'S NEW ANTICLERICAL POLICY

The main new wave of agitation at century's end began while the last colonial war still raged in 1897–98, for the republican press blamed much of Spain's woes in the Philippines on the influence of the religious orders. The latter did possess extensive estates in the islands on which about 2

---

1. One of Miralta's titles is worth citing in full: *Los secretos de la confesión: Revelaciones, misterios, crímenes y monstruosidades; sacrilegios, aberraciones y ridiculeces; miserias, problemas sociales o religiosos y extravagancias humanas; inmoralidades de la moral conservadora y ultramontana, y otros excesos o pecados oídos a los penitentes durante larga práctica del confesionario por Constancio Miralta (Presbítero)* (Madrid, 1886).

percent of the native population lived, and they also played a major role in Philippine religious life. After the collapse of the empire, several thousand *religiosos* were repatriated to the mother country, while the first of several thousand French monks and friars began to enter Spain to seek shelter from the new exclaustration laws of the French Republic. The agitation about Spain being overrun with monks and nuns, domestic and foreign, only increased in volume.

Many Catholics were convinced that Masonic conspiracy lay behind the reburgeoning anticlericalism, and during the previous generation they had carried on considerable propaganda of their own to "expose" the role of Masons as something other than a society of benevolence. Members of the Catholic extreme right introduced an unsuccessful motion to prevent the Grand Master of the Spanish Orient, Miguel Morayta, from assuming his elected seat in parliament in 1899, and eventually Catholics would be accused of suffering from a virtual "Masonic psychosis." There is no doubt that the Masons, who numbered about 65,000 in Spain during the 1890s, sometimes figured prominently in Spanish liberalism and republicanism, but their direct collective influence on both politics and anticlericalism has doubtless been considerably exaggerated.

Much greater controversy stemmed from the first Conservative "regenerationist" government in 1899, led by Silvela and his temporary political associate Polavieja. Alejandro Pidal, instigator of the earlier abortive attempt at Catholic political union, returned to the ministry of development and education, and altogether the Silvela administration presented the strongest neo-Catholic tint of any Spanish government since the Isabeline regime of the 1860s. When Pidal quickly produced regulations for the state secondary curriculum that would require some religious instruction, cries of "vaticanism" rent the air.

Anticlerical riots, the first in more than a quarter-century, broke out in several cities during the summer of 1899. Combined with renewed Liberal and republican opposition in parliament, this was an indication of mounting antagonism to any pronounced neorightist policy in Madrid. Silvela, the new Conservative leader, chose to return to a more moderate position. Polavieja, the "Catholic general," was dropped from the cabinet within a few months, followed by Pidal, who was replaced by a more neutral personality in the newly created ministry of education. As it turned out, Silvela had little appetite for confrontation, and despite high ideals and lofty goals, proved unable to provide the Conservatives with effective leadership.

Liberal party leaders pressed for a quick return to power, using the anticlerical banner as a rallying point. They were obviously inspired by the contemporary French government of Waldeck-Rousseau, which in

1899–1900 imposed a drastic policy of state control over Catholic orders, achieving the functional unity and political longevity of French Radicalism in the process. The elderly Práxedes Mateo Sagasta had led the Spanish Liberal party ever since its consolidation in the 1880s, but he was no Waldeck-Rousseau. Sagasta had seen three preceding Spanish regimes come and go. His own priorities were compromise and survival, and his nickname *El viejo pastor* (the Old Shepherd) testified to his long record of successfully holding together the centripetal members of his flock while guarding against the excesses of the more radical. He would have preferred a new liberal program geared primarily to the current economic problems of a country facing heavy government debt and domestic depression, but that could not equal the emotional effect of anticlericalism among the Liberal rank-and-file. A sudden outbreak by a few small bands of Carlist guerrillas in the Catalan back country, leading to a temporary suspension of constitutional guarantees, added to the alarm being generated among party activists. With some reluctance, Sagasta gave in and warily hoisted the anticlerical banner in the closing days of 1900.

The next phase was inaugurated by a cultural event, the opening in Madrid of the new anticlerical drama *Electra* by Benito Pérez Galdós on January 30, 1901. Spain's greatest living writer—and some might have said the greatest since Cervantes—Galdós was a personal friend of Menéndez y Pelayo but a bitter foe of the Church, and some of his major novels had featured vigorous attacks on Catholicism. The opening of the play coincided with major publicity given the hearing of a suit before the Supreme Court in Madrid brought by the mother of a young heiress who claimed that her daughter had been forced into a convent by clerical pressure—an argument parallel to that of the play. Emotions were intensified by the impending marriage of the princess of Asturias (elder sister of D. Alfonso, heir to the throne but still a minor) to an Italian aristocrat of Carlist background, whose Carlist father arrived in Madrid at this moment. The resulting riots and demonstrations in Madrid were echoed in some twenty of the largest cities in Spain. They continued with scant interruption for a full week, and were often directed against the Jesuits, for two centuries the prime single target of anticlerical animus. The outbursts were contained only by the declaration of martial law and the use of troops in a number of cities.

This breakdown of public order was the signal of doom for the governing Conservative administration, no longer headed by Silvela. In March 1901 Sagasta and the Liberals returned to power, forming a new ministry known to political wags as the "Electra cabinet." After a few minor anticlerical measures, it conducted new elections in which religion more than anything else was the issue. These did not produce decisive results. Under the still-oligarchic Spanish system the government normally won elections, but the modest Liberal majority was unimpressive by the standards of the day.

The main issue in the anticlerical struggle had become the size and number of the orders and their possible restriction or expulsion by the government, as in France. The Concordat of 1851 had authorized three male orders, two specifically and a third to be named subsequently. The identity of the latter was never stipulated, providing a legal loophole for the introduction of scores of orders in the second half of the nineteenth century. The Spanish law of associations of 1887 theoretically applied to religious orders, requiring their registration with the government, but orders had normally been recognized simply by an administrative order rather than by the registration procedure stipulated.

One of the chief Catholic defenses in this situation was that the Concordat had never intended to restrict the number of orders to the same three throughout Spain and that different third orders were to be permitted in different provinces. There were many other arguments. They included the interpretation that other orders were covered by Article 43 of the Concordat, referring miscellaneous issues to the "canonical discipline of the Church"; reference to the 1887 law, which excepted those orders that were approved by the Concordat; clear indication that the 1887 law was directed primarily toward secular associations; the historical sanction of legal recognition by Spanish government over the years; and finally, that Article 45 of the Concordat stipulated that "any future difficulty" was to be negotiated between the papacy and the crown rather than be made the subject of arbitrarily restrictive legislation.

Minor anticlerical demonstrations, including a few genuine riots, continued sporadically in a number of cities during the spring and summer of 1901. The Portuguese government instituted new legislation at this point, restricting Catholic orders in metropolitan Portugal; and the more severe new French law of associations was passed in July, stimulating the movement of further hundreds of French monks and friars into Spain. The Sagasta ministry followed suit with a measure in September 1901 to require all orders in Spain, save the two specified in the Concordat, to register with Spanish authorities within the following six months.

Sagasta nonetheless had no intention of presenting the Church with any drastic *fait accompli*. His aim seems to have been to use this initial legislation as leverage to negotiate some reasonable concession from the Vatican. Such ambition was a complete failure, for the papal representatives firmly stood their ground and advised the orders in Spain not to register. When the deadline passed without result, Sagasta's administration was reorganized, and a milder measure was introduced in April 1902 that still required the orders to register under the terms of the 1887 law but seemed to indicate automatic approval. This was the exact contrary of the wholesale suppression of orders that had begun in France.

The Liberal government hoped to make this part of a general Church reform project that might be negotiated with the Vatican. It proposed to attempt a slight reduction of the ecclesiastical budget, the closing of monasteries and nunneries with less than twelve residents, consolidation of parish structures, elimination of certain marginal establishments, and the use of 20 percent of the resulting savings to increase the income of the poorest parish priests. However reasonable some of these aims seemed, the papacy was in no mood to compromise, viewing them as the mere entering wedge of a new anticlerical assault. Only a few marginal concessions were admitted, and negotiations soon broke down altogether.

Old and ill, Sagasta had reached the end of his rope. He had no illusion that the Liberals could win in direct confrontation with conservative opinion. The more ardent anticlericals began to desert the government, claiming that the Old Shepherd had used the religious issue merely to gain the prime minister's chair, from which he then immediately raised a white flag.

THE CATHOLIC CONSERVATISM OF ANTONIO MAURA

The Liberal ministry collapsed in December 1902, to be replaced by the Conservatives under Silvela. Silvela lacked the nerve of leadership, however, and by the close of the following year had been replaced as prime minister by the bold, energetic, and imperious Antonio Maura, whose style was altogether different. Allegedly the descendant of Sephardic *chuetas* from Mallorca, Maura was an ardent Catholic and represented a new approach that aimed at economic modernization coupled with extreme legal and cultural conservatism. The program he established for the Spanish right would survive until the death of Franco in 1975. The adjective *liberal* had already been dropped from the name of the Conservative party, and henceforth it would become explicitly identified with Catholic interests and the defense of religion.

Maura did make an effort to settle the issue of registration by preparing to negotiate a new *Convenio* (Agreement) with the papacy. This would have stipulated free registration of all the orders in Spain without sanction or proscription. It would also have included a few minor concessions to the Liberals, such as full taxation of the orders' commercial activities and the closing of small monasteries with less than twelve residents. Before this proposal could be carried through, however, the government fell, over a minor political issue, and following two short-lived ministries under secondary leadership, the Liberals returned to power in 1905.

Since the death of Sagasta two years earlier, the Liberals had been severely divided. Factionalism stemmed primarily from personal rivalry between the various party leaders, though there were also minor programmatic differences related to degree of moderation or radicalism on key issues. The Spanish Liberal party remained an essentially nineteenth-century organization down to its demise in 1923, individualist on social issues, orthodox in finance, elitist and oligarchic in style and structure, and largely divorced from the masses. Since the factions could agree on little else, anticlericalism still served as its main rallying point. As several short-lived ministries under diverse factional chieftains succeeded each other in power from 1905 to 1907, complete liberty of civil marriage was restored in Spain and plans were drawn up for the resecularization of cemeteries and a new restrictive law of associations to apply to the orders. The latter touched off a major Catholic protest campaign during the autumn and winter of 1906–7. Large meetings were held in the northeast, and petitions of protest bearing hundreds of thousands of signatures were collected. The faithful had little to fear, for the Liberals lost power altogether early in 1907 and were replaced by Antonio Maura, now firmly in control of the Conservative party.

Maura's "long government" from early 1907 to late 1909 was probably the most successful of that era, passing scores of bills on new economic measures, attempting electoral reform, and legalizing strikes and lockouts in Spain. Maura hoped to rally all conservative and Catholic forces in the country behind his revitalized Conservative party, and at first he seemed to achieve some success in that endeavor. His government placed restrictions on the scope of civil marriage and indicated that it planned eventually to take measures to deal with the issue of registration and legalization of the orders once and for all. Liberal and republican foes charged it with "vaticanism" and suggested that an agreement existed for Catholic support of the Maura administration, though indeed no such formal understanding ever seems to have been reached.

Maura's strength and success, his broad conservative and Catholic backing, and his imperious manner and determined tactics were all alarming to the opposition. Republicans and some Liberals insisted that the government, because of its religious identity, domination of parliament, and vigorous law-and-order policy, was dangerously reactionary, despite its reform policies in social and economic affairs. A proposed new antiterrorist law of 1908 was blocked by a united front of Liberals and republicans as a threat to civil liberties. This marked the first occasion on which the monarchist Liberal party had joined with the republicans to thwart its Conservative counterpart, but this was justified on the grounds that Maura had abandoned the principles of compromise on which Cánovas had founded the system. The truth of such a charge is nonetheless doubtful. Spain's two-party system under constitutional monarchy had resolutely defended Catholic interests since 1875, and Maura merely continued that practice. The image sometimes projected by his rhetoric—and even more, that projected by his enemies—created the impression that he would make of the Conservative party a Catholic confessional group, but such was not the case. Maura in fact proposed to preserve the existing institutional structure as exactly as possible. What was new was the combination of a bolder policy of administrative and economic reformism with a determined ideological conservatism opposed to cultural change.

THE "SEMANA TRÁGICA"

His downfall was precipitated by colonial revolt against Spanish operations in northern Morocco in 1909. The weak and unprepared Spanish army felt it necessary to mobilize reserve regiments immediately and called up several contingents of troops from Barcelona and other centers. By late July this resulted in massive draft riots in the Catalan capital that took on quasi-revolutionary overtones, with the main focus on anticlerical incendiarism directed against church buildings, monasteries, convents, and schools. Military intervention was necessary to restore order after what became known as Barcelona's "Semana Trágica" (Tragic Week). Altogether, at least eighty religious buildings were burned, including twenty-one of Barcelona's fifty-eight churches, thirty of its seventy-five convents and monasteries, and some thirty buildings devoted to educational or service activities. More than a hundred deaths resulted, though more from the pacification than the initial disorders. Two clergy were killed, and another perished in one of the many fires set by the rioters.

The repression that followed was harsh and somewhat arbitrary. About 2,000 accused rioters were arrested and 5 subsequently executed. The most famous of these was the anarchist conspirator, pedagogue, and terrorist Francisco Ferrer. His case became an international *cause célèbre*, provoking protests and demonstrations against "inquisitorial Spain" throughout Europe.[2] The repression sparked a renewal of intense

---

2. Ferrer was involved in the riots, though not necessarily a prime instigator of them. A revolutionary propagandist and organizer of "rationalist" schools, he was, however, implicated in earlier acts of anarchist terrorism. For the Spanish authorities, his execution served a symbolic function.

opposition to Maura on the part of the Liberal-republican bloc, and the young king, Alfonso XIII, encouraged his resignation three months later, enabling the Liberals to return to power.

The events of the Semana Trágica, their causes, motivations, and consequences, have been a source of controversy for commentators and scholars ever since. From the very beginning, observers were struck by the fact that the lower-class rioters directed their rage against religious property rather than against the persons of the clergy, the government directly, the army or police, the upper classes, or the economic system. It has always been appreciated, however, that this is in large part explained by the fact that the dominant force in Barcelona during the early years of the century was not the Liberals, Conservatives, Catalanists, or anarchists but the Radical Republican party of Alejandro Lerroux. *Lerrouxismo* was a derivation of nineteenth-century French lower-middle-class radicalism, anticlericalism, and freethinking. It showed remarkable talent for opening neighborhood social centers and conducting active propaganda and electoral mobilization. Its ideological stock-in-trade was an unusually virulent form of anticlericalism that found full expression in the Barcelona riots. By contrast, anarchism had had only a marginal influence on the working classes of the Catalan capital up to that point.

The church burnings of the Semana Trágica also reveal the qualified and limited character of secularization in early twentieth-century Spain. It would be more than fifty years before the moral-religious structure was replaced by the secular adoration of leisure, mass consumption, and other forms of materialist reverence. Political and cultural controversy in Spain was still conducted in a moralistic frame of reference. Throughout the nineteenth century the "true spirit of Christianity" had been a standard watchword for anticlericals. Just as conservatives identified the social and political order with moral truth and religion, many middle-class and some working-class radicals invoked high principles of education and cultural development as the primary needs of society and the ultimate cures for its problems.

Even the most radical republicans taught that the solution to national problems lay in politics, culture, and education rather than in economic reform or social revolution. Barcelona workers were the more easily influenced by the *comecuras* (priesteaters) of *lerrouxismo* because of the class basis of religion in the larger cities. The clergy often found it physically and emotionally awkward even to approach workers, and their manner was often detested by the latter for its apparent condescension. Catholic schools and social centers were frequently scorned for snobbery, class bias, and lack of concern for workers' problems. Church property was therefore burned with great zest all over Barcelona as a protest against the failings of the clergy in their religious and social roles, but violence against persons was very limited. There was also a rather morbid interest in ransacking monasteries and convents to verify the stories concerning equipment for orgies, hidden treasures, and buried nuns. Some fifty mummified corpses of nuns were disinterred by the rioters in convents.

THE CANALEJAS GOVERNMENT'S "PADLOCK LAW"

The next Liberal government was able to bring together its diverse factions only on a general platform of civil liberties that included freedom of conscience and education, civil marriage, secular burial, and the control of religious associations. In February 1910 José Canalejas, the most coherent and forceful of the Liberal leaders, took over as prime minister and led his followers into general elections. The government returned the usual parliamentary majority in the lower house, but in the senate it was three votes short, thanks in part to the presence of the seventeen appointed prelates who safeguarded the Church's interests. Thus for its nearly three years of life the Canalejas government would lack a full majority, a situation henceforth endemic under the parliamentary monarchy. The institutions of nineteenth-century Spanish liberalism had resulted in a stalemated regime, as was the case throughout southern Europe at that time. They permitted the mobilization and expression of any number of protest groups, but the major institutional forces were too oligarchic and too entrenched either to be displaced or to be susceptible to further fundamental reform.

Canalejas was the last vigorous leader of historic Spanish liberalism, and was himself something of a paradox. Though a friend of the notorious Archbishop Cardinal Cascajares of the 1890s and a man who maintained a family chapel in his home, he had been a consistent anticlerical in politics since 1899 and achieved the direction of his party on that basis. He led the last major reformist government of the regime from 1910 to 1912, emphasizing social and economic legislation, yet met such unremitting opposition from the left that it threatened to undo his administration.

The Liberals had already canceled the right of the clergy to inspect the curriculum of non-Catholic private schools, and in June 1910 recognized the right of Protestant churches to exhibit external titles and emblems on their buildings, a practice previously forbidden. The main goals were to establish the long-sought state restrictions on religious orders, and secondly, to negotiate a reduction in the ecclesiastical subsidy. Ultimately, however, Canalejas realized that these measures could not be imposed by legislative will. They could only be arranged through negotiations with the Vatican, which refused all major concessions.

The Canalejas government countered by introducing the famous and controversial *Ley del candado* (Padlock Law), which proposed that no new religious community would be legally recognized in Spain within the next two years unless it registered with the ministry of justice and ecclesiastical affairs (Gracia y Justicia, as this Spanish ministry had been known for most of the period since 1851). Moreover, such permission would automatically be denied to orders if more than one-third of their members in Spain were foreigners (presumably French). Yet the force of this proposed legislation was considerably diminished by the fact that Spain already held nearly 4,000 communities of regular clergy and nuns, totaling nearly 55,000 religious, including representatives of every single order recognized by Rome. Furthermore, a subsequent amendment provided for the automatic lapsing of this regulation if a new law of religious associations was not passed within two years.

In July 1910, well before the presentation of this legislation to parliament, its mere announcement provoked the Catholic north to erupt in organized mass protest, officially endorsed by major municipal and provincial governments in the Basque country. By August, similar actions spread throughout Catalonia, leading to a major expansion of the network of Catholic Action there. In San Sebastián, center of mass demonstrations, the government eventually called out the troops and imposed absolute martial law.

There was little for Catholics to fear. Though the initial legislation was approved, the permanent measures on which it depended for any real effect were never codified. While an International Eucharistic Congress was held in Madrid in 1911 amid gala festivities, the government struggled against manifold foes. Further efforts to negotiate concessions from the Holy See proved fruitless, for the papacy saw no need to concede gratuitously what the Spanish administration could not obtain from its own parliament. The career of Canalejas was then abruptly ended by an anarchist assassin at the close of 1912. The Liberal party was never successfully reorganized, and managed only a temporary face-saving formula before allowing the Padlock Law to lapse altogether at the end of 1914.

Thus the direct achievements of the anticlerical offensive were few and limited. Liberal governments did manage to further liberalize and secularize the atmosphere of the state educational system, backward and inadequate as it was, and to broaden the terms of civil marriage. Their futile efforts to control the orders merely provoked countermobilization by Catholics. After 1914 their party was disintegrating, caught in the death throes of a stalemated parliamentary system. From that point on, severe social and economic problems, together with military and colonial issues, precluded further fixation on anticlericalism.

NEW ORGANIZATIONAL INITIATIVES
AND POLITICAL APPROACHES

Efforts at Catholic political organization were renewed after the turn of the century under the stimulus of the new anticlerical campaign. These first took the form of a number of Catholic "Juntas" or "Ligas" (Committees or Leagues), set up in various of the more strongly Catholic provinces between 1901 and 1903, partly at the initiative of the primate, Cardinal Sancha. The Ligas Católicas had the same general goals as the old Asociación de Católicas, staging rallies, distributing information and exordia, defending Catholic interests, and also, in a new departure, sometimes sponsoring independent Catholic candidates. Only one Catholic independent was elected in all Spain in 1905, but local candidates stood with somewhat greater success in the next contests, held in 1907. The papal nuncio steadily encouraged more political activism, along with expanded functions for such lay organizations as Catholic Action, which had originally been introduced in Spain in 1888. Engagement in politics was further encouraged by cancellation of the Vatican's requirement of electoral abstentionism for Italian Catholics. New parallel associations, called Comités or Centros de Defensa Social, were opened in Madrid, Barcelona and other large cities. Yet though the Ligas persisted for a number of years they eventually faded away, weakened by their ambiguous nature, which sought to be something more than a propaganda agency yet never tried to be a party.

A dramatic example of collaboration occurred in 1906–7 when Carlists, Catholic Catalan regionalists, and other Catholic groups joined with moderate republicans in the broad Catalan Solidarity regionalist coalition in opposition to the centralism of the liberal state. It completely swept the parliamentary elections of 1907 in Catalonia but did not survive long thereafter. During the next few years, Catholic activism in politics was represented directly only at the provincial level, as new alliances were negotiated to support independent candidates. Opposition to Canalejas' Padlock Law generated a wave of Catholic publicity and propaganda between 1910 and 1912, but this was primarily negative and oppositional. It did not produce any direct new Catholic alternatives.

The most productive new step in relation to public affairs during these years was probably the organization of an Asociación Católica Nacional de Jóvenes Propagandistas (ACNP; The National Catholic Association of Propagandists, the adjective "Young" soon being dropped) by the Jesuit Angel Ayala at the close of 1908. This became a major layman's activist group devoted to public information, propaganda, and the defense of Catholic interests. In 1911 it founded a daily newspaper in

Madrid, *El Debate*, which quickly emerged as the most important and sophisticated Catholic political voice, in increasingly close association with the Church hierarchy. The ACNP established La Editorial Católica in the following year and made it the largest Catholic publisher in Spain.

After 1912 the struggle between clericalism and anticlericalism began to wane, as the politics of regionalism and socioeconomic conflict absorbed more and more attention. These problems were in turn exacerbated by the outbreak of World War I. Though Spain maintained a consistent position throughout as the largest of the neutral European states, the war had a major impact, increasing internal tensions. Spanish attitudes toward the war itself reflected a sort of left-right split, as radicals and liberals favored the Entente and conservatives the Central Powers. Spanish Catholic opinion strongly supported Germany, seeing in the Central Powers the bulwark of conservative institutions as opposed to more liberal states such as England, France, and Italy, all of whom had led assaults on the Church.

The new pope, Benedict XV (1914–22), was hailed as the first in centuries to have had personal experience in Spain, where he had served earlier in the nunciatura. After Italy's entry into the war, the Spanish episcopate offered him sanctuary and refuge, should it prove necessary to flee a belligerent country.

In 1917, the year of the Russian revolution, Spain was also beset by attempts at three different dimensions of revolt: political, military, and social. Though each was isolated and doomed to failure, together they demonstrated the growing restiveness with established institutions. The religious issue played no role in any of them, which seemed to indicate that the antagonisms of the nineteenth century had been replaced by other concerns.

Regionally, the most effective pressure group within the higher clergy were the Catalans, now firmly in control of their regional Church. Catalans were culturally the most sophisticated of Spanish Catholics, and connections between ecclesiastics and the more conservative Catalanists were close. Yet the closely-knit, well-read, and culturally more advanced Catalan clergy were no more adept than any other section of the Church in bridging the gulf between the non- and anti-Catholic parts of their own urban industrial society. After 1917, Catalonia became the main focus of radical labor and revolutionary activity in Spain, and Catalan anarchosyndicalists were fanatically anti-Catholic, assassinating the cardinal archbishop of Tarragona in 1922.

The slow but steady disintegration of the political institutions of parliamentary monarchy after 1917 was naturally of growing concern to Catholic conservatives. That this paralleled the experience of all other south European countries could scarcely be a source of consolation, but only added to the alarm. The last effective leader of the regular Conservative party, Eduardo Dato, was murdered by anarchists in 1921, and by that point the two-party system established by Cánovas and Sagasta in the preceding century had ceased to function.

Only one alternative, and that of limited utility, appeared within the regular political spectrum. In 1913 Antonio Maura had resigned the leadership of his party on the narrowly interpreted grounds that King Alfonso and the dominant political forces were refusing to abide by the established rules of the game (an accusation for the most part exaggerated). After that point his own followers within the increasingly fragmented Spanish party system were known simply as Maurists. Maura himself never evolved beyond his own ideas and program of 1907–9, but some of his followers tried to project a new ideology of "Maurism." This was grounded in the principles of Catholicism, and while standing firmly for law and order, pressed for social reform, economic deveolopment, honest administration, and government decentralization. The Maurists also emphasized Spanish patriotism, almost a form of prenationalism, to a distinctly greater degree than the other main factions. They were the only regular parliamentary faction to form their own youth group, the Young Maurists, and altogether stressed a broad new set of doctrines and programmatic goals for Catholic political activism. Consequently *El Debate*, as the most eminent Catholic newspaper in Spain, usually supported Maurism, even though many Catholics involved in politics did not.

In 1919 a more liberal and social-minded group of ecclesiastics and intellectuals founded a new Grupo de Democracia Cristiana, to the left of the Maurists. The Group was not itself a party or a political faction, and actually amounted to little more than a study and propaganda association. Its significance lay in the fact that it was the first Catholic organization in Spain to espouse the nomenclature and some of the values of the Christian democratic parties organized in other Catholic countries.

Catholic political initiative and representation in general remained as fragmented and anomic as that of Spain's oligarchic political system. So long as the regular structure of conservative parliamentary monarchy endured, the Church seemed incapable of any effective response to new enterprises. In March 1922, for example, *El Debate* and the ACNP announced the start of a Gran Campaña Social in Madrid, a large fund-raising and mobilizing endeavor in support of a major Catholic university and broad new social and informational activities by Catholic groups. This had to be called off after only three weeks, because wealthy Catholics resented the pressure for contributions, and the crown and the established groups found the initiative an irritating complication.

The most original and suggestive new endeavor was the organization in December 1922 of Spain's first Christian democratic political party, the Partido Social Popular (PSP). Inspired by the success and doctrines of Don Luigi Sturzo's Partito Popolare Italiano, the PSP declared itself an officially Catholic political party that also accepted fully the legal order of parliamentary liberalism. Its membership was heterogeneous in the extreme, being composed of young Carlists, part of the Maurist Youth, the Grupo de Democracia Cristiana, and the promoters of new forms of social Catholicism among the laity and clergy. The PSP's members and supporters were far from unified, for some advocated advanced social programs while others were very moderate, just as some were radical democrats and others strong law-and-order people willing to accept the principle of emergency dictatorship. The PSP announced the aim of mass mobilization in contrast to the oligarchic clientelism of the established parties. It preached proportional democratic representation in parliament, a corporative senate, and decentralization of the national government. Despite or because of its contradictions, it was far too advanced for the great majority of Catholics, and thus it did not present a ticket in the last elections of the parliamentary monarchy in May 1923. Four months later the existing party system was abruptly replaced by the military dictatorship of General Miguel Primo de Rivera.

EDUCATION AND CULTURE

The dominant position of Catholic schools in secondary education was largely maintained through the 1920s, while the attention given by the religious orders to education continued to increase. Whereas in 1904 about 49 percent of the male orders and 34 percent of the female orders were devoted to teaching, by 1923 these figures had increased to 57 and 42 percent respectively. Further subsidies were provided by the state to open more Catholic elementary schools in regions where there were no public schools. The Catholic primary education system expanded, and some attention was given to increasing the small number of Catholic schools in the neighborhoods of urban workers.

By this point, however, state education was growing at a more rapid pace, contributing to the expansion of secularized attitudes in Spain. The advantage of Catholic schools lay perhaps in their lower student-teacher ratio, since so many of the state schools were single-teacher rural establishments or woefully understaffed urban institutions. By 1930, Catholic schools accounted for nearly one-third of the elementary schools in Spain and a slightly higher proportion of secondary ones.

One effect of anticlerical legislation was to reduce further the limited

Catholic influence in the public school system, influence that had never been as great as anticlericals supposed. Despite the Church's success in educating large numbers of the middle classes, it continued to lose ground among the poor and the urban workers and among the cultural elite.

The volume of Catholic publications in most categories continued to grow, and informational services were more abundant than ever before. There was a further expansion of the general Catholic press and of the more serious cultural reviews published by scholars in the religious orders. Yet the continued growth in Catholic publications was now merely one aspect of the expansion of cultural activities in a more literate and productive society. By the 1920s it could not arrest the marked tendency toward secularization and cultural and social materialism that were beginning to dominate large segments of Spanish society.

There was evidence of new growth and sophistication in Catholic scholarship by the 1920s, a modest Catholic counterpart of the flourishing of what literary specialists like to call the Silver Age of early twentieth-century Spanish culture between 1898 and 1936. Mention might be made of the relatively unknown Galician priest Angel Amor Ruibal, who taught in the seminary of Santiago de Compostela. Amor Ruibal, who died in 1930, produced a ten-volume work called *Los problemas fundamentales de la filosofía y del dogma*, a novel and eclectic attempt to work out a new understanding of philosophical truth, and possibly the most original such exercise by a Spanish cleric since the time of Ramon Llull.

By the 1920s, the Church leadership and the clergy in general were increasingly preoccupied with the growing informality of popular dress, behavior, and culture. Pastoral letters were issued on the sins of immodesty and the dangers of pornography, which was then being distributed in Spain in quantity for the first time. The growing popularity of oceanside vacations and the construction of swimming pools raised new problems. One aspect of the dilemma was met by confection of the notorious *traje de baño tipo Padre Laburu* (the Padre Laburu style swimsuit), a remarkable device—named for its inventor, a Basque priest—that clothed its wearer from neck to ankle, yet was loose enough to permit some movement in the water.

THE FRUSTRATIONS AND ACHIEVEMENTS
OF SOCIAL CATHOLICISM

The mounting intensity of what was widely known as the "social problem" in early twentieth-century Spain stimulated a variety of new efforts at "social Catholism" and worker organization. These were almost uniformly of very limited or no success. Only in the Catholic countryside did a religiously affiliated mass socioeconomic organization prove effective.

This was not for lack of benevolent foundations. The *Reseña Eclesiástica* for 1920 listed some 12,000, of which approximately 1,000 were located in Madrid and 800 in Seville but only 200 in Barcelona, the chief industrial center. Of these, about 3,000 were devoted to education and other adult or instructional activities, another 3,000 to charity, approximately 2,500 to medical care (including more than 2,000 hospitals or medical-assistance centers), and only about 1,800 exclusively to devotional activities. Problems were at least fourfold. Most of the foundations were small and lacked funds to expand their activities. Moreover, like religious devotion in general, they were geographically maldistributed. The effectiveness of their operation seems to have varied greatly. Some of the hospitals and charity centers revealed a high level of commitment and effective service, while others did not. The social approach in the larger cities sometimes exhibited superciliousness and class bias, or made assistance dependent on submission to religious instruction or devotional activities.

Verbal attention certainly increased. Some ninety pastoral letters from members of the episcopate, dealing in whole or in part with social problems, have been counted for the four decades 1891–1930. Catholic study groups on social issues multiplied, more and more publications appeared, and the amount of literature distributed to Catholics and workers alike greatly increased. A number of social assemblies for priests were held, and by 1914 a course in sociology had been established in almost every seminary in the country.

The lack of imagination and creative power in modern Spanish Catholicism encouraged a fascination with foreign models. If Italy provided the chief inspiration for progressive political Catholicism, the German Volksvereine and Belgian free Catholic syndicates filled much the same function for social Catholicism. The French Catholic "Social Weeks" were also imitated, one being held yearly in Spain between 1907 and 1912 to inform ecclesiastics about social problems.

A variety of new efforts were made at worker organization. The lack of accomplishment by Vicent's worker circles led to a search for other models, next discovered in the Catholic "Unioni Popolari" of Italy, recommended to the Italian episcopate in an encyclical of Pius X in 1906. Beginning in 1905, small Catholic "Uniones Profesionales" were formed in Bilbao, and later spread to a dozen other cities. The advantage of the UPs was that they were "pure," all-worker organizations, yet did not use the frightening name *sindicatos* (trade unions), and might thus be described as a kind of halfway gesture between mixed worker-employer circles and genuine trade unions.

Another departure was the organization of a network in Barcelona in 1907 called "Acción Social Popular." Its founder was the Jesuit Gabriel Palau, who figured prominently as the most active promoter of social Catholicism in Spain during the next decade. The ASP was neither a political party nor a trade union, but a social and cultural organization aimed at the dissemination of religious and social information. By 1915 this "Volksverein hispánico," as Palau sometimes termed it, had more than 27,000 members in Catalonia. It did more than any other Catholic group in Spain to try to raise the level of consciousness of Catholics about the social problem and that of workers about religion. It also organized a number of Uniones Profesionales and formed a small worker insurance and benevolence association. Since the UPs generally believed in avoiding conflict with management, however, they had scant economic success and few members, except for one notable Barcelona white-collar union (UPDEC).

Palau was ultimately defeated not by hostile anarchosyndicalists (who denounced his labor supporters as forming a "sacristy of scabs") but by rivals in the Catholic power structure. The Marqués de Comillas, the Catholic multimillionaire and promoter of multiple paternalistic welfare schemes, endeavored to generate a distinct set of Church and employer-controlled syndicates through a Catholic national council in Madrid. The current primate, Cardinal Aguirre, allowed himself to be persuaded that Palau planned to dominate social Catholic initiatives throughout Spain, while Jesuit rivals resented his prominence and following, limited though it was. Conservative Catholics complained that both the ASP and the weak Barcelona UPs were fomenting labor strife. In 1916 Palau was forced to resign and move to Argentina. His organization was replaced by a new, ultraconservative Acción Popular, heavily paternalistic and fully controlled by the Church hierarchy. Only in the small Catalan industrial town of Igualada did a handful of independent Uniones Profesionales survive with strong worker support.

In fact, the only successful initiative of social Catholicism in Spain's industrial capital during the early twentieth century was not a labor organization but the Barcelona Caixa de Pensions per a Vellesa i d'Estalvis (Old Age Pensions and Savings Bank). This was founded by a lay militant, Francesc Moragas, after the industrial strike wave of 1902. The Caixa's aims were eminently practical and it offered equal terms to all participants, irrespective of their spiritual condition or interest in formal devotions. It soon prospered, providing genuine assistance for many and becoming one of Catalonia's largest financial institutions down to the present day.

The concept of Catholic syndicates as distinct from mixed workers' circles, discussion groups, and benevolent associations started to take hold in several parts of the country in 1912, the year of the first apparent strike by such an organization. The most active leaders were two Dominicans, Pedro Gerard and José Gafo. Inspired more by the Belgian Catholic free syndicates than the employer-associated French Syndicats Jaunes or the Italian Unioni, Gerard organized a syndicate of vineyard and distillery workers in Jerez de la Frontera, while Gafo formed a syndicate of railwaymen in Madrid. Similarly, an Asturian priest, Maximiliano Arboleya, began to organize syndicates of miners and then of farm workers in his area. By 1916 Gerard and Gafo had brought together a Federación Nacional de Sindicatos Católicos-Libres, employing the adjective "Free" in the title of their unions to indicate that they were exclusively worker syndicates not subject to paternalistic employer control. Three years later the employer-dominated Confederación Nacional de Sindicatos Católicos Obreros that had been concurrently created by Comillas and the main ultraconservative "social Catholic" oligarchy attempted to arrange unification with the Católicos-Libres. Though Gerard had been forced to abandon his work and died that year (1919), Gafo and his followers walked out of the conference, insisting on independence and a more militant labor policy. Yet, though the Católicos-Libres were the most vigorous and "advanced" of the Catholic syndicates and had organized about 60,000 workers, even they attempted to avoid direct conflict with capital much of the time. Catholic emphasis was always placed on *La Paz Social* (social peace), name of the most influential social Catholic paper of the preceding generation. In the harsh world of Spanish labor relations, whose asperity was compounded by the violent tactics of the leftist unions, all the Catholic syndicates lacked the aggressiveness to achieve significant economic or organizational results, while some remained little more than fronts for management control.

A more effective organization, one that continues to flourish today, was the Solidaridad de Trabajadores Vascos (STV; Solidarity of Basque Workers), the Basque nationalist labor organization formed in 1911. The STV was not officially confessional like the regular Catholic syndicates, but it was composed almost exclusively of Catholic workers and was strongly Catholic in tone, like all Basque nationalist organizations in the early period. As the workers' arm of a major protest movement, it was less hesitant to engage in aggressive trade union activities. Even the STV at first relied on white-collar employees, however, and did not expand into a larger and more significant labor organization until after the coming of the Second Republic in 1931.

The only trade union movement originated by Catholics that even momentarily became a major Spanish labor federation was that of the Sindicatos Libres of Barcelona, not to be confused with the Sindicatos Católicos-Libres of Gerard and Gafo. The Sindicatos Libres of Barcelona were organized in 1919 by radical young Carlist blue- and white-collar workers, disgusted by the strong-arm tactics and heavy-handed domination that accompanied the organization of Catalan workers by the anarchosyndicalist CNT. At that point the CNT, an officially atheistic confederation, counted more than 700,000 members, the first mass labor movement in Spain of any hue.

The Carlist workers of Barcelona represented quite a different culture than that of the upper-class paternalists and ecclesiastics who normally promoted social Catholicism. Theirs was a grass-roots organization that stemmed from popular rural Carlism, which in Catalonia and elsewhere had combatted anticlericals and liberal capitalist politicians for a full century. While rejecting domination by anarchist goon squads, Carlist workers had little interest in embracing modern urban capitalism and its culture, whether liberal or conservative. They proposed an independently Catholic "people's syndicalism," not officially confessional, that would work for the improvement of labor at the same time that it combatted anarchosyndicalism. The Libres of Barcelona scorned most Catholic syndicates as artificial, with the sole exception of Gafo's Católicos-Libres.

In their early years, the Barcelona Libres dedicated themselves to a bloody street war with the CNT in which scores were killed. Favored by the military governor of the city in 1921–22, they momentarily gained physical dominance over their rivals and increased their membership in Catalonia to a purported 175,000 (about half as many as the CNT in that region). In fact, with the CNT temporarily outlawed, the Libres for the moment became the primary labor organization in Spain's largest industrial region, though their following was normally weakest in the larger factories. As their labor following increased, they adopted a more militant and aggressive policy toward management, conducting many strikes of their own, though almost always with greater moderation in economic tactics than the CNT. Their combination of left-wing economics and right-wing cultural attitudes struck many as protofascist, but the charge was an artificial one, for they remained a class-based organization, rejected nearly all radical modern culture, and had nothing to do with nationalism. By 1923, with freedom restored to the CNT, the Libres found themselves isolated and losing members, but they managed to sustain their strength in some areas nonetheless.

The history of the Sindicatos Libres of Barcelona was obviously quite distinct from that of confessional Catholic syndicalism. They were on good terms only with Gafo's workers' syndicates, which by the early 1920s had been reduced mainly to the Basque provinces and Navarre. Finally, in December 1923, the two groups merged, forming the Confederación Nacional de Sindicatos Libres de España, with little more than 100,000 members, mainly from the Barcelona Libres. The organization grew once more under the Primo de Rivera dictatorship, only to face virtual collapse with the return of freedom and the regional domination of the CNT.

There was, however, one large and reasonably successful socioeconomic organization that was officially confessional—the Confederación Nacional Católica Agraria (CONCA), initiated in Old Castile in 1912 and transformed into a national confederation five years later. The CONCA was a Catholic farmers' organization. Its leaders tended to be owners of large landholdings, and its membership was frequently structured around the local village priest. Its principal following was concentrated in Old Castile and Leon, in a northeastern zone centered on Navarre, Alava, and northern Aragon, and the eastern provinces of Valencia and Murcia. The CONCA sought to protect the existing social interests and property structure of northern Spain, where backward smallholdings predominated, intermixed with larger estates. Its success was due to several basic factors: the continuing Catholicism of the north Spanish countryside, the absence of competing organizations there, and the rewards generated by its socioeconomic activities. The CONCA established a sizable network of rural cooperatives (for both consumers and producers) and organized farm insurance programs and savings and credit organizations. Though it also promoted machinery rental cooperatives, its goal was not so much the modern transformation of agriculture as greater security and well-being under the existing structure. By 1922 it had enrolled more than half a million families, representing over three million people, and had as large a following as the CNT.

The CONCA played no role in the poverty-ridden, latifundist, and religiously tepid south. An organizational campaign in Andalusia during 1919–20 achieved little, despite a publicized drive to convince largeholders to give away a little of their property to landless peasants. Membership subsequently declined, but even after the collapse of the monarchy, when it had to face the enmity of a new Republican regime, the CONCA held much of its ground. Even though it later enrolled only about 200,000 families, the CONCA played an important role in maintaining the strength of social and political Catholicism in the northern countryside during the years that followed.

CATHOLICISM AND
THE PRIMO DE RIVERA DICTATORSHIP, 1923–30

Though the monarchy did not fall until 1931, parliamentary government came to an end in September 1923 with the establishment of the dictatorship of General Miguel Primo de Rivera. This regime lasted six and one-half years, until January 1930, and in the process won the active or passive support of the great majority of Catholics. Middle-class opinion in general at first favored this benignly authoritarian, almost bloodless new dictatorship, accepting its argument that internal disorder and political factionalism had made Spain ungovernable through normal parliamentary means.

At the very outset in November 1923, King Alfonso and Primo de Rivera made a state visit to Rome, during the course of which they rendered formal obeisance to the pope, the most important gesture of this sort made by any head of state since 1870. The dictatorship developed harmonious relations with the Church hierarchy and endeavored to favor Catholic interests in a number of ways. Though it did little to increase the ecclesiastical stipend, it provided further financial and administrative assistance to Catholic education. Conversely, when the Catalan episcopate combatted the regime's suppression of regional culture and the use of Catalan in religious services, the government was able to count on the tacit support of other groups of the hierarchy.

The most progressive sector of Catholic civic activists, the Partido Social Popular (PSP), divided over the issue of collaboration. Yet even within the PSP, only the most liberal minority resisted, a position otherwise shared among Catholic groups only by Basque nationalists and some of the liberal Catalanists.

The various institutions of social Catholicism generally supported the Primo de Rivera regime. The company unions of Comillas and his Jesuit associates (Sindicatos Obreros Católicos) rallied immediately, as did the CONCA. Gafo and the Libres lent their support and participation later on, despite their more radical position on economic issues.[3] Only a handful of social Catholics, such as the Asturian Arboleya, held fast to the position that political democracy must be consubstantial with social justice. Identification with the dictatorship would prove well-nigh fatal

---

3. Gafo declared that he favored partial socialization of property and worker participation in ownership, a position supported by a part of the Libres.

after 1930, when with the exception of the CONCA, the very modest achievements of social Catholicism would be largely swept away.

The main civilian collaborators of Primo de Rivera came from Catholic ranks. José Calvo Sotelo, former young Maurist and then militant of the PSP, became director of local administration under the dictatorship and prepared a broad new statute of local self-government. Later, after the initial Military Directory was replaced by a regular cabinet, Calvo Sotelo rose to be minister of finance. Many of his political colleagues filled lesser positions.

It was the ACNP which helped to take the initiative in 1924 in forming the Unión Patriótica, which became the regime's political front. The initial concept of the UP was, admittedly, based more on that of the Catholic Center in Germany—a broad civic group of Catholics willing to work with diverse forms of government. By 1926, however, the UP had become an official state movement. Two years later, when a largely nonelective National Assembly was convened to work out a possible constitutional reform, former militants of the ACNP and PSP such as Víctor Pradera took the lead in trying to establish terms of a more conservative and semiauthoritarian regime under the monarchy. This attempt completely collapsed, however, for lack of coherent leadership and authentic support.

Close association with the dictatorship would have disastrous consequences for the Church just as it had for the monarchy. Nor did its Catholic identity benefit the dictatorship in the long run, either, for this only stimulated a major new phase of anticlericalism whose passions were enlisted by the foes of the regime. Primo de Rivera's proposal to grant official recognition to degrees awarded by Catholic universities on the same terms as those given the state university system sparked the first open opposition to his government in 1928–29. This took the form of student demonstrations and riots, an important factor in helping to precipitate the dictatorship's downfall.

The confused course of Catholic civic and social action, with its mixture of progressive and authoritarian elements, altogether failed to reduce the divisions between Catholics and non-Catholics, and in fact the de-Catholicization of most of the larger cities and the south was accelerating. Even though so major a Catholic organ as *El Debate* had gone into opposition in 1928, the identity of Catholicism with a rightist authoritarian regime made the Church a prime target of the republican reaction that developed. After the experience of the seven-year dictatorship, the most liberal members of the middle classes were more convinced than ever that Catholicism was the bulwark of authoritarianism and reaction and hence the main obstacle to progress and enlightenment. In somewhat parallel fashion, urban workers and the southern rural proletariat saw the Church as the cultural and moral support of the possessing classes, the principal dike against revolution. Thus when the monarchy collapsed in April 1931, the Church would find itself even more exposed and vulnerable than at the start of the liberal regime.

6

From Anticlericalism to Revolution

THE INAUGURATION of the Second Republic in April 1931 initiated the most dramatic phase of the contemporary history of both Spain
and the Church. As a western European country whose intelligentsia and
juridical institutions were attuned to the most advanced norms of west
European liberalism, Spain had been consistently introduced to sophisticated forms of liberal representative systems for more than a hundred
years. It was customary for political innovation in Spain to precede social
and economic development or general cultural transformation. No other
country in the world at such a limited level of general national development persistently endeavored to sustain such advanced political forms.
To that extent, the introduction of a democratic republic in the midst of
the Great Depression was fully consistent with Spain's modern history of
"precocious liberalism."

Contrary to what has frequently been alleged by hostile commentators, the response of the Catholic Church was far from one of unremitting
animosity. As other governments moved steadily toward more pronounced forms of liberal and radical politics, a democratic republic with
reasonable guarantees of freedom for the Church would have been far
from the worst context for religious institutions. Recent experiences with
such diverse countries as the Soviet Union, Italy, and Mexico, combined
with the dismal collapse of the Spanish monarchy, did not leave the
Church leadership eager to engage in combat with the new Spanish
system.

That the Republic decided to launch a frontal assault on the Church
was due to the temporary preponderance of the left, combined with the
frustrations and abuses of the preceding generation. The radicalization of
anticlerical feeling that developed after 1931 was of such an intensity that
it often seems difficult to comprehend. The extreme Spanish anticlericalism of the Republican decade built of course on the classical nineteenth-
century anticlerical doctrines and the attempted moderate anticlerical
offensive of the years 1901–12. At first it seemed no more than a victorious Spanish variant of the standard hard-line anticlericalism adopted or

attempted by most west European or Latin American Catholic countries in the transition to liberalism. The deadly virulence of Spanish anticlericalism probably stemmed, however, from its dual dimensions: the cultural/political anticlericalism of the middle-class extremist or "left" Republicans and the total revolutionary anticlericalism of the mass revolutionary movements.

The cultural and political anticlericalism of the middle-class left Republicans was rooted in the standard Enlightenment/rationalist critique of Christian theology in general and the Catholic clergy in particular. As has been seen in the preceding chapter, this was exacerbated in Spain, as in certain other Catholic countries, by the reestablishment of a strong bond between the Church and the parliamentary monarchy, together with the Catholic religious revival and the prominent place of the Church in middle-class secondary education. Such sources of antagonism were only broadened and sharpened by the experience of the Primo de Rivera dictatorship, which seemed to provide final proof that the Church was in league with repression and reaction and therefore must be brought to its knees.

The mood of the revolutionary movements was more extreme yet. It has already been suggested that anarchosyndicalism, the largest of the Spanish revolutionary worker movements, was dominated by a moralistic and dichotomous or manichean ideology that assigned great weight to the cultural and educational underpinnings of the dominant oppressor society. The fact that in the neo-Catholic Spanish society the principal palliatives of the capitalist system in social welfare were administered by the clergy reinforced the conviction that the latter represented the most insidious aspect of the existing structure, legitimating it and providing motivation and inspiration. Thus to a Spanish anarchist the burning of a church held greater value, both practical and symbolic, than the bombing of a capitalist factory.

Anticlericalism also became much more salient for the Socialists, the other mass revolutionary movement. The intensification of anticlerical policy among them also seems in considerable measure to have been a consequence of the example of the dictatorship, which seemed to prove that the Church was a more important part of the capitalist system than Spanish Marxists had given it credit for. It also followed the expansion of the Socialist party and its trade union affiliate into much broader organizations comprising more heterogeneous (and illiterate) supporters, with whom anticlericalism of the most extreme sort was quite popular. Added to this was a great renewal of anticlerical propaganda after 1930, which partly accounts in itself for the growing hatred.

All this in turn created the logical sequence of self-reinforcing mutual hostilities. The assault on the Church soon produced a massive defensive reaction on the part of Catholics which Republicans and leftists alike then saw as their chief political threat. This only seemed to them to confirm their original diagnosis and to give the conflict a more lethal quality. It was no longer a matter of culture and education but of revolution and counterrevolution, of life and death. In 1909 and 1931, anticlerical rioters concentrated on the burning of buildings; by 1934 revolutionaries were beginning the categorical murder of priests as an ineluctable concomitant of revolution.

The new wave of Republican and leftist anticlericalism provoked such a powerful reaction among Catholics that it has often been blamed for the eventual breakdown of the Republic and for the Civil War. At least insofar as the breakdown itself is concerned, this seems a considerable exaggeration. The religious issue certainly made a major contribution to anti-Republican sentiment, but strictly political and economic factors were equally important. The Civil War of 1936 should not be confused with those of 1822, 1833, or 1872. Rather than a traditionalist/liberal struggle like the latter, it was one of the major revolutionary/counterrevolutionary wars of the twentieth century. It was not primed by liberal anticlericalism but by the immediate rise of a powerful mass revolutionary left that conservative forces chose to confront before it was too late.

The Second Spanish Republic represented an attempt at democratization in the very moment that the direction of political change in the rest of Europe was toward authoritarianism, whether conservative, fascist, or communist. It ended with the dismal spectacle of the only country in the history of the twentieth century whose polity completely broke down into revolutionary/counterrevolutionary civil war without experiencing major involvement in foreign war, colonialism, or outside intervention.

This was the fault neither of clericalism nor of anticlericalism but of two other aspects of the Spanish situation. One of these was the inherent conflict between the country's political precocity—combined with the advanced cultural and institutional norms of its modern elites—and its social and economic backwardness. A maximally explosive combination was produced: optimal freedom and opportunity for the development of sociopolitical conflict contrasted with very limited means for its deflection or resolution. There were countries in eastern Europe that were equally underdeveloped, but not so free, democratic, or politically precocious. They simply repressed their problems, something that liberal Spain was incapable of doing. The advanced states that were equally liberal and democratic did not suffer such social and regional division or economic stress.

Another primary conditioning factor was Spain's independence, amounting almost to isolation. Neutral in the First World War and little involved in contemporary empire, Spain did not feel the international pressures that induced movements of unity or nationalism at home and determined or foreshortened the responses of many other countries. This left its domestic factions free and unfettered, with opportunity to develop their mutual competition to the utmost. In Spain the left-right dialectic of modern politics was therefore carried out to its final and most destructive consequences.

THE SECOND REPUBLIC

The first government of the Second Republic was made up of representatives of the diverse Republican parties, ranging from moderate to extremist, and of the Socialists, who suddenly expanded into a mass movement for the first time in their history. They had not been voted in by direct referendum, but the Republican-Socialist coalition had resoundingly defeated monarchist candidates in the larger cities in the municipal elections of April 12, 1931. This victory, which provoked the departure of Alfonso XIII, probably held as much plebiscitary value as was conceded to it at the time.

The coalition's electoral manifesto declared: "Catholics: the maximum program of the coalition is freedom of religion. . . . Only religious liberty can emancipate us from discreditable clericalism. . . . The Republic . . . will not persecute any religion. Tolerance will be its theme."[1] Though a deliberate deception on the part of the majority of the coalition, this propaganda was obviously accepted by many Catholics. All indications were that the great majority of politically conscious Spaniards approved the new regime, whether or not with any degree of enthusiasm. A more calm and bloodless transition has rarely occurred in any land.

The Church leadership similarly accepted the new regime without formal complaint, hoping for a continuation of the favorable terms of the existing Concordat under a democratic regime. Catholic opposition to the Republic in any official or organized sense cannot be said to have existed. Even though Primo de Rivera had appointed a number of ultraconservative bishops of Integrist or Carlist background, these also held their peace, save for private complaints and murmuring.

The first discordant note from the Church was struck on May 2, when the *Boletín Oficial* of the archdiocese of Toledo published a pastoral letter from the primate, the very conservative Cardinal Pablo Segura, in praise of the departed king. Segura declared that it would have been less

---

1. Quoted in José M. Sánchez, *Reform and Reaction* (Chapel Hill, 1964), 74.

than just to fail to note his constant devotion to the Catholic faith and the Holy See, and his consecration of Spain to the Sacred Heart of Jesus. Though the pastoral did not attack the Republic directly, its praise of Alfonso XIII was interpreted as such. Republican authorities pressured the papal nuncio to have Segura recalled to Rome, which occurred within eight days. The papacy of Pius XI sought no quarrel with the new regime, a particularly accommodating attitude being shown by the secretary of state, Cardinal Pacelli (the future Pius XII). On the day before his departure, however, a meeting of archbishops in Toledo agreed to issue a public protest against the anticlerical policies already announced by the new government.

Immediately afterward, on May 11, there occurred the notorious *quema de conventos* (burning of convents). Over a period of three days, anticlerical mobs in Madrid, Seville, and five other cities sacked and burned approximately one hundred religious buildings. The political identity of the rioters and the groups responsible remains a matter of controversy; extremist Republicans may have been as active as anarchists. At any rate, Republican authorities proved most reluctant to provide police protection, taking the position that Church institutions were not worth any risks to security forces. This event was the first sign of Republican radicalization and sent a chill of terror down the spines of devout Catholics. A few days later, Mateo Múgica, the bishop of Vitoria, the only prelate to have given outward evidence of hostility against the new regime, was exiled from Spain, as was Segura by formal action a month later.

The parliamentary elections of June 1931 were completely swept by the various Republican groups and the Socialists, who emerged as the largest single political party in Spain. Republican candidates still rode the crest of a wave of high expectations, while potential opposition was both disorganized and disheartened. The governing coalition had thus been given complete power to write the terms of the new constitution as they pleased. They produced in most respects a model liberal democratic charter, guaranteeing electoral democracy, civil rights, and due process of law. The constitution also provided a mechanism for the extension of regional autonomy, and its only radical socioeconomic provision was the one setting theoretical terms for state confiscation of property when public interest should dictate.

The primary controversy surrounding the new constitution lay in the drafting of the famous Article 26 dealing with religious affairs. The interim prime minister, Niceto Alcalá Zamora, was a practicing Catholic and a veteran of the old Liberal party under the monarchy. He hoped for a moderate solution providing for a free Church in a free state, and some of the more prudent Republicans agreed. The great majority, however, were ardent anticlericals who demanded much more than mere separation. Their ally, the Socialists, had historically not stressed the anticlerical issue; Pablo Iglesias, the Marxist founder of the party, regarded religion as epiphenomenal and primarily the concern of petit bourgeois. The experience of the dictatorship and the reign of Alfonso wrought a change, however, convincing most Socialists that the Church was an important support of capitalism and reaction.

In mid-September the prime minister, Alcalá Zamora, met with the papal nuncio, the archbishop of Tarragona, and the Socialist minister of education to establish terms for a free Church in a free state. According to Alcalá Zamora, this formula was approved by the council of ministers on September 20 by a vote of 11 to 1, with only the Socialist minister of public works opposing, but the cabinet subsequently refused to stand by this decision.

The leader of the debate on Article 26, and indeed the new "revelation" and strong man of the Republican government, was the minister of war, the liberal writer Manuel Azaña. Though not a very original or creative literary figure Azaña was a cosmopolitan intellectual of considerable power and an admirer of French-style radical liberalism. He hoped to model Spain in the image of the Third Republic and was convinced that this required a drastic solution to the problem of the Church.

Though he gained a reputation of being the leader of the forces of anticlericalism, Azaña in fact moderated the original proposal produced by the Socialist-extremist Republican majority. This would have eliminated every form of legal immunity for churches, prohibited all financial contributions save those by individuals, and abolished all religious orders and nationalized their property. The final version, approved by parliament on October 13, by a vote of 178 to 5 (with most Catholics abstaining or walking out), was somewhat more moderate.

As approved, Article 26 made no mention of the Concordat, which was de facto unilaterally annulled. It separated Church and state for the first time in Spanish history, and stipulated that a subsequent law was to be passed to regulate the complete extinction of the state ecclesiastical budget within two more years. Moreover, it specified the automatic dissolution of any religious order that required, in addition to the three regular canonical vows, a special vow of obedience to an authority other than the state. This particular provision was aimed directly at the Jesuits, as that unfortunate revolving-door order braced for its fifth expulsion.

Moreover, Article 26 provided that all other orders would become subject to supplementary legislation that must meet requirements specified as follows:

1. Dissolution of those whose activities endanger the security of the state.
2. Inscription of those permitted to remain in a special registry of the Ministry of Justice.
3. Prohibition against acquiring or maintaining, either by themselves or through third parties, more property than that which, following verification, is required for maintenance or immediate fulfillment of their activities.
4. Prohibition against participating in industry, commerce, or teaching.
5. Liability to all taxes.
6. Obligation to submit annual reports to the state concerning the investment of their goods in relation to the work of the association.

The property of the religious orders is liable to nationalization.[2]

The intent of Republican policy was thus much more than mere separation of Church and state. It was the subjugation of the Church and the suppression of Catholic culture through the elimination of Catholic education, virtually all of which was carried on by the orders. The following Article 27 stipulated further that all public manifestations of religion were subject to authorization by the state.

Even the small minority of moderate Republicans were not pleased with the legislation. Alcalá Zamora and one other Catholic minister resigned, while José Ortega y Gasset, Spain's most famous and prestigious intellectual, at that time a Republican deputy, warned against "taking tactics of sudden liquidation for combating the past." In his words, such persecution was an "armed cartridge" that might produce a "delayed detonation."[3]

The position of the Republican-Socialist majority was that its religious policy was both necessary and democratic because, in the words of a famous speech by Azaña, "Spain has ceased to be Catholic." This was a most ambiguous proposition. After a hundred years of liberalism and a growing climate of mass secularization, Spain was obviously not the monolithic Catholic country of a century earlier. Protestants had increased to more than 20,000 in number, but the main change had been in the direction of agnosticism or atheism, with a kind of liberal Deism or revolutionary ideologies serving as the chief replacements of religion. Withal, the great majority of the population still recognized a formal or nominal religious affiliation, and there was little doubt that many more

---

2. *Gaceta de Madrid*, December 9, 1931.
3. Quoted in James R. O'Connell, "The Spanish Republic: Further Reflections on its Anticlerical Policies," *The Catholic Historical Review* 57:2 (1971), 275–89.

Spaniards genuinely believed in Catholicism than believed in any other position or doctrine. Catholicism had lost the support of the cultural and political leadership and the government, and that of large organized masses of Spaniards, however, and no longer possessed the unthinking cultural reinforcement of tradition. In this sense Spain had ceased to be Catholic in the traditional way, though perhaps not to the degree that Azaña supposed.

The only concession by the government to any form of Catholic opinion was parliament's election of the Catholic moderate liberal Alcalá Zamora as the first president of the Republic, at the close of 1931. Subsequent legislation in 1932 dissolved the Society of Jesus once more, legalized divorce, secularized the cemeteries, and prohibited any transfer of Church property to third-party ownership. The first of these measures brought the immediate closing of two universities, three seminaries, two astronomical observatories, twenty-one of Spain's most sophisticated secondary schools in the classical curriculum, and a number of other educational centers, as well as the confiscation of millions of dollars of property. The supplementary law on religious associations was passed in June 1933, implementing the terms required by the constitution. This declared all Church property to be property of the nation and thus subject to state restriction, and required that all teaching by the orders end in secondary schools by the following October 1 and in primary schools by December 31. Moreover, lay instructors were forbidden to take their places, sounding the death knell of Catholic education. Educational expansion was in fact one of the primary goals of the Republic, yet such limited funds were available that the closing of Catholic schools, which educated at least 20 percent of all Spanish children registered in schools, would have greatly reduced educational opportunities throughout the country.

Formal legislation was accompanied by a campaign of petty harassment and persecution absolutely incomparable to anything experienced by Republicans under the monarchy.

> In Seville, two priests were arrested for conducting a funeral procession and charged with violating the law prohibiting public manifestations of religion. One pastor was fined for saying Mass in his church, the roof of which had been destroyed by lightning, as a public display of religion. Priests were fined for allowing "royalistic" music to be played during services and for alluding to the "Kingship of God" in their sermons on Christ the King. In some towns the tolling of church bells was taxed, in others the wearing of crucifixes as ornamental jewelry was forbidden.[4]

---

4. Sánchez, *Reform and Reaction*, 145.

Random violence and arson against churches and other religious build-ings continued, encouraged by the attitude of Republican authorities, though no major attacks occurred.

Republican policy paralleled earlier anticlerical programs in such Catholic countries as France, Portugal, and Mexico. Of the three, the other Republican experience most comparable to that of Spain was Portugal. There the separation of Church and state effected by the Republic had endured, but Republican politics had ended in virtual chaos, followed by dictatorship. It had been necessary to seek a partial compromise with the Church long before the demise of the Portuguese First Republic in 1926. Given the Spanish indifference to Portugal, bordering on scorn, this example was of course ignored, but it was a most instructive one that the Spanish Republican leaders would have done well to heed.

THE CATHOLIC REACTION

The Catholic response to the anticlerical legislation of 1931 to 1933 was shock and outrage in the highest degree. Republican policy revital-ized lay militancy and reawakened a sense of Catholic identity that had apparently lain dormant in hundreds of thousands of people, verifying the old adage that the blood of the martyrs is the seed of the Church. Though very little blood was shed in the anticlerical offensive, its con-sequence was to elicit a powerful Catholic resurgence and opposition that was simply nonexistent in 1931.

In the short run, one of the most pressing needs of the Church was financial, for the scheduled extinction of the ecclesiastical budget at the close of 1933 would eliminate most of the support for more than 30,000 secular clergy as well as many vital Church functions. In 1931 state assistance amounted to 66 million pesetas (about 7 million dollars), reduced to about 29 million for the following year and only 5 million in 1933. A report presented to the parliament in October 1931 listed the capital wealth of the Church as 11,921 units of rural property, 7,828 units of urban real estate (including religious buildings), and 4,192 *censos* or bonds, amounting to an estimated capital value of 129 million pesetas or about 14 million dollars. Assuming the approximate accuracy of this evaluation (and that is somewhat uncertain), it provided little measure of the remaining income of the Church, since much of this property was not commercial real estate invested at a market rate of return. Meanwhile, state auditors devoted themselves to the confiscation and evalution of the sizable properties of the Jesuits, wealthiest of the orders.

By early 1932 the Church was under severe financial pressure, which became even more intense in the following year. Though a few properties could be sold to generate income, the only adequate recourse was to start a major campaign for private contributions. This was something to which Spanish Catholics were completely unaccustomed, and the response was frankly discouraging. Cardinal Ilundain, archbishop of Seville, asked for a single peseta per month (ten or eleven cents) from each family in his archdiocese to support the clergy and the services, but was quite unable to obtain it. Zeal for financial contribution was in no way commensurate with the ardor of political fulmination against the Republic exhibited by the great majority of the faithful. A Catholic parents' association did, however, manage to organize some 50,000 parents to seek alternative means of education for their children in the face of the threatened closure of Catholic schools.

Despite the sense of outrage, the Church's official position remained moderate, correct, and conciliatory. In April 1933, Segura was replaced as primate by Isidro Gomá y Tomás, former bishop of Tarazona, an ultraconservative monarchist (like most Spanish prelates) but diplomatic in comportment. His first pastoral letter on assuming the archbishopric of Toledo recognized numerous shortcomings in the Church's past policies and conceded that the great majority of Spaniards lacked deep religious convictions. Gomá called attention to the paucity of serious Spanish Catholic thought, and urged a renewal of the kind of genuine piety that was also in short supply among Spanish Catholics. He suggested that the present situation would not have developed had it not been for the laziness and irresponsibility, as well as the cowardice, of many Catholics.

The climactic measures of anticlerical legislation in June 1933 provoked a collective pastoral letter by the Church hierarchy, which protested vigorously and in detail, particularly with regard to the restrictions on the orders. This was followed by an encyclical of Pius XI, *Dilectissima nobis*, which discussed the Spanish case at length and roundly condemned the new legislation.

It was the Republic that finally served as the catalyst for creation of the mass Catholic political party which some had sought for half a century. The lead was taken by Angel Herrera, editor of the influential newspaper *El Debate*, and fellow activists of the Asociación Católica Nacional de Propagandistas (ACNP). They first organized a small national group called Acción Popular to present candidates who would stand for the defense of Catholicism in the first Republican elections of 1931. This initial effort was weakly organized, and only six of their first thirty-nine candidates gained seats in parliament. During the following year, support multiplied many times over. By October 1932, when Acción Popular held its first national congress in Madrid, it had enrolled 619,000 members, the largest mass base of any political organization in Spanish history to that point. It had also acquired an outstanding young national leader in the thirty-four-year old law professor José María Gil Robles, who had first gained a university chair at the age of twenty-four. Extremely hard-working and a brilliant orator in the classic Castilian style, Gil Robles exhibited a personal energy and vigor of conviction that would make him the undisputed leader of political Catholicism during the Second Republic.

Acción Popular was strongest in the firmly Catholic regions of northern Spain, where the CONCA farm network was used to rally support. It was paralleled by several other regional Catholic groups, by far the most vigorous of which was the Derecha Regional Valenciana in the Spanish Levant, led by Luis Lucia. Whereas Acción Popular was strongly conservative and quasi-monarchist in orientation, the DRV was under Christian democratic direction of a more liberal cast. These and other Catholic political groupings finally came together in Madrid in March 1933 to form a broad national alliance, the Confederación Española de Derechas Autónomas (Spanish Confederation of Autonomous Rightist Groups), commonly known from its acronym as the CEDA. Gil Robles and the other *cedista* leaders were fully justified in their confidence that the next parliamentary elections would reveal their new confederation to be the largest single political force in Spain.

The ultimate weakness of the CEDA was certainly not its voting base, but the fact that it was defined more by what it was against than by what it was for. From the beginning, the primary function of the CEDA was defense of Catholic interests. Its concrete political goals were less clear, in part because they varied widely from one subgroup or region to another. The Vatican and the papal nuncio strongly encouraged a broad and unified Spanish Catholic party similar to the German Center party. Thus Gil Robles and Herrera carved out a "possibilist" position with respect to form of government, hoping to embrace cooperative monarchists and conservative Republicans at the same time. About all that was clear was the CEDA's commitment to legal, parliamentary tactics and its espousal of conservative principles on most issues. With the exception of the strong progressive group in Valencia, most of its members and supporters were rather more conservative than the leadership and by 1933 more promonarchist as well.

The CEDA was immediately denounced by the left as a form of "clerical fascism." There was never much more substance to this charge than antipathy to the confederation's Catholic and often ultraconservative origins. In most of Europe, antifascism preceded fascism and excelled it in strength. This was certainly true in Spain, where by 1933 most of the left, modeled on foreign patterns, judged political developments by analogy to such countries as Italy, Germany, and Austria. Since there was no significant fascist movement in Spain, the CEDA, emerging as the main foe of the left, was conveniently cast in that role.

Some greater substance to the charge of fascism could be detected in the case of the Juventudes de Acción Popular (JAP), the CEDA youth movement. The latter adopted much of the external style of fascism—which of course was almost equally that of the revolutionary left—and advocated authoritarian solutions. Like fascist and left-revolutionary groups, the JAP adopted special shirt uniforms and engaged in bellicose posturing. For them, however, it was largely imitation and play-acting. Their formal salute was a caricature of the fascist gesture, raising the arm only halfway and then drawing it back across the chest. Like well-brought-up middle-class Catholic boys, they carefully avoided engaging in street violence with the left.

Extreme right-wing Catholicism was as usual represented by the Carlists, whose activities were greatly revived and stimulated by the legislation of the left-liberal Republic. The Carlists soon managed to reunify their ranks and reorganize themselves as the Comunión Tradicionalista. They reawakened strong support in Navarre and organized new nuclei in several other provinces, so that by 1933 they gained the backing of nearly 5 percent of the Spanish electorate.

At the beginning of the Republic, the Carlists had formed a *vasconavarro* bloc with the Basque nationalists that represented the three Basque provinces and Navarre and provided the Church's most vigorous defense in the Constituent Cortes. At first the Carlists also cooperated with the Basque nationalists in an effort to gain regional autonomy for their area, but by 1932 came to a parting of the ways. Rural Navarre had little in common with the industrial Basque provinces, and Carlists were unwilling to make any concessions to the atheistic Republic by way of compromise. By 1933 they were drilling party militia in Navarre and preparing for radical confrontation.

Conversely the Basque Nationalist party (PNV), which had begun on the right, moved to the democratic center under the Republic. It became a mass movement in the two northern Basque provinces only with the advent of the new regime, finding in democratic mobilization and cooperation with the Republic the first opportunity in its history to achieve regional autonomy. The Basque Nationalists remained strongly Catholic save for one liberal and anticlerical offshoot, and continued a very close association with much of the local clergy in their region, some of whom frankly served as party organizers. The place of the Basque population within the broader framework of Spanish spirituality is illustrated by the fact that in 1920 the Basque provinces and Navarre, containing only 4.8

percent of the Spanish population, provided 33.4 percent of the membership of Marian congregations (major devotional associations) in Spain. Strong emphasis on social reform, trade unionism, and economic welfare also became hallmarks of Basque nationalism under the Republic, as the Basque movement did more to adopt the principles of social Catholicism than any other large political organization in Spain. Though it did not normally use the nomenclature or title of Christian democracy, the PNV had in fact become the first successful Christian democratic party in Spain.

A much smaller but even more advanced counterpart existed in Catalonia in the form of the Unió Democrática de Catalunya (UDC). This was a Catalan regionalist party that specifically espoused the principles of Christian democracy and also adopted a rather drastic program of social reform, emphasizing trade unionism and a general policy of welfare and redistribution. The UDC was a tiny group doomed to isolation. Its norms of Christian conduct and moderation prevented association with either left or right, and it had no influence on the practical course of affairs.

SPANISH CATHOLICISM AND CORPORATISM

Since the nineteenth century, the most common Catholic reform doctrine for modern state and society had taken the form of corporatism. In 1931, amid the Great Depression and the growth of radical new political and social solutions, Pius XI referred to corporatism as one appropriate Catholic approach to modern social problems in his famous encyclical *Quadragesimo anno*. Sometimes referred to as the "other ism," corporatist doctrine has often been even vaguer than that of socialism and has assumed several quite distinct variants. Its root concept propounds the harmonious internal organization of individual sectors of society or of economic function in broad, organically associated structures of representation and cooperation. Economic corporatism differs from syndicalism in combining the organization of both capital and labor within the internal association of each major economic sector. Political corporatism adopted the theory of representation by functional groups or economic and professional units in an "organic" (functionally and structurally related) system, as distinct from the atomistic, individually separated, mutually competitive parliamentary system of liberalism. To its advocates, the advantage of corporatism lay in its decentralization of function and group—avoiding statism—and in its "natural" and harmonious system of representation as contrasted with the individual competition and factionalism of liberalism.

The original Catholic theories emphasized societal corporatism from the bottom up, avoiding the centralized control of a powerful state. By the early twentieth century, however, other corporative theories were adopted by secular nationalists and authoritarians who stressed the very reverse—statist doctrines of corporatism under which the government would dominate the organization and functioning of a corporative system in place of parliamentary liberalism. This became part of the basis for Italian Fascism after World War I.

Nineteenth-century corporatist theories were first echoed in Spain during the 1870s, and later were commonly featured in many of the reform plans for local and national government from the 1890s on. No changes of this sort were ever actually instituted, however. The only political group to espouse corporatism as a primary doctrine was the dominant group of Carlists, whose theoretician Juan Vázquez de Mella elaborated a broad doctrine of Catholic societal corporatism.

Under the Second Republic, various leaders of the CEDA showed considerable interest in corporatism, although the CEDA never officially endorsed any brand of corporatism as an alternative to the existing political system. Carlist doctrines were further updated in Víctor Pradera's El estado nuevo (1935), which outlined a decentralized corporatist framework of government to replace the Republic.

Falange Española (FE; the Spanish Phalanx), the small Spanish fascist movement of the period, embraced a variant of corporatism which it called "national syndicalism." The Falange declared itself officially Catholic and affirmed traditional Spanish culture, but it rejected all the Spanish right and emphasized its own brand of "national revolution." Fascism consequently had very little support among Spanish Catholics until 1936, for it seemed too radical and too little Catholic when compared with a broad confessional movement like the CEDA.

In addition to Carlism and Falangism, there emerged a new-style Spanish radical right led by José Calvo Sotelo, the sometime young Maurist who had served as Primo de Rivera's finance minister. Its organizational base was a new non-Carlist monarchist party called Renovación Española, which Calvo Sotelo temporarily expanded into a coalition Bloque Nacional. Renovación Española also proclaimed itself an ardent defender of Catholic interests, but its main goal was to establish a modern authoritarian regime on a corporative basis. Calvo Sotelo's radical right differed from the CEDA in its frank appeal to dictatorship, and from fascism in its reliance on the military and on traditional elites. It eschewed mass mobilization and was fully identified with the existing social and economic structure. Much more than the Falange, Calvo Sotelo and his associates were the true ideological progenitors of the right-wing Catholic authoritarianism of the subsequent Franco regime.

This sector was responsible for developing the main theoretical organ of the radical right in Spain, the monthly journal *Acción Española* (named after the *Action Française*). The most important writer featured in *Acción Española* was Ramiro de Maeztu, a former liberal of the Generation of Ninety-Eight who had turned to traditionalism and nationalism during World War I. In 1934 he published *Defensa de la hispanidad*, the most articulate and elaborate resurrection of the traditional Spanish ideology written during these years. For Maeztu, all Hispanic culture and history was defined by its close identity with and service to Catholicism, a categorization which he also projected (much less convincingly) to Spanish America as well. Maeztu propounded the restoration of pan-Hispanic unity, and the development of a transatlantic Catholic corporative bloc to preserve the Hispanic world from Anglo-Saxon liberalism and Asian Communism.

SOCIAL CATHOLICISM UNDER THE SECOND REPUBLIC

The five years of the Second Republic were the most intense period of agitation and mobilization yet seen in Spanish history. The major Catholic response took the form of political mobilization, while social endeavors, as usual, lagged. Catholic syndicalists continued to be divided between progressives and ultraconservatives. Gafo remained active, and during the first years of the Republic labored unsuccessfully to convince the Church hierarchy that Catholic syndicates would be more effective if not required to be officially confessional.

The most genuine achievements of Catholic syndicalism took place in the Basque provinces and Navarre. The Basque nationalist STV blossomed into a broad organization. Gafo reorganized the rump of his former Católicos-Libres as the Basque-Navarrese Confederation of Professional Worker Syndicates (CVNSOP), and claimed nearly 25,000 members once more by 1934. In Catalonia the UDC formed a Christian democratic trade union group, Unió de Treballadors Cristians de Catalunya (UTCC), but like its parent organization it languished, with scarcely 3,000 members.

After the revolutionary insurrection of 1934 (discussed in the next section), an effort was made to bring all the diverse Catholic syndicates, with the exception of regional nationalists like the STV and UTCC, together in one confederation. The result was a new Confederación Española de Sindicatos Obreros (CESO) by 1935, which claimed to have 273,000 affiliates, though this number was open to doubt.

One of the most original developments of the Republican years was the organization of the Federació de Joves Cristians (FJC; Federation of Christian Youth) in Catalonia in 1931. The FJC was emphatically a youth group, not a political party, dedicated to spiritual devotion, religious proselytizing, and attention to social problems. Its sincerity and authenticity were uncommonly high. Though the FJC counted 7,000 members in 1936, it suffered much the same fate as did the UDC, a different sort of specifically political organization, so that its significance probably lay more in its exemplary quality than in its immediate influence or success.

Thus the most noteworthy avatars of social Catholicism were to be found in very small groups or semi-isolated individuals. The Grupo de Democracia Cristiana, for example, continued to function, and revived the practice of informational *Semanas Sociales* under the Republic. Clearly the most significant cultural enterprise of Catholic progressives was the intellectual journal *Cruz y Raya* (1933–36), directed by José Bergamín, which published the first work of such subsequently major figures as Julián Marías and José Antonio Maravall.

COLLAPSE OF THE REPUBLIC

The original Republican coalition exhausted itself in internal disputes and inept administration by the middle of 1933, leading to new elections in the fall. The Republican system was not based on proportionate representation but favored large coalitions. The CEDA was able to form a series of practical alliances, sometimes with the right and sometimes with the center, and returned 115 deputies, the largest number of any single party. By contrast, the Socialists were greatly reduced and the left-wing Republicans almost wiped out.

After 1933 there was no natural majority in the Republican parliament (rather like Germany after 1930). The Catholic president, Alcalá Zamora, therefore called upon the only large center group, the Radical Republicans (who were the second largest party), to form a government with whatever support they could muster. Alejandro Lerroux, the Radical leader, was nearly seventy years old and not the same demagogue who had promoted incendiary anticlericalism in Barcelona thirty years earlier. Though his party was still anticlerical (but much more moderately so), it represented middle-of-the-road Republicanism primarily, resting on an opportunistic coalition of veteran political manipulators and job-seekers.

The Radicals could not maintain power without the support or acquiescence of the large CEDA bloc. As the price for that support, the new government restored part of the ecclesiastical budget and at the close of 1933 rescinded the ban on Catholic education, just as it was to have gone into effect. Moreover, some effort was made during 1934 to consider terms of a new, more limited concordat with the Vatican, but the latter insisted on revision of the anticlerical legislation first, which was farther than the Radicals were willing to go. In fact, they had no particular program other than to enjoy the spoils of office, and therefore Republican government completely stagnated during 1933–34.

Though the CEDA's position was that it had no interest in entering the government, representing a new citizen mobilization for which the time was not yet ripe, the stagnation of 1934 forced a change in policy. By the autumn of 1934 it became clear that without direct CEDA participation the Radicals would doze and porkbarrel their way through the entire term. Yet this in turn constituted a grave problem, for all the left insisted that the CEDA was a subversive, "clerical fascist" party which, despite the fact that it was the largest in Spain, must never be allowed to share power.

Gil Robles and some other CEDA leaders had officially denounced the principles of fascism, condemning statism and authoritarianism and the politics of violence in general. Even though a distinction was clearly drawn between Catholic culture and radical fascist culture, and even though the nationalism of the CEDA was in fact fairly moderate, the position of the entire left was categorical. Spanish politics were already polarized by 1934.

At the beginning of October 1934 three *cedistas* entered the cabinet, two of them from the most liberal and progressive sectors of the party. This became the signal for a mass revolutionary insurrection by the Spanish left. It achieved a momentary success in the mining region of Asturias, where the revolutionaries held sway until quelled by major military intervention. Revolutionary atrocity became the order of the day and among the victims were thirty-four ecclesiastics. This was followed by a harsh and extensive repression.

Once the principles of electoral democracy and parliamentary government were rejected by the very forces that had initiated the Republic and written its constitution, the system had little chance to survive. Nor did the right-center governments of 1934–35 manage to implement any alternative policy of their own. The strange alliance of Catholic *cedistas* and anticlerical Radicals that had sparked the revolutionary outbreak was too contradictory and unstable to govern effectively under Radical leadership, but the Republican president refused to allow Gil Robles, who briefly became minister of war in 1935, to form a government of his own. After four years, Republican politics were not only polarized but also stalemated.

One ultimate goal for the CEDA was constitutional reform to alter at least part of the terms of Article 26. This could not be completed without an effective parliamentary majority, which was still lacking. Consequently the parliament of 1934–35 managed to frustrate all sides. The left was excluded from power and saw part of its work undone, yet the right lacked the strength and institutional cooperation to govern and institute its own policy directly.

At this juncture the arbiter of the Republic's destinies was Alcalá Zamora. Though he shared the CEDA's ambition to revise the anti-Catholic provisions of the Republican constitution, Alcalá Zamora was also determined to preserve the democratic regime. He suffered from a strong personal antipathy to Gil Robles of the sort common among rival Spanish politicians, and fearing a strongly reactionary policy, refused to allow the CEDA to form a government. Instead, he took the gamble of calling new elections for February 1936, hoping desperately to reconstruct a Republican center. The Radical party had thoroughly discredited itself through corruption and inactivity and had disintegrated, while the parties of the left, Republican and revolutionary, formed a broad Popular Front. In the Republic's final elections, the Popular Front won a popular plurality of one and one-half percent, but the majority bloc system of awarding seats gave it two-thirds of the deputies in the new parliament. Though the CEDA increased its vote slightly over 1933, it was placed in a hopelessly minority position, while the democratic center was eliminated almost altogether.

During the spring of 1936 a prerevolutionary situation inexorably developed. The Socialists refused to participate in another "bourgeois" government, leaving a minority left-Republican ministry to try to administer the country. Alcalá Zamora, the last guarantee of moderation, was deposed in order to elect Azaña to the presidency, and the leftist monopoly of power was complete. This did not lead to strong government but rather to incipient chaos, as the revolutionary forces engaged in massive strikes, frequent acts of violence, and in several areas wholesale seizures of property. Anticlerical outbursts were merely one feature of the violence and disorder that pervaded much of Spain. In a parliamentary speech on June 16, Gil Robles charged that in the four months since the elections, 160 churches had been totally destroyed and 251 partially wrecked. During the course of the spring, enforcement of the original legislation of 1933 banning Catholic education began in a haphazard way, and an undetermined number of schools were shut down in various provinces. Some religious buildings were confiscated, and a few of them unilaterally occupied by the revolutionary parties, with the benumbed acquiescence of the left Republican government. The latter could conceive of no policy other than to tolerate the aggression of the left while blaming it on, and to some degree repressing, the right.

The revolt against the left Republican government on July 17, 1936, that precipitated the Civil War was essentially a movement by dissident groups of the military. Its authors were not primarily moved by senti-ments of religious piety to take arms against an impious regime, but were motivated by strong emotions of nationalism and patriotic conservatism to take arms against the revolutionary left and the regional separatists before such forces became fully dominant. Issues of politics, economics, and institutional privilege predominated over those of religion. General Emilio Mola, the chief planner and organizer of the rebellion, proposed to follow the example of the contemporary Portuguese regime and main-tain separation of Church and state, though always with the understand-ing that a right-wing military government would be much more solicitous of Catholic interests than the leftist Republic.

Catholic activists thus played only a very secondary role in the con-spiracy and revolt, though most of them hoped increasingly for some such military response as the prerevolutionary spring of 1936 wore on. The CEDA lost much of its following after the elections, particularly among the youth who, disillusioned by the democratic process, turned in large numbers to the fascistic Falange. This was happening even in the DRV, the most liberal and democratic wing of the CEDA. Most of the military conspirators, however, had a low opinion of Catholic and nearly all other civilian parties. Leaders of the CEDA and the monarchist groups were eventually given limited information about the revolt, but the support sought from them was almost exclusively financial. Only at the last instant was an understanding reached with the Carlists of Navarre to commit their civilian militia to the revolt.

THE REVOLUTION

The irony of the Spanish military rebellion of July 1936 was that it provoked precisely what it was designed to avoid: the outbreak of full-scale revolution by the left. At first only about a third of the country was occupied by the rebels; in most other areas the residual authority of the Republican government collapsed, to be replaced by local councils and committees of the revolutionary parties. The degree of social and eco-nomic revolution varied considerably from district to district, as did the extent of the terror that accompanied it.

The Spanish Civil War quickly acquired a grisly reputation, much of it fully deserved, for large-scale atrocities and mass murders by both sides. In this it was similar to all other revolutionary/counterrevolutionary civil wars of the century, which have usually been fought with little quarter. While the exact number of political murders on either side will probably never be known with full precision, they were not generally dispro-portionate to the casualties in other such struggles in Russia and Finland during the preceding generation, or in East Asia and Greece in the years following.

The terror in Spain resembled that in the Russian Civil War insofar as the clergy became a major target of the violence in each case. The persecution inflicted on the Catholic Church was greater than that ever seen in the history of western Europe, even at the height of the French Revolution. The number of clergy slaughtered, nearly 7,000, was roughly proportionate to the Communist massacres in Russia, given the different sizes of the population involved, though gruesome tortures seem to have been somewhat more common in Russia.

The anarchists had the most violent anticlerical reputation among the revolutionaries, but large-scale killing also occurred in areas like south-central Spain where the anarchists were weak. The secular clergy suffered most, losing 4,184 victims to the terror, nearly one priest in every seven in Spain, or more nearly one in every four in those provinces controlled by the revolutionaries. Among the orders, 2,365 monks and 283 nuns were also killed, for a grand total of 6,832 dead.

The slaughter was proportionately most extensive in the district of Barbastro, quickly overrun by Catalan anarchists, where nearly 88 percent of the diocesan clergy were killed. The figure for the Catalan province of Lérida was 66 percent and for Tortosa 62 percent. In the Barcelona district only 22 percent of the secular clergy were killed, for anarchists never had such a free hand there as in some other provinces. The Socialists were not reluctant to make their contribution to the hecatomb. In the rural province of Ciudad Real south of Madrid, where they predominated, 40 percent of the clergy were slaughtered, and similarly in Toledo, nearly 48 percent were killed. There has been much comment on the irony that the great majority of these victims were simple, poor parish priests of modest background, scarcely any wealthier or more privileged than the supposed "class enemies" who killed them.

In addition to loss of life, enormous destruction was wrought on Church property of all kinds, but especially church buildings, and especially in the northeast. In Barcelona and some other parts of Catalonia and eastern Aragón, nearly all churches were wrecked or burned either in whole or in part. In hundreds of localities all over eastern and southern Spain, priceless historical art objects were lost to this wholesale vandalism.

The only Catholic group to participate actively on the Republican side were the Basque nationalists, and even this was uncertain during the first weeks of the Civil War. Some former nationalists deserted in the face of the revolution and turned to Franco's movement. The adherence of the Basque nationalists to the Republican cause was assured only after the rump Republican parliament voted an autonomy statute for the three provinces in September 1936, and by that time only the key industrial province of Vizcaya had escaped the control of the insurgent forces. Vizcaya was thus the only province in the Republican zone where churches remained open and few of the clergy were molested.

In fact, the ecclesiastical supporters of Basque nationalism remained almost as active as ever, continuing to play key political roles. During the first months of the conflict, Spanish Nationalists shot fourteen captured Basque nationalist priests whom they accused of subversive political activities, and over sixty more were imprisoned. Intervention by the papal nuncio secured their transfer to a monastery under guard. Some were later pardoned and transferred to pastoral work in southern provinces where the customarily short supply of parish priests had been reduced to drastic levels by wholesale killings under the short-lived revolutionary regime.

Strictly for political reasons, the wartime Republican government tried to maintain diplomatic relations with the Vatican throughout the conflict, even though the Madrid nunciatura was vacant after November 1936. The major ploy in this regard was to include a devout Basque nationalist Catholic, Manuel de Irujo, as minister without portfolio in the first Popular Front cabinet, formed in September of that year. In May 1937 Irujo became minister of justice for eleven months in the government of the Socialist Juan Negrín. The tiny Catalanist Christian democratic group UDC also tried to foster political contacts between Republican authorities and liberal Catholics. A few individual Catholics, such as the prominent Republican generals Miaja and Rojo, continued to serve the leftist regime throughout the year.

Republican political gestures produced scant effect. In August 1937 the Republican government declared freedom of "private worship" for the first time, and six months later began to consider the possibility of the public reopening of one church in Barcelona as a propaganda device. The "Thirteen Points" peace maneuver of Negrín on April 30, 1938, promised citizens full civil rights and freedom of religious practice. This was something that the Spanish left had consistently refused since 1931, but imminent military defeat produced a feeling of desperation. All these maneuvers failed, and in the summer of 1938 the Negrín government moved to the left once more, intensifying repression and resuming political executions. The bishop of Teruel, seized by Republican forces at the beginning of 1938 in their only successful offensive of the war, was finally shot a year later in the Republican evacuation of Catalonia.

The savage persecution by the Spanish Revolution was possibly the most intense single trial suffered by Spanish Catholicism in its long and eventful history. Both the ordinary faithful and the clergy bore their sufferings with courage and stoicism. Scarcely a single apostasy was registered among the latter in the face of their tormenters. The courage with which both clergy and laity withstood the most intense persecution was, sad to say, not equaled by corresponding mercy, charity, and justice among the triumphant Catholics of Franco's Nationalist zone.

7

National Catholicism

DURING THE early twentieth century, Spanish Catholicism had clung to its highly conservative culture and had played little or no role in movements toward renewal in the Church as a whole. Yet it did demonstrate a modest capacity to respond to new political and social patterns, and in 1931 its leaders showed greater willingness to coexist with the Republic than did the Republican politicians to accommodate the Church. Opportunity for a just and equitable separation of Church and state was squandered by the government, and the resulting confrontation with and partial persecution of the Church reawakened a militant, adversarial spirit among many of the faithful. By 1936 the tone and attitudes of Spanish Catholicism were much more conservative and even reactionary, producing a spirit of religious restoration highly susceptible to the political movement of the military rebels. General Franco, leader of the new military regime, took advantage of this to reestablish a partial symbiosis of Church and state. The resulting "national Catholicism" of the Franco regime produced, at least for a decade or so, the most remarkable traditionalist restoration in religion and culture witnessed in any twentieth-century European country.

COUNTERREVOLUTIONARY CIVIL WAR AS CRUSADE

The military revolt that touched off the Spanish Civil War was organized almost exclusively by sectors of the Army officer corps. It represented a nationalist and rightist reaction against the revolutionary forces and the Kerenskyist policy of the Republican government, with the goal of installing a more authoritarian and conservative military-dominated regime. Religion played no official role in this enterprise. Some of the military activists had little concern for the defense of Catholicism, while others were reluctant to complicate the situation further by giving a religious coloring to their movement. The insurgents hoped for extensive middle-class support and had no interest in antagonizing moderate anticlericals. Thus their first pronouncements during the early days of the conflict made no particular reference to the religious issue. Indeed, the head of the rebel Junta de Defensa Nacional, formed on July 23, 1936, was the senior general Miguel Cabanellas, well known as a moderate liberal and Freemason. Only four of the Junta's ten members could be identified as political supporters of Catholicism in previous years.

The counterrevolutionary goals of the rebellion nonetheless made conservative Catholics its natural allies from the very start. As was indicated in the preceding chapter, some Catholic rightists, primarily Carlists, participated marginally in the preparation of the revolt. More important, with few exceptions the revolt was initially successful only in those provinces where public opinion supported the right. As news of the explosive revolution and mass atrocities in the Popular Front zone crossed the lines, the volume of popular Catholic support eventually became overwhelming. This in itself was hardly surprising; only a diametrically opposite response would have been remarkable. As it was, Catholic backing in terms of political support, military volunteers, financial assistance, and—perhaps above all—spiritual motivation and cultural legitimization became the most important single domestic pillar of the Spanish Nationalist movement.

As the revolt stalled militarily, then broadened into full-scale civil war, the military leadership moved to take advantage of Catholic backing. By the end of July General Mola, the organizer of the rebellion, used the phrase "the true Catholic Spain." In a radio address of August 15 he hailed "the cross that was and remains the symbol of our religion and our faith,"[1] pledging to raise it above the new state. Such pronouncements thenceforth became increasingly frequent. The first formal disposition in recognition of the new regime's Catholicism came on September 4, when it was ordered that school textbooks in the Nationalist zone be revised in accordance with Catholic doctrine and that educational activities be segregated by sex.

Within thirty days of the outbreak of the conflict Church leaders began to speak in favor of the military movement. Bishop Mateo Múgica of Vitoria, issuing a pastoral instruction written by the primate, Gomá, denounced Catholic Basque nationalists for establishing a political entente with leftist revolutionaries in two of the Basque provinces. Bishop Olaechea of the city of Pamplona, center of the fervently Catholic province of Navarre whose volunteers poured into the insurgent cause from the beginning, declared on August 23, 1936, "This is not merely a war that is being waged but a crusade."[2] When General Franco, soon to be

---

1. Felipe Bertrán Güell, *Preparación y desarrollo del alzamiento nacional* (Valladolid, 1939), 243; Manuel Tuñón de Lara, *El hecho religioso en España* (Paris, 1968), 134–35.
2. Quoted in José Chao Rego, *La Iglesia en el franquismo* (Madrid, 1976), 26.

named Nationalist commander-in-chief, moved his headquarters to Salamanca in the following month, Archbishop Pla y Deniel handed over the archdiocesan residence for Franco's official use. In a pastoral, "Las Dos Ciudades," issued on September 30, Pla recited the long record of Republican persecution and stressed that the Church could not be criticized "because it has openly and officially spoken in favor of order against anarchy, in favor of establishing a hierarchical government against dissolvent communism, in favor of the defense of Christian civilization and its bases, religion, fatherland and family, against those without God and against God, and without fatherland. . . ."[3]

After Franco assumed the powers of head of state on October 1, this tendency became accentuated. Franco himself had shown little indication of religious faith or interest as a young officer in Morocco, but developed a Catholic identity after marriage, and by the time of the Civil War gave every evidence of believing that the faith and Spanish nationalism were consubstantial. He fully subscribed to the traditional Spanish ideology, though curiously his new regime first appears to have officially labeled itself a "Catholic state" in a minor decree of October 30 establishing the *plato único* (a day of the week in which restaurants would serve single-course meals to save food). The role of military chaplains was officially restored in the Nationalist Army on December 6, though they had served with some volunteer units (mainly Carlist Navarrese) from the beginning.

During 1937 relations between the Church and the new state began to be regularized. Wartime conditions precluded special resumption of the old ecclesiastical budget—and in some respects required ecclesiastical assistance to the state—but a lengthy series of measures were adopted to enforce Catholic norms in most aspects of culture and education and to foster religious observance. The Marian cult and all traditional symbols were restored in public schools, Corpus Christi was declared a national holiday once more, and Santiago was restored as patron of Spain. More and more regulations followed, not to be fully completed for nearly a decade.

Cardinal Isidro Gomá, archbishop of Toledo and primate, strongly supported the Nationalist movement from the first days of fighting. With part of his archdiocese still in the hands of the Popular Front, he published a pastoral, "El caso de España," on November 24, 1936, that specified, "This most cruel war is at bottom a war of principles, of doctrines, of one concept of life and social reality against another, of one civilization against another. It is a war waged by the Christian and Spanish spirit against another spirit. . . ."[4]

---

3. *Iglesia, Estado y Movimiento Nacional* (Madrid, 1963), 21–23.
4. Ibid., 25.

Several weeks later, Gomá traveled to Rome to argue in favor of Vatican support for the Franco regime. Though the Vatican, like most Catholic opinion around the world, naturally favored those who defended Catholicism against one of the most remarkable persecutions in its history, Pius XI also found it impolitic to have to take sides formally. A small number of devout Catholics had remained with the Popular Front regime, the Catholic Basque nationalists had just concluded a political deal with the Republic, and the Spanish Nationalists, accused of many murders and excesses of their own, could not but inspire some caution. However, when Gomá returned to Nationalist Spain on December 19, he was named "confidential and semi-official [oficioso] representative" of the Holy See to Franco's government.

Though the Vatican remained reluctant to commit itself, Franco urged the Spanish Church hierarchy to issue an official statement in order to dispel false impressions abroad. Gomá was himself eager to have the leadership of the Church in Spain take an official stand through a collective pastoral. On March 10, 1937, Cardinal Pacelli, Vatican secretary of state, wrote to Gomá, "The Holy Father leaves it fully up to your prudent judgment."[5] Pacelli's letter opened the way for the negotiation and writing of the famous "Collective Letter" of the Spanish hierarchy that was published on July 1, 1937, soon after the final collapse of Catholic Basque resistance in Vizcaya.

This major document, forty-two pages long, provided a long and detailed statement of the Spanish Church's position on the war, accompanied by a carefully argued justification. It catalogued the deficiencies of the prewar Republic and the latter's failure to observe democratic procedure or maintain civil rights, then discussed in detail the onslaught of the unique Spanish anarcho-Marxist revolution, which it termed simply Communist. The hierarchy rejected the often-heard interpretation that the Civil War was essentially a class war, terming it primarily an ideological conflict, a war of ideas. They pointed out that all the wealthier provinces of Spain, those with the highest per capita income, were dominated by the left, while the Nationalist movement was based primarily on the poorer and agrarian regions, whose predominant philosophy was Catholic, not collectivist/materialist.

The hierarchy disclaimed any desire for conflict with the left. They observed that the Church did believe in the doctrine of just war and in the past had helped to organize armed crusades, but emphasized that this was not their position. "The Church" they said, "has neither desired nor sought this war, and we do not think it necessary to vindicate it against the

---

5. Quoted in Hilari Raguer, *La espada y la cruz* (Barcelona, 1977), 103.

charges of belligerence with which the Spanish Church has been censured in some foreign newspapers."[6]

In these circumstances the Church leaders believed that Catholics had no alternative but to support the "civic-military movement," as they termed it, of Franco. The adjective *national* as applied to Franco's forces was deemed fully justified. The Spanish prelates held that the values of the insurgents corresponded to the Spanish national spirit and were shared throughout Spain, and that the insurgents were also national in their aim of restoring the culture and ethos of Spanish society in consonance with its own history.

Thus, with the exception of three dissident prelates who refused to sign, the Spanish hierarchy endorsed the struggle of Franco's regime in the Civil War. What it did not do, however, was to endorse the Franco regime as a specific form of government or as an end in itself.

> With respect to the future, we cannot predict what will take place at the end of the struggle. We do affirm that the war has not been undertaken to raise an autocratic state over a humiliated nation but in order that the national spirit regenerate itself with the vigor and Christian freedom of olden times. We trust in the prudence of the men of government, who will not wish to accept foreign models for the configuration of the future Spanish state but will keep in mind the intimate requirements of national life and the path marked by past centuries.[7]

The Collective Letter made it clear that the Church leadership had no intention of endorsing any specific form of authoritarianism. Apparently with Fascism and Nazism in mind, it warned against the influence of "foreign ideology on the state that would tend to divert it from Christian doctrines and influence."[8] The nascent Franco regime had not yet fully defined itself in mid-1937, and was seen by the Spanish hierarchy, by no means incorrectly, as above all a right-wing traditionalist-nationalist regime.

From the very beginning, Franco had made evident his intention of creating a new state on national-authoritarian foundations. Though he had used the term *totalitarian*, he had also made clear in his first speeches and interviews that such a description was not in itself imitative of foreign regimes, since the example of a Spanish "totalitarian" regime that he preferred to cite was that of the "preeminent," though not fully absolute,

6. Cardenal Isidro Gomá y Tomás, *Pastorales de la guerra de España* (Madrid, 1955), 147–89.

7. Ibid.

8. Ibid.

monarchy of the Catholic Kings, Fernando and Isabel. Certain aspects of Fascist style such as the Roman salute were nonetheless employed from the very beginning, and were occasionally used by Church prelates themselves.

Franco raised the war-swollen Falange, a movement generically fascist in doctrine, to the rank of official state party in April 1937, but in the process merged it with all the other nonleftist political parties in the Nationalist zone. There was little protest against the absorption or reduction of major Catholic secular organizations. The CEDA simply ceased to exist, while the general Catholic trade union federation (CESO) and the abortive Carlist Obra Nacional Corporativa were disbanded and absorbed into the Falangist state syndical system in 1938. The Catholic university student group, Confederación de Estudiantes Católicos, survived only one year longer, until it was similarly subsumed by the Falangist student organization, the SEU. Of all Catholic political and social groups, only the agrarian organization, CONCA, endured into the post-Civil War period with its identity and independence at least partially intact, though reduced in support and range of action.

Yet though the Falangist program was adopted as the official state program, Franco stressed in his formal announcement that this was not the final and complete doctrine of the new Spanish state but simply a point of departure. The incipient Franco regime had clearly become semifascist or partially fascist, but its structure remained highly syncretic and its full future definition undetermined. This was made clearer the following summer, when the statutes of the new Traditionalist Spanish Phalanx, as the state party was now termed, were published. These went well beyond the merely respectful acknowledgement of Catholicism in the original Falangist program. They declared the goal of the movement to be restoration of Spain's "resolute faith in her Catholic and imperial mission." The first article recognized "the Christian freedom of the person," while Article 23 stipulated the naming of a national director of religious education and attendance. This was but part of the beginning of a trend that the German ambassador found quite alarming in its "reactionary" and "clerical" quality. Indeed, when Franco emphasized that Spanish "totalitarianism" would be derived from the monarchism and cultural policy of the Catholic Kings, he was not merely coining a symbolic phrase. The Franquist regime was embarked on the most traditionalist, indeed reactionary, cultural policy of any twentieth-century western state, bar none. It was an enterprise virtually without parallel.

Though this was not fully defined in explicit political philosophy, it was enough for nearly all Church leaders and the great majority of Catholic laymen. Perhaps the nearest thing to a discussion took place in the influential Jesuit journal *Razón y Fe* in October 1937. José Azpiazu, discussing the concepts of "the traditional state and the totalitarian state," inquired:

> What is the concept of the totalitarian state and what does it represent? Above all—in Spain more than anywhere else—it represents a strong and complete type of state, shorn of the weaknesses and hesitations of the liberal and socialist state, a power representing all the vital forces of the nation. . . . For many—though mistakenly, in our judgment—the totalitarian state means a state that takes into its hands the direction and control of all the affairs of the nation. Such a concept is totally false and one must expunge it. If that were true, the totalitarian state would be equivalent to the socialist state or at least very similar to it.
>
> . . . The state must assist the Church in achieving her most holy goal of the salvation of man to the greatest degree possible. This is not different from the goal of the state but simply superior to it. So that if we should try to define the essence of the totalitarian state in a single phrase, we would say that the Spanish totalitarian state should not be totalitarian in the objective sense—that would be equivalent to a socialist one—but in the subjective sense of a total and sovereign power, strong and not limited, directive and not frustrated. . . . If it were thus, let us have the totalitarian state, for that would be equivalent to the total resurrection of the pure and authentically traditional Spain, without shadows of foreign systems nor the mixture of non-Catholic doctrines.[9]

Azpiazu correctly introduced the distinction between a structurally totalitarian socialist system of the Leninist-Stalinist pattern and the essentially Mussolinian type of political dictatorship of limited scope that employed the rhetoric and coined the phrase of totalitarianism. What he failed to do altogether was to define the structural, philosophical, or functional nature of a Spanish totalitarianism as distinct from that of Fascist Italy, beyond the general insistence that Spanish nationalism could only be exclusively Catholic. Totalitarianism therefore merely stood for some form of an authoritarian system—though not at all structurally totalitarian in the comparative empirical sense—and for cultural

---

9. J. Azpiazu, S.J., "Estado tradicional y estado totalitario," *Razón y Fe*, 37:477 (Oct., 1937), 186–87, in J. J. Ruiz Rico, *El papel político de la Iglesia católica en la España de Franco* (Madrid, 1977), 67. It might be noted that Padre Azpiazu was perhaps the leading authority in the Spanish clergy on the theory of corporatism. He had earlier published *El Estado Corporativo* (Madrid, 1936), and later brought out *El Estado Católico* (Madrid-Burgos, 1939).

and religious unity. Unity was, in fact, the common theme of both religious and secular commentators.

In the same number of *Razón y Fe*, a well-known Jesuit writer, Constantino Bayle, engaged in similarly fuzzy qualifications. He argued that the National Movement, as Franco's state party was now called, was not necessarily fascist, since it was also pluralist. For Bayle, there was no clear content to the term fascist. If fascism were to mean law and order and the resurrection of the national spirit, he was for fascism. "If that is meant by fascism, then we are in agreement. . . . And, carefully examined, the party or organization for whom the term is least ill-suited [the Falange] stands for nothing else [no otra cosa es]."[10]

There were a few ideologues in the new system who specifically espoused the term fascism and also made its definition in Spain consubstantial with Catholicism. Probably the most influential new book of political doctrine published in Spain was José Pemartín's *¿Qué es lo nuevo?*, which opined that "fascism is, in brief, the Hegelian fusion of state and nation. Consequently, if Spain is to be national, and is to be fascist, the Spanish state must necessarily be Catholic."

Much more common, however, was the public invocation of the Nationalist cause in the Civil War as a crusade pure and simple.[11] A considerable literature in this vein developed in 1937–38, devoted to justifying the cause of revolt, the concept of the just war, and the crusading quality of the Nationalist movement.[12] Conversely, there was no trace of self-criticism or any public sign of concern over the harshness of Nationalist policy, which involved extensive political executions, ultimately reaching into the tens of thousands. There may have been an occasional instance of private intercession by an individual priest or prelate, but it never went beyond that.

Cardinal Gomá remained adamant throughout the war in his faith in

---

10. Quoted in Ruiz Rico, *El papel politico*, 68.

11. Merely to cite six samples noted by one religious historian: the archbishop of Valladolid: "The most holy war witnessed by the centuries" (Mar. 30, 1937) and "[Nationalist troops are] crusaders for Christ and for Spain" (Mar. 28, 1937); the archbishop of Granada: "We find ourselves once more at Lepanto" (Oct., 1937); the archbishop of Córdoba: "The most heroic crusade registered by history" (Dec. 30, 1937); the bishop of Tuy: "This is not a civil war but a patriotic and religious crusade"; the bishop of Tenerife: "Of all the just and holy wars known to history, none is more sacred and just." Chao Rego, *La Iglesia*, 26, 377–79.

12. Fray Ignacio González Menéndez-Reigada, *La guerra española ante la moral y el Derecho* (Salamanca, 1937); Julio Meinville, *¿Qué saldrá de la España que sangra?* (Buenos Aires, 1937); Constantino Bayle, *Sin Dios y contra Dios* (Burgos, 1938); Juan de la Cruz Martínez, *¿Cruzada o rebelión?* (Zaragoza, 1938); A. de Castro Albarrán, *Guerra santa: El sentido católico de la guerra española* (Burgos, 1938).

the righteousness of the Nationalist cause, a faith equally certain that the Crusade would lead to a profound spiritual awakening in Spain. At the May 1938 International Eucharistic Congress in Budapest, he declared that the Civil War could not end in compromise but that the left must surrender completely. Near the conclusion of the fighting, his pastoral "Catolicismo y Patria" intoned, "Let us give thanks to God that he has willed to make of Spain a Christian people from the heights of [state] power. This is declared, moreover, by the new legislation of the state, informed by Catholic spirit in its broad trajectory. And our hope is confirmed, dear diocesans, by the undeniable religious resurgence that we have observed in the liberated portion of our beloved archdiocese."[13]

Formal derogation of some of the principal Republican anti-Catholic legislation was nonetheless delayed by the Franco regime until the spring of 1938, when both its military dominance in the war and the recognition and support of the Vatican seemed assured. In March of that year obligatory religious instruction was restored in public schools, crucifixes mandatorily reinstalled in all classrooms, the validity of religious marriage emphasized, and plans announced for a new religiously inspired secondary-school curriculum. The only lingering expression of anticlericalism took the form of occasional minor verbal outbursts or street gestures by the radical wing of the Falange that were quickly squelched.

During the Festival of Victory held in Madrid's Church of Santa Bárbara on May 20, 1939, Franco offered the public prayer: "Lord God, in whose hands is right and all power, lend me thy assistance to lead this people to the full glory of empire, for thy glory and that of the Church. Lord: may all men know Jesus, who is Christ son of the Living God."[14] It was a most unusual invocation of empire during the era of the Second World War, though one fully consistent with the traditional Spanish ideology.

NATIONAL CATHOLICISM DURING WORLD WAR II

The complete triumph of Franco in 1939 seemed to assure total reidentification of Church and state. Franco was ready and eager to resume the regalist powers of the Spanish state along the lines of the Concordat cast aside by the Republic in 1931, but the Vatican remained cautious in its official dealings. The papacy had waited until a score of governments around the world officially granted diplomatic recognition to the Franco regime before it followed suit in May 1938. The experience

---

13. *Iglesia, Estado y Movimiento Nacional*, 35–37.
14. Ibid., 45–46.

of the previous decade with the Mussolini system had led to quite different results from those anticipated by Pius XI's concordat with the Italian government in 1929, and the former Cardinal Pacelli, the Vatican secretary of state who became Pius XII in 1939, was apparently determined not to concede as much to Franco as had been granted Mussolini. The Spanish state abolished divorce in September 1939 and officially resumed the former ecclesiastical budget two months later, but a general agreement with the Vatican was not worked out until 1941, and it was well short of a concordat. The new agreement did grant the Spanish government the right to make presentations to the episcopacy, but specifically withheld the broader authority over other Church appointments conceded under the former Concordat.

Whether or not the regime regained traditional regalian rights, it was not reluctant to impose the controls and censorship of twentieth-century authoritarianism. It is true that to some extent the censorship of ecclesiastical publication was exercised through and in agreement with the Church leadership, but this was not always the case. During the Civil War, for example, Pius XI's anti-Nazi encyclical, *Mit brennender Sorge*, was suppressed, appearing only in the diocesan bulletins of the bishops of Calahorra and Mallorca, and then in the Jesuit journal *Razón y Fe* by express order of the Vatican. The Pope was censored by radio as well. His radio message to Spain of April 15, 1939, felicitating the Nationalists on their victory, contained a passage urging kindness and goodwill toward the defeated that was cut off the Spanish broadcast.

Cardinal Gomá found the first year of life in the new postwar re-Catholicized Spain profoundly disillusioning. The religious revival was outwardly impressive, but seemed to redouble the traditional emphasis on external manifestation rather than inner spiritual experience. Shortly after the Civil War ended, Gomá confided to the British ambassador, Sir Samuel Hoare (who was Catholic), that Franco's triumph had not produced the true spiritual renewal that Gomá had anticipated. What it had produced was the "autocratic state" which Gomá had overconfidently refused to recognize as a danger in 1937. Catholic student associations were absorbed by the Falange's SEU, Catholic social groups repressed if they competed with the state syndicates, priests forbidden to use the regional vernacular in Catalonia and the Basque provinces (despite Gomá's intercession), and a pastoral of the primate himself suppressed as too indulgent of the opposition and obliquely critical of the government. Gomá died in August 1940 a politically disillusioned prelate.

Gomá was nonetheless exceptional among the Spanish Church leaders of his day. His strong conservative personality defended the integrity of the religion in a more direct and independent manner than did most of the rest of the episcopacy, who in general were strongly identified with the regime despite its excesses. With the liberal Catalan Cardinal Vidal i Barraquer condemned to exile until his death in 1943, only the extreme traditionalist Cardinal Segura, at the opposite end of the spectrum, remained to speak out on behalf of the Church's independence.

Following his exile by the Republic, Segura had spent five years in Church administration in Rome and was then appointed to the archbishopric of Seville during the Civil War. He detested Falangists as heterodox fascists, and his defiance of the regime in Seville became legendary. Segura curtly refused requests, after the war had ended, for the celebration of *misas de campaña* (open field masses) at Falangist rallies, observing that this was a political spectacle which profaned holy services in a sacrilegious manner. His cathedral in Seville was said to be the only major church building in Spain that did not bear the names of fallen Falangists on its walls. During the course of a public sermon in 1940, he had the audacity to inform his listeners that the Spanish term *Caudillo* (used in the Franco regime for the head of state as equivalent of *Führer* or *Duce*) had signified in classical literature the leader of a band of thieves, and that Loyola's *Spiritual Exercises* classified such a figure as a demon. This outburst provoked such wrath that Franco's ministers could barely restrain him from ordering Segura's second exile.

The outbreak of major war in Europe had some tendency to divide Catholic opinion, though it created no major problems. Catholic moderates on the one hand and some religious rigorists on the other feared closer association with Nazi Germany, while the Catholic sectors of the Falange generally supported a pro-Nazi policy. The clearest opposition was expressed by Fidel García Martínez, bishop of Calahorra, who issued strongly and categorically anti-Nazi pastorals in 1942 and 1944. As it developed, the regime's prudent diplomacy skirted this problem with considerable skill.

Antagonism between the Church and the state party, the Falange, was nonetheless sometimes extreme. While the hierarchy avoided major confrontation, its close support of and identification with the regime could not have withstood any full-scale fascistization of Spanish government. The decline of the Axis in 1942–43 was the major and final factor impelling the regime in the opposite direction. Between 1942 and 1947 it had progressively to readjust to the triumph of the democracies in western Europe, and it underwent a new phase of institutionalization. This included introduction of a corporative parliament, a Spanish Bill of Rights (Fuero de los Españoles), and the legitimization of the regime as a monarchy, institutionally, with Franco as regent for life.

Within the government, the ministries of justice and education were specifically reserved for ultra-Catholics so that religious norms would be brought to bear on the legal and educational systems. Franco's first education minister, the Catholic monarchist Pedro Sainz Rodríguez, introduced a new secondary education curriculum in 1938 to restore the primacy of Catholic teachings and the traditional humanities. A new law of university organization in 1943 recognized "as supreme guide Christian dogma and morality and the authority of sacred canons with respect to teaching."[15] The subsequent law of primary education went even further to bring every aspect of elementary education in line with Church doctrine.

While Catholic standards were ubiquitous in the instruction of the innocent, Catholic moral direction was also broadly introduced into the extensive new prison system. A quarter-million Republicans languished in the regime's jails during the immediate aftermath of the Civil War, though their number was steadily reduced during the 1940s. The clergy were given broad powers of spiritual supervision, and made extensive though generally ineffectual efforts at the conversion of "Reds," involving compulsory attendance at mass and catechizing in many prisons. It was claimed, no doubt correctly, that the highest rate of success was scored in securing repentance and last-minute conversion among the thousands who were executed during the Civil War and the first years that followed.

Within the state syndical system, an ecclesiastical advisor of syndicates was appointed in 1944. Similar religious advisory agencies were established under a number of other ministries and state institutions. They became a standard feature of Spanish institutional life for the next quarter-century.

Though Gomá may well have been right about its absence of spiritual depth, the decade after the Civil War brought a marked revival of most aspects of religious life. Church attendance increased greatly, church buildings were reconstructed on a large scale, and virtually every single index of religious practice rose. By 1942 a new series of "popular missions" of mass evangelizing were in full swing, continuing on a broad scale for more than a decade. In terms of the absolute number of people nominally involved, these may have been the largest evangelistic exercises yet seen in the twentieth century anywhere in the world. In large industrial cities like Barcelona, there were sometimes nearly a quarter-million people lining the streets during such mission campaigns, though the lasting effects were probably not much greater than St. Francis Xavier's mass baptisms of Asians in the late sixteenth century. Seminary

---

15. Quoted in Víctor Manuel Arbeloa, *Aquella España católica* (Salamanca, 1975), 275.

facilities were expanded throughout Spain, though the number of seminary students did not increase markedly until about 1945, after the new religious acculturation had had more time to shape young vocations.

One of the most remarkable features of post-Civil War Spain was the general resacralization of most formal aspects of life.

> Religion was a natural part of social life: Christmas, with its nativity scenes and processions of the Wise Men; Lenten lectures and open or closed spiritual exercises; Novenas; the processions of Holy Week; Eucharistic processions and the viaticum to the sick; rosaries at dawn; the processions of the Sacred Heart of Jesus; pilgrimages to the Virgin; festivals of patron saints; the religious activities of charitable guilds and confraternities and spiritual brotherhoods. . . . The entire year was accompanied by some form of public religious manifestation.[16]

This resacralization of Spanish life affected all public affairs and institutions and was strongest in those regions and sectors of society that had never undergone secularization in the first place: the Catholic north with its predominantly religious rural society, and significant portions of the middle and upper classes. Conversely, it was much weaker and had much less effect among the former bastions of the revolutionary cause: the poverty-stricken rural south and the urban workers. Yet even in the latter areas there was some change during the 1940s, as a minority of the formerly indifferent returned to church attendance and certain forms of piety, whether under duress or from conviction or a new sense of social conformity. For a few years during the 1940s the Catholic Spain of tradition seemed once more to have been restored.

THE APEX OF NATIONAL CATHOLICISM, 1945–60

Catholicism proved of decisive assistance to the Franco regime in two distinct phases, the first during the Civil War and the second during the crucial survival phase of the regime at the close of World War II. By the last years of the world conflict, opinion within the Church hierarchy concerning the regime had become more divided. Several bishops had grown increasingly hostile, producing the first "social pastorals" in a few widely separated dioceses that condemned the abuses and injustices of the prevailing economic structure, particularly in the countryside. This current culminated in the first collective social pastoral by the bishops of

---

16. Rafael Gómez Pérez, *Política y religión en el régimen de Franco* (Barcelona, 1976), 156.

eastern Andalusia in October 1945, which recommended separate worker and management associations instead of the state vertical syndical system. Much more typical, however, were the post-Integrist prelates who still strongly defended the regime and opposed any drastic change, though only one—Eíjo y Garay, the "blue bishop"[17] of Madrid—had gone so far as to identify himself with the Falange.

During the closing moments of World War II the regime strove to intensify its symbiosis with religion in order to confirm a nonfascist identity, and thus more than ever before tried to make of Catholicism its central ideological foundation. Enrique Pla y Deniel, Gomá's successor as primate, cooperated fully in this enterprise, writing in *Ecclesia*, organ of the Church hierarchy, on March 21, 1945: "It must be said with perfect clarity: The World War has nothing to do with the Spanish Civil War." His pastoral "Al terminar la guerra" ("On the Ending of the War"), issued on August 28, 1945, defended the regime from charges of being either statist or totalitarian. It reemphasized the classic doctrine of the right of rebellion against tyrannical regimes such as that of the Popular Front and insisted that "the episcopacy and the clergy did not exceed the limits set by the Roman pontiff. Not a single priest performed military service in the Civil War, and the ecclesiastical hierarchy blessed one of the belligerent groups only after the character of the Civil War of the first moments was transformed into a crusade."[18] In February 1946 he defended the Nationalist cause as a genuine crusade before the College of Cardinals in Rome.

At the same time, the Church leadership expected the regime to undergo major reform in the direction of moderation and the institutionalization of traditional legal norms. Pla's pastoral of May 8, 1945, synthesized the position of the hierarchy when it endorsed the regime but also urged it to acquire "solid institutional bases in conformity with our historical traditions and compatible with present realities." During the next two years, Pla hailed the regime's new institutional formulations and urged Catholics to participate in the system.

During the 1940s and 50s the most influential Catholic group was the Asociación Católica Nacional de Propagandistas (ACNP), which had played a vigorous role under the monarchy and in the organization of the CEDA during the Republic. Reorganized after the Civil War, the ACNP counted only about 600 members, but among these were the most influential lay leaders and activists. During the first months of 1945 several key laymen played prominent roles in making diplomatic and religious

---

17. Blue was the color of the Falange.
18. Quoted in Arbeloa, *Aquella España Católica*, 248.

contact abroad to try to reduce the extent of Spanish political isolation. The two most active figures were Alberto Martín Artajo, national president of Catholic Action, and Joaquín Ruiz Giménez, president of the international Catholic organization Pax Romana.

On July 18, 1945, one day after issuing the Spanish Bill of Rights, Franco installed his first new cabinet of the postfascist era. Its most prominent personality was the Catholic Action head, Martín Artajo, as foreign minister. He was to retain that post for twelve years, representing the regime to the world of western democracy. Another Catholic Action militant occupied public works, while a longtime Franquist Catholic retained the post of education. In all, only three of thirteen ministers could be identified as primarily Catholic as distinct from primarily Franquist in either a Falangist or quasi-monarchist sense, but in that time of international ostracism the ministry of foreign affairs was unusually significant. Later, in 1951, the Pax Romana leader Ruiz Giménez took over the ministry of education, though its authority, in anticipation of his reformist bent, was then somewhat reduced.

The new institutional framework built the Church hierarchy into the senior advisory state leadership for the first time since the early nineteenth century. The primate theoretically became one of the three members of the new Regency Council. In the Council of State (the regime's highest consultative body) he sat ex officio, while another prelate was one of the seven appointive members. Seven bishops were appointed by Franco to the new Cortes, and two priests were among the corporatively elected deputies in its first session.

José Antonio Girón, Falangist minister of labor and usually considered a representative of fascism within the regime, declared in his own capacity in 1945 that the revolution of Falangism was directed above all to fulfillment of the Catholic spiritual mission of Spain. Near the end of his state-constructing labors after nearly ten years, Franco told his corporatist parliament on May 14, 1946: "The perfect state is for us the Catholic state. It does not suffice for us that a people be Christian in order to fulfill the moral precepts of this order: laws are necessary to maintain its principles and correct abuses."[19] By that time the broadest assortment of religious regulations seen in any twentieth-century western state had been established in Spain.

The climax of the neo-Catholic orientation came in August 1953 with the signing of a new Concordat between the Spanish state and the Vatican. This arrangement was more eagerly sought by Madrid than by Rome, and Spanish Catholics played a major role in convincing the

---

19. *Iglesia, Estado y Movimiento Nacional,* 75–76.

Vatican of its desirability. The Concordat provided the fullest recognition of the regime by the Church, reaffirmed the confessionality of the Spanish state, and recognized the right of presentation of bishops by the head of state. It also affirmed the juridical personality and independence of the Church and the full authority of canonical marriage, and restored the legal privileges of the clergy that had been partially abolished in Spain in the mid-nineteenth century. Coming immediately before the military and economic pact between Spain and the United States one month later, it served to consummate the relative international rehabilitation and partial acceptance of the regime. The neo-Catholic tactic adopted in 1945 had produced a bountiful harvest, while the moderating and liberalizing changes that the new Catholic ministers had hoped to introduce into the regime had for the most part never taken place.

Other important public gestures followed: the reconsecration of Spain to the Sacred Heart by Franco in 1954; the supervision of foodstuffs sent under the new American pact by Caritas, the principal Catholic charity association; and the suppression of legalized prostitution in 1956, abolishing the licensing of brothels begun fifteen years earlier (though this step was probably prompted by the requirements of entry into the United Nations and its affiliate organizations). The obverse of state religious policy were the sharp restrictions imposed on Spain's nearly 30,000 Protestants. The 1945 Spanish Bill of Rights guaranteed them freedom of private worship along the lines of the 1876 constitution, but all public activity and announcements were prohibited. Moreover, Protestants were subjected to a variety of legal harassments, and there were occasional acts of violence against their meeting places. Even so, some Catholic prelates still found Protestant infection a major source of danger and railed against it in public pronouncements.

During the 1940s and 50s Catholic schools not only regained but improved upon their earlier position within the general framework of Spanish education. Forty-nine percent of all secondary students attended Catholic schools at their high point in 1961. For adult laypeople, the new movement of Cursillos de Cristiandad (religious retreats), initiated in 1949, reached its apex during the 1950s, involving tens of thousands of men and women in new Christian education and spiritual rededication. The Cursillos were so successful that they were later copied by both Catholics and Protestants in many other countries.

The role of Catholic publications also reached its zenith during this period. Thirty-four of the 109 daily newspapers being published in Spain in 1956 could be defined as Catholic organs, and more than 800 other periodical publications were being brought out by either the clergy or Catholic lay associations. Subsequently, a new agreement with the state in 1962 freed official Catholic publications from prior censorship, while certain Church officials continued to participate actively in the general state censorship.

Growth in the number of religious vocations continued through the mid-1950s, as an all-time record number of new priests for the modern era (more than 1,000 per year) were ordained between 1954 and 1956. The clergy continued to be drawn from roughly the same predominantly northern social sectors as in preceding generations. It was now more urban, and even more working-class, in social background than before, however, while at the same time drawing more new members from the upper classes (table 7.1).

Yet the decade of the 1950s, which witnessed the height of neo-Catholicism, also revealed the first indications of a new decline in religious devotion. Some indicators of religious activity had in fact begun to go down as early as the close of the 1940s. The number of seminary students remained at nearly 8,000 from 1951 to 1963, but the annual total of new ordinations started to drop slowly after 1956, even though the number of priests reached its peak for contemporary Spain at 34,474 (counting regular clergy serving as priests) in 1963. In the three main "Red" cities of Madrid, Barcelona, and Valencia, where the need for urban missionary work was greatest, the number of priests increased by more than 10 percent during the 1950s but by 1960 still had not regained the level of 1931. Although this was not clear to many at the time, the urban, industrial, and consumer-oriented society of the 1950s was inaugurating a new phase of secularization. This "development society" did

TABLE 7.1
Social Origin of New Religious
Vocations, 1934–57

	1934	1947	1957
Urban worker	8.7%	11.6%	13.3%
Farm worker	17.6	9.8	5.5
Landholder	43.5	42.7	32.1
Urban middle class	28.6	33.7	41.9
Upper class	1.5	2.2	7.2

Source: *Adapted from Severino Aznar,* La revolución española y las vocaciones eclesiásticas *(Madrid, 1949); and R. S. Azaceta, "Les vocations dans les seminaires espagnols" (Institut Social, 1958), 75, in P. Iztueta Armendáriz,* Sociología del fenómeno contestatario del clero vasco *(Donostia, 1981), 124–25.*

not nurture as many religious vocations as in the 1940s. Response to popular missions was similarly in decline, and fewer new missions were undertaken, even on a more modest, less obtrusively public basis.

There were significant signs of change within the clergy and lay organizations as well, as they began to be affected by the liberalizing influences of postwar Europe. The combined membership of the youth and adult branches of Catholic Action, which stood at 373,000 in 1947, increased to 532,000 in 1956, and along with this growth came further diversification of activity. Those who insisted on a unitary leadership and format lost out to the pluralists, who insisted on diversified branches of autonomous activities. Dissonant initiatives were undertaken by four social groups: the Juventud Obrera Católica (JOC; Catholic Worker Youth), the Vanguardia Obrera de Jóvenes (VOJ; Worker Vanguard of Youth), the Juventud Rural de Acción Católica (JARC; Rural Youth of Catholic Action), and especially the Hermandades Obreras de Acción Católica (HOAC; Worker Brotherhoods of Catholic Action), small Catholic blue-collar workers' groups founded in 1946, whose activities were restricted by the regime. The HOAC slowly expanded and became much more militant in political and economic attitudes by the mid-1950s. Catholic students resumed autonomous activity within the SEU, the state university student organization, and began to align themselves with moderates in the opposition. By the early 1950s Spanish laypersons were participating actively in all the principal international organizations of the Catholic Church.

After the signing of the Concordat, friction between the government and Church leadership actually increased, aggravated by the three issues of censorship, the freedom of Catholic workers' groups, and the slowness of further institutional change withing the regime. Cardinal Archbishop Pla y Deniel had never actually filled the seat reserved for him on the Council of State. For some years the only prelate willing to serve Franco in this capacity was Eíjo y Garay, the Blue Bishop. The position of the Church hierarchy and of the leaders of Catholic Action on HOAC was that these groups were religious organizations of workers, not Catholic trade unions, and should in no way be molested by the state. The regime's syndical bosses correctly perceived that in the long run the HOAC represented a new form of competition in workers' organization and continued to restrict and harass them.

Some of the clergy also began to speak out more directly on certain social and cultural issues that had direct political overtones. By the late 1950s this was most notable in Catalonia and the Basque provinces, where they actively resumed their longstanding identification with regional culture and interests and hence provided significant stimulus for the revival of Catalan and Basque nationalism. Individual prelates in certain other districts also assumed the initiative more frequently on behalf of local social and cultural causes.

TECHNOCRATIC AUTHORITARIANISM AND THE FINAL PHASE OF NATIONAL CATHOLICISM

The middle phase of the Franco regime, based on neo-Catholicism and a sort of limited reformism partially associated with Catholic Action, came to a close in 1956–57. After attempting a few overt measures of liberalization that displeased key members of the regime while failing to placate the opposition, Ruiz Giménez was dismissed from his post as minister of education. Falangists then pressed for a neo-Falangist reform of the regime that would give institutional dominance to the party (National Movement). This move in turn was blocked by the military and other sectors of the right, including the Church hierarchy. Franco sought some new alternative that would not involve drastic political change, and in 1957 appointed a new cabinet of military men and technical experts, most of the latter either members or associates of the Catholic secular institute Opus Dei.

The leader of the new orientation was a lawyer and administrative specialist, Laureano López Rodó. He had served as technical administrative secretary to Admiral Carrero Blanco, who was in turn minister-secretary to the presidency of the Spanish state and Franco's chief political lieutenant and advisor. López Rodó and his fellow technocrats introduced sweeping changes in Spanish economic policy in 1959–60, liberalizing much of its structure and opening up the country to large-scale foreign investment and mass tourism. This replaced the semi-autarchy of the regime's first two decades with a new orientation toward a market economy, incomplete though it was. The new strategy aimed for rapid economic development accompanied by minimal political change, the former intended in large measure to substitute for the latter.

During the 1960s the presence of members of Opus Dei in several key ministries, flanked by friends and sympathizers in others, gave rise to a new alarm—sometimes even within Catholic ranks—about the "domination of Opus Dei" in government. No such domination existed, though the neoliberal economic plans of the 1960s were administered by key personnel whose association had begun, at least in part, with their membership in the institute.

Opus Dei (Work of God), which originated as a diocesan association, was a new and unique Catholic organization in post-Civil War Spain and indeed in the Catholic Church as a whole. It developed from a small

nucleus organized by the Aragonese priest José María Escrivá de Balaguer in 1928. Recognized by the Vatican as a community institute in 1943
under the name Sociedad Sacerdotal de la Santa Cruz (Opus Dei) (Priestly Society of the Holy Cross), Opus Dei became the first secular institute
within the Roman Catholic Church four years later. It would expand to a
worldwide membership of approximately 72,000 by 1982, when Pope
John Paul II would recognize it as the Church's first "personal prelature."
As a secular institute, Opus Dei is composed of three categories of
members: clergy who have taken full ecclesiastical vows (a very small
proportion of the total), lay members who have taken monastic vows
(numeraries), and lay members who marry and raise families (super-
numeraries).

The mission of Opus Dei is the sanctification of the secular world. As
conceived by its founder and leaders, this labor of disseminating spiritual
values can be most effectively performed through the key professions of
late-industrial society such as university teaching, business, finance, and
higher levels of management. The fact that a disproportionate number of
the institute's members have careers in these areas has given Opus Dei a
reputation for elitism, while the reserve displayed by leaders and members about their own association as an organization and their interrela-
tionships has created a certain air or appearance of secrecy.

During the first years after the Civil War, members of Opus Dei were
in general less closely connected with the regime than were those of
Catholic Action. The institute's work and emphasis seemed more progressive and modern than did that of the typical Spanish Catholic organization of the 1940s, and thus it was supported and encouraged by
several wealthy Catholic modernists, particularly in Catalonia. Conversely, Falangists attacked and opposed the institute and its members
almost from the very start.

Opus Dei came to notice as scores of its members gained university
professorships during the 1940s and 50s. Some alleged that by the 1950s
as many as 25 percent of the teaching positions in Spanish higher education were held by institute members. In 1952 Opus Dei opened what soon
became the first completely developed Catholic university in the country,
the University of Navarre at Pamplona. Other members came to prominence in business and financial affairs, and some were interested in
pursuing a political role (while others opposed such activity). Though
there was more than a little divergence of opinion on political affairs
among members of Opus Dei, one sector of lay members and activists
decided to collaborate in a technical modernization of the Spanish regime, and it is reasonable to conclude that their common membership in
the institute was a major factor in bringing them together in government.

Economic freedom and prosperity were almost inevitably calculated to sooner or later bring much greater cultural and political freedom in their wake, since in the great majority of cases the one follows the other. López Rodó himself later announced that after Spain's average income reached two thousand dollars per capita (at the 1965 price level), the country would be ready for western-style democratic reform. Certainly a "development dictatorship" geared to the materialist goal of rapid economic development could not easily remain a sacralized national Catholic state in the manner of the 1940s and 50s. Slowly but steadily during the 1960s, the form and rhetoric of the regime itself began to shift.

8

Democratization and Secularization

SPANISH CATHOLICISM emerged triumphant from the most savage persecution ever unleashed against religion in a western country during modern times. In conjunction with the Franco regime it proceeded to a formal resacralization of Spanish life that was equally unprecedented. So long as its social base and cultural values remained intact, direct assault seemed not to weaken the traditional faith so much as in some respects to make it stronger.

The challenge to traditional religion during the 1950s and 60s was of a totally different sort. In late Franco Spain the faith could never be formally challenged, much less overtly attacked. It was, instead, undermined, diverted, and ultimately in considerable measure transformed by the most rapid process of social, economic, and cultural change that ever took place in any single generation of Spanish history. The decision to "open up" Spain economically produced not only rapid industrialization and a marked growth in cities but also powerful new social and cultural trends. Full employment and steady, unprecedented increases in income for nearly all social sectors created the first experience in mass consumerism in the life of Spain. The possibility of a new society oriented toward materialism and hedonism, never remotely within reach of the bulk of the population, quickly emerged. Rural and small-town society was progressively uprooted, drawn into the vortex of the large cities, industrial zones, and burgeoning European labor market abroad. Despite continuation of an attenuated state censorship, foreign cultural influences entered Spain on the broadest scale ever witnessed. Mass foreign tourism, combined with the movement of hundreds of thousands of Spaniards abroad, exposed much of Spanish society to styles and examples widely at variance with traditional culture but often most seductively attractive. This was accompanied by mounting bombardment from the contemporary media and mass advertising. The transformation of cultural environment was thus absolutely without parallel.

The clergy itself was not immune to this process. By the 1950s more Spanish priests and religious began to go abroad for study and training than ever before. During the preceding decade there had been very little interest in new theological or other religious studies, but by the late 1950s and 60s a great deal of attention was being given new Catholic thought and Church programs in other parts of Europe. New religious programs also encouraged a more innovative and critical approach. The Cursillos de Cristiandad (Short Courses in Christianity) that organized numerous religious retreats for laymen also emphasized a more personal approach to religious life. For the first time since the early sixteenth century major emphasis was placed on the distribution and reading of the Bible. During the last twenty years of the Franco regime, probably more Bibles were distributed than in all the rest of Spanish history.

Catholic laymen took advantage of the partial tolerance shown them by the regime to adopt increasingly militant and subversive positions. The most radical layman was an activist, Julio Cerón Ayuso, who organized a nominally Catholic but semi-Marxist clandestine revolutionary group called the "Frente de Liberación Popular." He was later tried by court-martial and sentenced to eight years for military rebellion. By the late 1950s several other laymen, in rapport with the start of "liberation theology" in Latin America, espoused only slightly less radical revolutionary goals and had to flee into exile.

Much more important than these first nominal "Catholic Marxists," however, were the organized efforts of the HOAC and its counterpart Catholic Action youth groups. For the first time in the history of the regime, the election of local syndicate leaders in various provinces was openly contested by the HOAC in 1960. Though technically this contradicted the Church hierarchy's earlier defense of HOAC, which had taken the position that these were primarily religious not trade-union organizations, the Primate Pla y Deniel did not hesitate to write directly to Franco protesting their repression by the police. The leader of the Church hierarchy warned Franco that he could not expect to continue to govern Spain with the same arbitrary and authoritarian tactics more than twenty years after the Civil War had ended, and insisted that the labors of HOAC were necessary if Spanish workers were not to turn to Marxism. By that time HOAC activists were cooperating with worker militants of the Spanish Communist Party (PCE) in building new resistance units called Comisiones Obreras (CCOO; Workers' Commissions) to provide alternative leadership for industrial workers. They organized several large strikes, and in 1962 the national president of HOAC was fined for distribution of illegal propaganda. This time *Ecclesia* spoke out indirectly in support of what had become a Catholic leftist worker opposition movement. Even as concern about the Opus Dei domination of government reached full force, several members of that secular institute also took up political positions in opposition to the regime, both to its right and left.

THE IMPACT OF VATICAN II

During this period the attitude of the Vatican toward the Franco regime shifted almost 180 degrees. It is true that Pius XII never overcame his personal reservations about Franco, even after the signing of the Concordat, but his later years were dominated by concern over the Communist menace abroad and the threat of Catholic liberalism within. The Spanish Church seemed a rock of conservatism and reliability in a sea of troubles, and both Spanish official media and the ordinary Spanish faithful demonstrated a marked degree of affection for this "Pope of the Spanish," as he was sometimes called in Spain.

His successor, John XXIII, took a very different approach during a five-year pontificate (1958–63) that prepared the way for the dramatic changes which occurred in the Roman Catholic Church during the 1960s. Relations with the Spanish state, however, were relatively calm and unchanged during his reign. The same could not be said of Pope Paul VI, who followed in 1963. This pope was well known as a reformer and liberalizer; little more than a year before his election, he had sent a letter to Franco in his previous capacity as archbishop of Milan protesting an imminent political execution in Spain. Just as some Integrists had prayed for Leo XIII in the 1890s in the hope that he would return to their concept of Catholicism, the extreme conservative sector of Spanish Catholicism in 1963 recoiled against the election of this "Communist pope." Their fears were intensified when he announced that he intended to continue the work of the great Church reform council, Vatican II, initated by John XXIII.

Franco's most informed biographer has observed that of all the reverses suffered by Franco during his long career, by far the most serious was not inflicted by domestic foes or hostile foreign powers but by the Roman Catholic Church through the reforms of Vatican II. The tone was set by John XXIII's final encyclical *Pacem in terris* (1963), which warmly espoused peaceful coexistence and western civil rights such as freedom of speech, publication, and association, as well as the freedom of political choice in government representation. To many in Spain, it seemed directed as much against the Spanish regime as against Communist systems. The Council, which came to a conclusion in December 1965, made no alterations in formal theology, yet fundamentally altered many Catholic practices and principles. Its most important changes had to do with Church-state relations, the role of the laity, drastic reform of the liturgy, the relaxation of ecclesiastical discipline, new approaches to political issues, and the espousal of ecumenicism. In most aspects save theological dogma, the Council accepted the modernist critique of the Church and espoused many of the values of secular liberal society. One of its basic documents, *Dignitatis humanae*, advocated religious liberty, which was partially denied in Spain. The constitution *Gaudium et spes* oriented the Church toward service in the contemporary world in a democratic framework aimed at social and cultural reform, recommending freedom from association with the state. Another document, *Christus Dominus*, "urged with all delicacy" that civil authorities "honor themselves by voluntarily renouncing rights or privileges of election, nomination, presentation or designation to the episcopal ministry," thereby implying the abrogation of one of the main terms of the Spanish Concordat of 1953.

The Spanish episcopacy by and large represented the extreme right of the prelates assembled in Church council. Only the Polish hierarchy, suffering under the trials of Communism, proved equally conservative, and the new pope began systematically to pass over the elderly, aging Spanish bishops (most of them ordained, in fact, before the Civil War) in higher Church appointments.

Yet there was a modest reformist tint even to some of the Spanish prelates' speeches at the Council, and steps were taken immediately afterward to liberalize several aspects of Church administration in Spain. Priests and to some extent local lay groups received greater autonomy, and in 1965–66 the role of the primate and his council of metropolitan archbishops was replaced by the organization of the Spanish Episcopal Conference, composed of all bishops and archbishops. Henceforth it would democratically elect its own episcopal president.

Though the Spanish hierarchy had not yet renounced the creed and institutional advantage of national Catholicism, and largely maintained its regular relationship with the Spanish state, a major reorientation was setting in whose implications would have as much political as religious impact. The struggle between traditionalism and modernism in the Church was clearly being won by modernism. The effect on the nature and tone of Spanish religion, the role and attitudes of the clergy, and the Church's relationship with state and society would be profound.

THE POLITICAL REVOLT OF THE YOUNGER CLERGY

In no Catholic society did the dramatic new doctrines of Vatican II have such a marked effect as in Spain. Even before the Council, there were signs of a kind of generational split appearing in the Spanish clergy.

The middle-aged ranks had been decimated by the Civil War, while thousands of young priests had entered the clergy during the late 1940s and 50s. Their reading matter was drawn not so much from traditional Spanish works as from translations of foreign Catholic writers, who were frequently more liberal and progressive than the Spanish. Whereas in 1950 approximately 75 percent of religious works published in Spain were by Spanish authors, this had fallen to only 52 percent by 1965, at which time only 17 percent of the works published on dogma were by Spaniards.[1] The younger clergy, particularly, were influenced by the new reformist doctrines of progressive Catholicism, though their impact varied considerably in different parts of the country.

It has been observed by Guy Hermet and others that in the twentieth century the Spanish Church has consisted of three rather distinct ecclesiastical configurations: the "Castilian" or main sector, the Basque and the Catalan. The Spanish clergy as a whole retained most of the general characteristics and physiognomy developed during the Catholic revival of the preceding era. They were still drawn disproportionately from the rural society and small towns of the Catholic north, and often had little rapport with the social structure of certain other areas. A sizable part of the Castilian clergy still remained generally conservative, though this was less the case among younger priests.

The Catalan clergy, by contrast, was much more urban in origin, and much more drawn from the urban middle and working classes. The Catalan clergy tended to reflect their regional culture not merely in their support of Catalanism but in their more sophisticated education and their interest in advanced, even radical, theological and ideological positions. When a small group of "Christian Marxists" later emerged among the clergy, they were concentrated primarily in Catalonia.

The Basque clergy differed from both the general Spanish and Catalan norms in their relatively close identity with their regional society, rural and urban, and in their espousal, at various times, of divergent extremes as a consequence. They were generally closer to the whole of a complex society than the clergy in any other part of Spain, and had the loyalty of a broader social following than the ecclesiastics of any region save those of the less developed, much more rural Castilian districts on their border. In the nineteenth century the Basque clergy had been largely traditionalist and Carlist, just as was Basque society. As modern nationalism developed during the twentieth century, the clergy tended increasingly to identify with it and in fact played a major role in its

1. According to Noel Anglois, "Le drame du clergé espagnol," *Etudes* (April, 1968), 570–71, in Iztueta Armendáriz, 246–47.

diffusion. For nearly two decades Basque culture and the Basque clergy as an autonomous unit were vigorously repressed by the regime, but as soon as the repression eased, Basque priests, especially the younger generation, resumed their active role in the struggles of their home provinces.

The revolt of the Basque clergy against the regime may be officially dated from May 30, 1960, when 339 priests signed an open letter to the regional bishops protesting the Church's close alliance with Franco's state, whose structure and practice they denounced. Though the letter was formally rejected by the Basque bishops, political insurgency began to spread through ecclesiastical ranks in the three Basque provinces. By the following year the Franciscan monastery of Aránzazu, one of the principle monastic residences in the region, had become a kind of general headquarters for Basque protest. One of the Franciscans was expelled for giving a sermon in which he was quoted as saying that "we shall not become disciples of Christ . . . until we recognize a brother in that separatist, in that Communist. . . . "[2] Oppositionist activities were supported by other monasteries of diverse orders and by much of the diocesan clergy in the region. By the last years of the decade the younger clergy were in a state of almost constant agitation, a few even providing asylum to the armed squads of ETA, the revolutionary Marxist Basque nationalist movement.

In Catalonia, the center of the dissident clergy during the 1960s was the famous Benedictine abbey of Montserrat, the region's most prominent religious site. The abbot, Dom Aureli Escarré, delivered a direct public attack on the regime in November 1963 on the occasion of the government's preparations for its "Twenty-five Years of Peace" celebration. This was by far the most critical public commentary by a senior figure of the Church to date, and the elderly Escarré was subsequently forced to retire. That changed nothing, however, and in the following years younger Catalan clerics became increasingly militant. The adoption of new regulations by the Church in 1964 that once more permitted use of the Basque and Catalan vernacular in religious services only expedited the process.

THE RADICALIZATION OF LAY ORGANIZATIONS

The liberalization and radicalization of lay organizations had begun earlier than that of the younger clergy and proceeded farther and faster.

---

2. "Un religioso vasco da una lección al episcopado español," *Eusko Deya* 26:458 (Sept.–Oct., 1961), 1, quoted in Guy Hermet, "Los precursores de la oposición clerical a Franco (1958–1969)," *Historia 16* 6:58 (Feb., 1981), 19–26.

Activists of HOAC and JOC tightened their association with Communists and other leftists in labor protests to the extent that the conservative hierarchy no longer found it possible to defend them from the regime but tried to restrain their activities, frequently without success. In the Basque provinces of Vizcaya and Guipúzcoa, the Juventud Rural de Acción Católica (Rural Youth of Catholic Action) had virtually transformed themselves into a Marxist organization, forming one of the bases for the expansion of ETA, the subsequently terrorist organization. All the while, members of Catholic Action grew more restive, eager to participate in political and social activities on their own. Following the conclusion of Vatican II, they pressed for new reforms in the spirit of the Council, reforms that would have granted them internal autonomy. These they were largely denied, and the 1966 national congress of Catholic Action was canceled. In the following year, when the annual congress was to select delegates for the upcoming World Catholic Action Congress, the Church hierarchy imposed a delegation of moderates and conservatives, excluding all representatives of HOAC, JOC, and the even more radical Vanguardias Obreras (Workers' Vanguard). A counter-delegation of liberals and radicals, led by Ruiz Giménez, was then selected by the laity.

By that time the Church leadership judged that Catholic Action and various of its collateral organizations had gotten completely out of control. Attempts to reorganize and bring it under tighter discipline in 1967–68 led to massive resignations and the virtual collapse of Catholic Action as an organization. By 1972, it was calculated that all the diverse chapters and affiliates of Catholic Action combined had only about 100,000 members, compared with, a decade earlier, over half a million members in the main organization and a grand total of nearly a million in all the affiliates combined.

DIVISION AND CHANGE WITHIN THE CHURCH HIERARCHY

Though the episcopacy and senior members of the clergy remained much more conservative than the younger priests, attitudes among the prelates continued to shift. Pope Paul VI (and to a lesser extent John XXIII before him) endeavored to strengthen reformist elements by designating a new series of auxiliary bishops, thirty-seven altogether, whose appointments under the terms of the Concordat did not have to be negotiated with the regime. After the conclusion of Vatican II, no vacant sees were filled for three years, and when regular appointments were resumed in 1968 the government no longer found itself in a position to force the selection of conservatives but only to veto the most liberal.

By that point the number of moderate reformers and moderate liberals in the hierarchy was almost equal to that of the arch-conservatives, and key new liberal appointments were made by the Vatican with each passing year. The aged Primate Pla y Deniel died in 1968 and an internal struggle arose over his successor. The Vatican ruled out a conservative but did not wish to offend the regime to the extent of appointing a clear-cut liberal. The choice was Vicente Enrique y Tarancón, archbishop of Oviedo, an outstanding theologian who had written three books in support of Vatican II but had prudently avoided public controversy with the regime. Early in 1969 he became primate and archbishop of Toledo. The Episcopal Conference met almost concurrently to elect its president for the next three-year term, and three ballots were needed before the incumbent conservative Archbishop Morcillo of Madrid was able to defeat Tarancón. The latter became vice-president and henceforth stood as the leader of moderate reform within the Spanish Church. Shrewd, tactful, an eloquent speaker with a flair for generating publicity, Tarancón would play the major role in the transformation of Spanish Catholicism during the 1970s.

THE VOCATIONAL CRISIS OF THE CLERGY

The most sweeping era of reform in Catholic history since the Counter-Reformation did not stop with major changes in Church policy and administration or even with a drastic political realignment of much of the clergy. Combined with the profound influences of contemporary materialism and hedonism, it had a traumatic effect on the sense of vocation and identity of many ecclesiastics, particularly the younger ones. More than a few seemed to lose interest in spiritual exercises and to seek the role of social activist instead. Social homilies often replaced religious sermons. Abuses in the administration of the sacraments grew increasingly common among an "enlightened" clergy, and arbitrary changes were sometimes introduced into the Mass. Parishioners in large cities were sometimes told to stop saying their rosaries and not to bother having their infants baptized, and were discouraged, occasionally forebade altogether, from coming to confession.

Renunciations of religious vocation and resignations from the priesthood multiplied by ten during the mid-1960s, then tripled once more by the end of the decade. In 1963 only 167 priests abandoned their vocation in Spain. By 1965 the figure reached 1,189 and then hit the all-time high of about 3,700 in 1969–70, as the total number of diocesan clergy steadily declined. The most commonly expressed motive for renouncing the priesthood was dissatisfaction with the vow of celibacy. The volume of senior seminary students, which had reached a record of about 8,000 during the 1950s, declined precipitously, falling to some 2,100 in 1971 and less than 1,800 by 1972–73. The Jesuit order, in the avant-garde of ecclesiastical radicalism, may have been the hardest hit of any single sector. More than one-third of the Jesuits in Spain had renounced their vows by the early 1970s, the membership of the order falling from 4,717 in 1966 to 3,077 in 1975 (though this was still 10 percent of the Jesuit membership worldwide).

Even in the Basque provinces, which always displayed the highest indices of religiosity in Spain, the clergy seemed as troubled as in Barcelona or Madrid. A *Diagnóstico sociológico de los conflictos sacerdotales* published by the Diocese of Bilbao in 1971 reported that nearly 50 percent of the priests in that diocese were uneasy with their office, that many suffered from serious doubts and questions of faith, and that quite a few were disenchanted and embittered. Between 20 and 30 percent were seeking new ideals or leadership. About 45 percent were of the opinion that current Spanish political conditions hindered spiritual work, and most opined that the Church should take resolute positions on current social and political problems. About 15 percent believed that the Church should directly and overtly oppose the established political structure, while 4 percent thought that the clergy should support violent revolutionary groups as well.

The crisis of vocations began to stabilize by 1971, for by that time most of the disaffected clergy had already renounced their vows. The annual total for secularizations dropped from 413 in 1971 to 386 in the following year and then to 352 in 1973. In 1974 there were only 330 new priests ordained, however, and the grand total of parish priests declined by more than 1,700 between 1969 and 1974.

TABLE 8.1
Number of Secularizations
among the
Regular Clergy, 1966–71

1966	305
1967	344
1968	446
1969	552
1970	532
1971	460

Source: *J. M. Vazquez*, Los religiosos espanoles, hoy *(Madrid, 1973), 193.*

Simultaneously within the Church there developed a partial revolt of radical younger clergy and a small portion of the laity. Several parishes in Madrid organized in 1968 their own Asambleas Cristianas to determine questions of policy and elect their own candidates to local Church offices. At about the same time 530 Basque priests dispatched a joint letter to the Vatican complaining about the conservatism of their regional hierarchs and of various Church policies. During the following year a national Federación de Asambleas Cristianas was organized, while radical laymen in several of the larger cities began to form their own independent parish networks, called *comunidades de bases*. In reaction, conservative ecclesiastics eventually organized a Hermandad Sacerdotal (Priestly Brotherhood), and a group of Jesuit traditionalists threatened to form a completely separate section of the Society of Jesus.

In an attempt to improve communications among the various ranks of the clergy, the hierarchy had authorized in 1967 the convening of full diocesan synods of all sectors of the diocesan clergy. These provided forums for new expressions of discontent and urgent requests for further reform. The boldest step toward a restoration of unity and harmony in the Church was taken in 1971, when a large Asamblea Conjunta (Joint Assembly) of prelates and representatives of all sections of the secular and a small portion of the regular clergy was convened in Madrid. Though it did not take up further administrative or structural reforms within the Church, the Joint Assembly affirmed a forthright stand on major issues. It advocated separation of Church and state, condemned conditions of "unjust capitalism," and recommended that prelates give up all state posts. The final report also spoke out in favor of full civil rights and a political system of free representation. A disavowal of the Church's role in the crusade of 1936–39 carried by majority vote but failed to get the two-thirds support necessary for inclusion in the final report. It concluded, "Thus we must humbly recognize and ask pardon for the fact that we failed to act at the opportune time as true "ministers of reconciliation" in the midst of our people divided by a war between brothers."[3]

The Assembly was preceded by the two largest opinion surveys ever conducted among the Spanish clergy and laity. The first, carried out in 1969–70, sampled approximately 18,200 members of the diocesan clergy on a variety of issues and obtained a response level of some 85 percent. The second was conducted among a varied sampling of 749 male regular clergy, 1,645 nuns and 7,686 Catholic laypersons. The first revealed considerable confusion among the secular clergy on issues of theology

---

3. Secretariado Nacional del Clero, *Asamblea Conjunta Obispos-Sacerdotes* (Madrid, 1971), 159, 161.

and morality, with 39 percent of the priests who were asked expressing some degree of uncertainty on various theological propositions, and an even greater proportion—51 percent—revealing their insecurity or uncertainty on questions of morality. Conversely, only about 10 percent—though 18 percent among those under 30 years of age—confessed to suffering from serious problems of religious faith itself.[4]

Equally revealing were the responses to the query "What ideology or sociopolitical form do you most favor?" (see tables 8.2 and 8.3).

These responses lay about halfway between the results of a major independent national survey conducted in 1969 (the FOESSA study) and the freely expressed preferences of Spanish people as a whole in the first new democratic elections of 1977. The extent to which the clergy, above all the younger ones, had approximated the positions of the predominantly leftist and semi-Marxist Spanish intelligentsia as a whole was particularly striking. Save for a comparatively small minority, the right-wing clergy had ceased to exist. In contrast, the male clergy as a whole was more pro-leftist than the laity sampled (whose numerical distribution by sex was not reported), save for a somewhat larger minority of "Catholic Communists" (2.0 percent among the general laity compared with 0.6 among the diocesan clergy) at the extreme left.

THE CHURCH AS THE AMBIVALENT PROTAGONIST OF POLITICAL CHANGE, 1969–74

By the end of the 1960s the situation of Spanish Catholicism had become contradictory in the extreme. The formal structure of the religion remained largely intact, but its cultural and spiritual bases were being drastically transformed, and large numbers of the clergy were either in revolt or abandoning the Church. The formal association of Church and state persisted under the Franquist system, but the Vatican clearly indicated that it wished a complete change, and in fact the clergy had become active leaders of the domestic political opposition. From petitions in the early 1960s they had moved to protest marches in Barcelona in 1966 and then to occupations of buildings and independent politicized assemblies, all of this accompanied in the larger cities by inflammatory sermons and agitation by individual priests. A few of the most radical proclaimed the need to put an end to capitalism and solemnly declared that "exploiters" could not expect to receive the sacraments in a state of grace. Christian-Marxist dialogues, either clandestine or conducted outside of Spain, became all the rage with these clergy. Hundreds were involved in political

---

4. *Asamblea Conjunta*, 643, 651, 653, 696.

TABLE 8.2
Political Preferences of 15,449 Spanish
Diocesan Clergy, 1970 (%)

	Under 30	*Over 64*	*Total Sample*
Socialism	47.2	3.9	24.8
Communism	0.9	0.5	0.6
Anarchism	0.6	1.3	0.4
Workers' movements	15.3	9.7	12.6
Monarchy	3.6	51.2	21.7
Falange Española	1.0	3.4	2.4
Republic	7.1	1.7	6.0
Regional autonomy	4.2	4.7	4.9
Present situation	4.2	11.5	10.5
No response	16.0	12.1	15.7

Source: *Secretariado Nacional del Clero,* Asamblea Conjunta Obispos-Sacerdotes *(Madrid, 1971), 109.*

TABLE 8.3
Political Preferences of Regular Clergy
and Catholic Laity, 1970–71 (%)

	Regular Clergy	*Nuns*	*Members of Apostolic Associations*	*Other Catholic Laity*	*Total Sample*
Socialism	23.0	9.0	17.6	21.8	18.7
Communism	0.5	0.6	1.0	2.0	1.4
Anarchism	0.8	0.4	0.5	0.7	0.6
Workers' Movements	7.7	10.4	7.5	6.1	7.3
Traditional or constitutional monarchy	13.9	7.2	9.1	6.4	7.8
Falange Española	3.1	3.3	5.2	6.1	5.2
Republic	6.1	1.3	4.9	7.8	5.9
Regional autonomy	7.1	1.3	1.5	1.7	2.0
Present situation	20.2	39.9	33.1	31.1	32.2
No response	17.6	26.5	19.6	16.3	18.9
Total sample	(749)	(1,645)	(2,511)	(5,175)	(10,080)

Source: Asamblea Conjunta, *707.*

activities that a quarter-century earlier would have brought immediate imprisonment, beatings, and long prison terms to laymen. Since, however, the clergy enjoyed special juridical privileges under the Concordat, they were treated with kid gloves. Only the most salient were arrested for civil (that is, political) offenses, and even then it was necessary to consult with the ecclesiastical superior. Eventually a special *cárcel concordataria* (lit. "Concordat jail") was set up in the Leonese city of Zamora, housing more than a score of inmates by 1969. While the hierarchy generally attempted to hold the wave of agitation in check, at least to some extent, this became less and less true with each passing year. When the liberal José Ma. Cirarda was appointed bishop of Bilbao on the death of the ultraconservative incumbent near the close of 1969, the insurgent Basque clergy of Vizcaya in effect had one of their own as leader. The regime declared a temporary state of emergency at the beginning of 1969 because of Basque political violence, bringing a delegation from the hierarchy to the ministry of justice to urge that it be lifted as soon as possible.

All this provoked a new kind of anticlericalism never before seen in Spain—the anticlericalism of the extreme right. Publications of old-line Falangists and other ultrarightist groups were given relative license in their verbal attacks on the "red clergy," and there were occasional physical assaults as well. In July 1971 the Minister of Justice publicly protested the "Marxistization" of the Church, echoing the language of a report presented by the Minister of the Interior six months earlier concerning the penetration achieved by subversive groups and ideas.

The leader of the right and principal supporter of the regime among the Church hierarchy was Msgr. José Guerra Campos, former auxiliary bishop of Madrid, an appointive deputy in the Cortes and currently secretary of the Episcopal Conference. He had delivered possibly the most notable and effective Spanish address at Vatican II on the theme of Christianity and Marxism, but Guerra Campos could count on no more than about 15 percent of the votes in the Episcopal Conference to support a direct proregime position. His public gestures on behalf of the government and the policies of the preceding generation drew the adherence of only a small minority of like-minded clergy and right-wing laity.

There were several efforts to form new rightist Catholic lay groups. The most extreme were the strong-arm squads known as the Guerrilleros de Cristo Rey (Warriors of Christ the King), which in turn were fully repudiated by the Church leadership.

The peak of clerical activism was reached in the early 1970s. Support from the highest stratum of the Church was demonstrated in 1972 when Pope Paul's liberal nuncio, Msgr. Luigi Dadaglio, indicated that it was appropriate to have offered church sanctuary to a group of 111 priests, students, and workers pursued by police for having demonstrated on behalf of Basque revolutionary terrorism. At the beginning of 1973 the Spanish foreign minister López Bravo (a member of Opus Dei) gained an audience with the Pope to present a personal letter of protest from Franco, but this elicited no significant change. Not long afterward the

Spanish hierarchy released a document, "La Iglesia y la Comunidad Política" ("The Church and the Political Community"), that came out in favor of democratic pluralism. During the same year a group of leftist laymen and clergy formed a group called Cristianos por el Socialismo, while the newest appointee as bishop of Bilbao, Antonio Añoveros (who was even more liberal than his predecessor, Cirarda), conducted an official ceremony of excommunication against a number of policemen who had beaten up an activist priest in his diocese. In November 1973 the ecclesiastics held prisoner in the *cárcel concordataria* at Zamora staged a prison riot, wrecking much of the furniture and other appointments, and were supported by demonstrations of sacerdotal solidarity in various parts of the country. Tension climaxed at the point of the assassination of Carrero Blanco, Franco's prime minister and chief lieutenant, in late December. At the state funeral that followed, Cardinal Tarancón, the new leader of the Church in Spain, was greeted by cries of "Tarancón al paredón!" (Tarancón to the firing squad) from the regime's supporters. By that point even the more liberal prelates realized that the time had come to try to avoid further confrontation, and some effort was made to restrain the activists during the months that followed.

One final crisis erupted in the late winter of 1974. Bishop Añoveros of Bilbao, who had earlier achieved some prominence through his social concerns in Andalusia, delivered three sermons on problems of Basque culture. In one of them he called explicitly for cultural autonomy for the Basque provinces, leading to an immediate sentence of house arrest. For several weeks the "Añoveros affair" threatened to explode completely the structure of Church-state relations, as the government considered officially expelling him from Spain and part of the hierarchy, meeting in Madrid, urged preparation of articles of excommunication against leaders of the government. Cooler heads prevailed on both sides, and the crisis subsided for the remaining months of Franco's life.

THE LAST PHASE OF FRANQUISM: NEGOTIATIONS FOR A NEW CONCORDAT

The central issue in Church-state relations during the final decade of the Franco regime, aside from the general question of freedom of expression,[5] was that of a new concordat or relationship which would

---

5. One measure of liberalization by the regime that was not entirely applauded by all sectors of the Church was the initiative in 1967 by the foreign minister of that period, Fernando Ma. de Castiella, to promote a new law of toleration for religious minorities that would improve the regime's image abroad. Though never subjected to severe physical

grant the Church greater autonomy. Throughout the reform period, both the Vatican and the Spanish Church were concerned to remove the Church's close institutional association with the state, particularly the government's partial control of the selection of bishops. Most of the clergy seemed willing to renounce their juridical privileges in favor of a new political and institutional framework that would provide greater freedom for all Spaniards. Insofar as a specific reform was concerned, however, there were various practical problems, not least of which was that of the ecclesiastical subsidy, and this restrained the Church from denouncing the Concordat directly. From the point of view of the government, the cost of the subsidy was a small price to pay for the residual benefits of the Concordat. Its proportionate expense had dropped from about one percent of the total state budget in 1940 to only about one-half of one percent in 1970.

When Archbishop Morcillo was elected president of the Episcopal Council in 1969, he was required to give up his official position in state agencies, and yet the formal connubium continued to exist on the surface. Leading prelates still took part in various public ceremonies, and despite the fact that the Church had become the regime's number one domestic political problem, Franco and his ministers continued to reaffirm publicly their total dedication to the national religion, expressions publicly climaxed during these last years by the reinauguration of the great statue to Christ the King by Franco on the Cerro de los Angeles outside Madrid in 1969.

The last phase in which Catholic elements played a major role in the regime was the so-called *monocolor* government of 1969 to 1973. It was handed that label because most of it cabinet positions had been given to friends and associates of the economic technocrat and head of state planning López Rodó. The fact that the governing group was in large measure made up of members and associates of Opus Dei raised alarm over Opus Dei domination to its all-time height. It also seems to have led to some internal conflict within the institute itself and to the resignation of several of its more liberal members. Yet the Opus Dei members and associates exerted little influence after the death of their chief patron, Admiral Carrero Blanco, who was assassinated at the close of 1973.

---

persecution like Christians in Communist countries, Spain's nearly 32,000 Protestants (roughly one-tenth of one percent of the population) had always suffered from discrimination and legal disabilities that varied somewhat from one denomination to another but always hampered freedom of religious expression. Such restrictions were largely removed by the law of 1967. Motivation for this reform—never fully complete until after the death of Franco—stemmed from both the new standards of tolerance adopted by Vatican II and the expectations of western European opinion.

During the final two years of the regime (1974–75), they were replaced by a mixture of right-wing Catholics (drawn from the lay activists of the ACNP) and regime ultras, with the latter predominating. Several of the Catholic members resigned, and there were few left in the cabinet during the regime's last year of power who had an overt Catholic identity.[6]

During this final phase of Franquism, tensions between Church and state eased slightly. The Church hierarchy was at pains to adopt a neutral and centrist position before the impending demise of Franco and possible change of regime. It looked toward restoration of the monarchy under Prince Juan Carlos to direct Spain's path toward peaceful reform and liberalization. Such happily proved to be the course of events, confounding left and right alike.

The Vatican had begun negotiations for a new concordat in 1968 but the regime dragged its feet. Church leaders favored a series of limited agreements on specific issues rather than a revised concordat in the old form, but Franco and his ministers had little interest in a new relationship, the old one having suited their purposes optimally. Yet the regime could not completely resist personal pressure from the Pope, and a draft sketch of a possible new concordat was released by the government at the beginning of 1971. This turned out to be unsatisfactory to the Church, for it resulted in only limited liberalization.

From that point on the Papacy became even more assertive with the regime, virtually dictating the choice of new prelates by offering only one nomination for each new vacancy, in technical violation of the Concordat. Franco had little alternative but to swallow such treatment in his declining years, and in most cases the Vatican did select new candidates from among centrists.

Even so, the Franco regime sustained its traditional national Catholic identity to its dying day, continuing on frequent public occasions to reaffirm its own peculiar theology, as if the position of the Roman Catholic Church in general had not changed since 1939 or 1953. Despite

---

6. The best composite analysis concludes that about one-fourth the ministers of the Franco regime could be identified politically as primarily Catholic, so long as one includes in that general designation a number of the military ministers of somewhat ambiguous identity. Ten ministers (7.7 percent of the total) came from Catholic Action or the ACNP. Fourteen of the "technocratic" ministers of the era of the 1960s were of Catholic background, members of or otherwise identified with Opus Dei, and accounted for 11.9 percent of Franco's ministers. To these may be added four Carlists, four military ministers either with CEDA connections or closely associated with other ministers who were members of Opus Dei, and five neo-Falangist ministers during the early years of the regime who were originally connected with the CEDA. Guy Hermet, *Les Catholiques dans l'Espagne franquiste* (Paris, 1980), 1:336–37.

the acute political tension between some portions of the clergy and the government, most members of the hierarchy continued to play the same ceremonial roles on public occasions. Three bishops sat as Franco's personal appointees in the regime's last parliament, and an archbishop sat in the government's Council of State and Council of the Realm to the very end.

STRUCTURE AND SCOPE OF SPANISH CATHOLICISM DURING THE TRANSFORMATION ERA

The Spanish Church had not played a major role in worldwide Catholicism since the seventeenth century—with the partial exception of key Spanish prelates at the Vatican during the episcopate of Pius X—but it produced a comparatively numerous clergy, at least before the decline in the late 1960s. Though Spanish Catholics as a whole numbered scarcely 5 percent of the worldwide Catholic population, their average of more than 25,000 diocesan priests during the 1960s represented a considerably higher proportion of the worldwide clergy. If the nearly 10,000 *sacerdotes religiosos* (priest-monks) are included, the total would amount to more than 10 percent of the worldwide Catholic clergy engaged in diocesan and evangelistic work. The more than 100,000 Spanish monks and nuns made up 15 percent of the entire number of Catholic religious throughout the world.

Yet worldwide comparisons can be somewhat misleading because of the shallowness of Latin American Catholicism, which generates very few religious vocations. European-wide ratios of clergy to the total number of Catholic inhabitants are higher, and thus, compared with other European Catholic countries, the number of parish priests in Spain even during the pre-Conciliar period was well below the average (see

TABLE 8.4
Size of the Spanish Clergy, 1945–76

Year	Priests	Monks	Nuns	Total
1945	22,913	15,953	48,904	87,770
1955	22,811	18,221	73,978	115,010
1961	24,910	28,452	72,783	126,145
1968	26,190	24,148	85,060	135,398
1971	24,492	31,022	97,000	152,514
1976	24,160	31,308	80,242	135,710

Source: *Guy Hermet*, Les Catholiques dans l'Espagne franquiste *(Paris, 1980), 1:44;* Guía de la Iglesia en España 1976 *(Madrid, 1976).*

TABLE 8.5
Number of Catholic Inhabitants per Priest
Engaged in Parish Work, 1959

Switzerland	766
Holland	907
Ireland	917
Belgium	974
France	1,090
Italy	1,109
Germany	1,125
Spain	1,336
Austria	1,578
Portugal	2,311

Source: Sociología del catolicismo europeo *(Barcelona, 1967), 111, in Fundación FOES-SA*, Informe sociológico sobre la situación social de España *(Madrid, 1970), 459.*

table 8.5). Only in the large numbers of its regular clergy and nuns did Spain truly stand out when compared with other regions of Catholic Europe.

The vocational crisis did not begin to diminish the number of diocesan clergy until 1969, though since that time the decline has been steady and unabated. The decline in the number of religious did not effectively set in until the early 1970s. The rate of decline in new ordinations and novitiates was about average for Catholic Europe during the 1960s and 70s, and as the ranks of the clergy in general began to thin and the average age to increase, a more normal distribution of age developed, helping to overcome the generation gap. During the 1970s the decline in vocations was most noticeable among nuns, until the drop-out rate among the diocesan clergy accelerated once more in the latter part of the decade. The decline in new vocations further accentuated the Church's reliance for recruits on the rural society and small towns of the north, who by the 1970s were providing an even greater proportion of seminarians than before. The only exception to this trend came in Catalonia among the urban middle classes, where there was some increase in new vocations.

During the past generation the role of Spanish prelates in the international Church leadership has been considerably smaller than the proportionate size of the Spanish clergy within world Catholicism as a whole. This was true even under Pius XII, but was accentuated under his liberal successors. When Vatican II convened in 1962, there were a grand total of 127 Spanish bishops and heads of religious orders, about 5 percent of the total in the Roman Catholic Church, but those with sees or appointments inside Spain accounted for only about 3.7 percent and were only slightly more numerous than the leaders of much smaller Catholic populations in Canada and India. By 1967 the grand total of 80 Spanish cardinals, archibishops, and bishops accounted for only 2.6 percent of the number of Roman Catholic prelates in these categories.

Spanish appointees became even fewer proportionately during the liberal pontificates of John XXIII and Paul VI. In 1959, after the reign of Pius XII, the five Spanish cardinals then comprised 6.3 percent of the College of Cardinals. By 1973 the College had been nearly doubled, but the number of Spanish cardinals remained the same, dwindling to only 3.5 percent of the total. By that time, only one of the thirty-two top Vatican administrators was Spanish.[7] Spanish religious, however, continued to play a much larger role in the leadership of the orders.

In general the Spanish Church remained a noteworthy missionary force within Roman Catholicism. The approximately 20,000 Spanish priests, religious, and lay ecclesiastical workers in Latin America in 1970 accounted for more than half of all foreign Church workers there and approximately equaled the number of native Latin American clergy. The number of Spanish Church workers in other European lands was not insignificant, and other missionaries served in Africa and Asia. Yet this labor, too, has been affected by the decline in vocations. Whereas 146 new missionaries were dispatched to Latin America in 1966–67, only 19 entered the field there in 1974–75.

Despite the collapse of Catholic Action as a result of political disputes, the volume of membership in lay organizations was still important. In 1970 the nominal membership in all lay groups in Spain combined was not far from two million. Since about 1960, Spanish lay leaders have played disproportionately influential roles on the international level of Catholic lay organizations. The conservative nature and immobilism of the Spanish hierarchy had tended to disqualify it in the Vatican's eyes for positions of greater influence during the reform era, but the relative success and progressive attitudes of Catholic Action and other lay associations brought Spanish lay leaders into much greater prominence in succeeding years.

When the post-Franco era began, the place of Catholic education, publishing, and communications remained imposing. The Church still operated 25 percent of all the schools in Spain, though its role in higher education remained exiguous. It possessed its own news agency and its own radio network, with some 50 outlets. There were 700 Catholic

---

7. These data on the Spanish role in the international Catholic heirarchy are drawn from Guy Hermet, *Les Catholiques dans l'Espagne franquiste* (Paris, 1980), 1:25–27.

TABLE 8.6
Religiosity of Various Professional Groups in 1969

Self-description	Housewives		Secondary School Graduates		University Students		Professionals		Workers and Employees	
Indifferent	1		6		15		10		12	
Non-practicing	5	}22	8	}44	12	}56	7	}48	22	}64
Not very practicing	16		30		29		31		30	
Practicing Catholic	64		47		35		46		22	
Very good Catholic	13		7		7		5		12	
Believer in other religion	0		2		2		1		2	
No answer or don't know	1		0		6		3		0	
Total sample	(3,896)		(196)		(250)		(231)		(420)	

Source: *Fundación FOESSA,* Informe sociológico sobre la situación social de España *(Madrid, 1970), 443.*

journals and periodicals, one-fourth of all those in Spain. Eight daily newspapers were being published.

Spain remained one of the Catholic countries with relatively high levels of church attendance. The massive FOESSA sociological study of 1969 revealed this clearly (table 8.6), for the average attendance figure of 34 percent for workers and employees was higher than the national norms of some of the formerly Protestant countries of northern Europe. Though attendance by young people dropped during the 1970s, impressionistic evidence indicates that general church attendance in Spain has continued to compare favorably with most other European lands.

Though the changes in Spanish Catholicism could be seen most dramatically by 1970 in the drastic mutation in Church-state relations and the crisis in ecclesiastical vocations, a major effort was made in certain sectors and in some parishes to work a change in spiritual orientation as well. One of the most notorious statements in this regard was made by the Jesuit José Ma. Díez Alegría, whose book *Yo creo en la esperanza* (1972) gained considerable attention. Díez Alegría claimed to have "discovered true religion," which involved replacing the "ontological-cultist" (or formalist-liturgical) form of traditional Spanish Catholicism with the "ethical-prophetic" religion of true Christianity. Fortunately most of the Spanish clergy were much less presumptuous than Díez-Alegría in claiming any possible grasp of the prophetic mode, but there was more emphasis among all on a personal relation to religious faith, and more concern that those who came to Mass should do so as the expression of faith and not as the result of conformity or social convenience. This concern was

TABLE 8.7
Church Attendance
by Region, 1965–74

Region	Population Attending Sunday Mass (%)
Andalusia	22.4
Aragon	61.2
Catalonia	21.7
Balearics	58.3
Canaries	22.4
New Castile	17.6
Old Castile & León	65.3
Extremadura	26.7
Galicia & Asturias	40.8
Valencia & Murcia	30.2
Basque Country & Navarre	71.3
National Average	34.6

Source: *Rogelio Duocastella et al., in Guy Hermet,*
Les Catholiques dans l'Espagne franquiste *(Paris,
1980), 1:309.*

accompanied by an unprecedented openness to Protestantism and Judaism, the holding of special Bible days and meetings with members and leaders of other churches.

Certainly the new political independence of the Church and the emphasis on individual conviction and social concerns had diminished the old sense of anticlericalism, even among the most antagonistic regions and social classes. Though many might put this down to the effects of secularization, which simply made traditional religious concerns and values seem less important, there was also positive evidence of a shift in perception. A national survey conducted by the Instituto de Opinión Pública in 1975 found that the proposition that "the clergy are on the side of the rich" drew more disagreement than agreement (35 to 25 percent), something that would probably not have been the case forty years earlier. At the same time, despite the Church's own drive for disestablishment, hostility to the state ecclesiastical subsidy was relatively muted (opposed by 25 percent compared with 38 percent in favor).

THE CHURCH DURING THE DEMOCRATIZATION, 1975–80

The death of Franco from advanced age in November 1975 opened the way for one of the most remarkable processes of national democratization in contemporary history. Under the expert tutelage of his successor, the shrewd and courageous King Juan Carlos, Spanish government and institutions were peacefully transformed from the inside out, the very mechanisms, laws, and institutions of an authoritarian system being employed to inaugurate a system of democratic elections in 1977. The process was fraught with much difficulty and tension, compounded by world recession and domestic economic stagnation, with mounting unemployment. Intense demands for regional autonomy added a new dimension of cleavage that only made consensus and democratization more difficult, as domestic terrorism—primarily from the Basque left—provided Spain with the grim distinction of overtaking Italy in the incidence of political violence.

The Church leadership under Cardinal Tarancón could derive satisfaction from having supported a successful new transition for the first time in a century (since the Restoration of 1874–75), for the outcomes achieved under Juan Carlos were largely those sought by the Church. During the years of democratization there was less tension between Church and state than at any time since the 1920s, because the new regime eagerly accepted the proposition of a free Church in a free state, and during the transition was even willing to bend over backwards in certain kinds of concessions, particularly of an economic nature. The new democratic state did not seek a concordat, and in June 1976 Juan Carlos wrote to the pope that the Spanish government was willing to give up the right of presentation that it had held for nearly half a millennium.

Tarancón's leadership proved optimal during the transition. His discretion, moderation, command of communications, and tactful dealing with both the government and its major opposition avoided unnecessary conflict and helped to ensure that the experiences of the Second Republic would not be repeated. First elected president of the Episcopal Conference in 1972, he received strong support for reelection three years later, only twenty of the eighty votes going to a conservative rival. Meanwhile, the papacy also became more reserved, tactful, and moderate in its policy in Spain from 1975 on. As the process of democratization got underway, new appointments became somewhat more conservative in tone to avoid any imbalance.

During the 1970s, the Spanish Church was led, essentially, by moderate liberals. The extreme liberal faction remained a distinct minority, its most conspicuous representative being the auxiliary bishop of Madrid, Mgr. Iniesta, who had come close to being exiled during the last year of the Franco regime for organizing an independent Christian Assembly of workers in one of the poorest districts of Madrid. The new national atmosphere of democratization did make it all the easier for the lay *Comunidades de base* to carry on their independent quasi-religious activities and in certain cases to expand, just as for several years there was especial interest in several of the marginal radical groups such as Cristianos por el Socialismo. At the opposite, the neotraditionalist Hermandad Sacerdotal continued its work, and claimed to hold the allegiance of a large minority of the clergy.

The first parliamentary elections were held in June 1977 to form a constitutent assembly that would write a new democratic constitution. Most sectors of the Church were careful to observe scrupulous neutrality in accordance with the new spirit. The hierarchy refused, for example, to lend explicit endorsement to the two principal Christian Democratic groups, one more radical and the other moderate, that presented themselves for the contest. To the surprise of some, Spanish Christian Democrats did very poorly, gaining scarcely more than 2 percent of the vote and virtually disappearing as a political force. Compared with Italy and Germany after 1945, the democratization of Spain had occurred late, during an era of intensive secularization. This, combined with the lack of Church endorsement and the political contradictions within and between the Christian Democratic groups themselves, further condemned them to impotence. Victory went to the newly constituted Unión de Centro Democrático (UCD), led by the prime minister, Adolfo Suárez, and representing the right-center. While the Church hierarchy carefully refrained from endorsing any specific group, its own position in politics was more nearly represented by the UCD than by any other, and a certain degree of indirect assistance was accorded the new centrist party. Its close competitor on the left was the rejuvenated and reorganized Spanish Socialist Party (PSOE), which also assumed the identity of leader of a muted, definitely not extreme or polarized, anticlericalism. Direct clericalism was espoused only by the parliamentary right, which won less than 10 percent of the popular vote. The newly legalized Spanish Communist Party (PCE), interestingly, planned to reverse its policy of the 1930s and hoped to make use of the new pseudo-"prophetic" and anticapitalist agitation of the radical sector of the clergy to legitimize Communism among the middle classes and widen its base of support, an ambition largely doomed to frustration. Though the Church hierarchy stayed out of the electoral campaign, in February 1977, four months before the balloting, the Episcopal Conference did issue a statement saying that Christians should be careful not to support groups "incompatible with the faith," especially those advocating "a concrete model of society" in which "fundamental rights . . . are suppressed,"[8] which was taken to be a warning against the PCE.

---

8. Quoted in Richard Gunther and Roger A. Blough, "Religious Conflict and Consensus in Spain: A Tale of Two Constitutions," *World Affairs* 143:4 (Spring, 1981), 366–412.

Compared with the treatment of the religious issue in the 1931 Republican constitution, which began a process of polarization and breakdown, the deliberations for the 1978 constitution were a model of reasonableness and political skill. The 1931 constitution had simply been imposed on the rest of Spain by an artificial and rather spurious leftist parliamentary majority, while that of 1978 was negotiated between all the major political forces. The chief problems had to do with the exact nature of the state's relationship with Catholicism and with education. The principle of complete freedom for all religions was easily agreed upon, as was the formula that "no confession will have a state character." Church leaders did, however, object to a preliminary draft which took no cognizance of Catholicism, and the Socialists eventually agreed to the declaration that "the public authorities shall take into account the religious belief of Spanish society and will maintain the consequent relations of cooperation with the Catholic Church and other confessions."[9]

The character and degree of support for education was the major bone of contention. The Socialists demanded that state support go exclusively to laic public schools, whereas the Church sought for equal subsidies to both Catholic and public schools. The solution eventually worked out in the Constitution provided for "freedom of education" as sought by Catholics, with the state guaranteeing equal per capita assistance to private schools based on enrollment, but the state was given authority to inspect and license all schools in Spain, which in turn were required to be "democratic" in accordance with self-management. (The latter formula represents standard Spanish Socialist Party doctrine, its meaning quite unclear.)

The Constitution did not deal with the issue of abortion, took no stand on divorce, and made no provision to continue an ecclesiastical subsidy. A separate agreement was reached with the Church by the government to continue the existing ecclesiastical subsidy for two more years and then to replace it with an obligatory special levy on Spanish taxpayers in the fiscal year 1980–81, though this arrangement drew criticism from the left.

---

9. Article 16 of the new Spanish Constitution reads:

"1. Ideological freedom and freedom of religious faith and worship are guaranteed to individuals and to communities, with no limitation on their expression other than that necessary for the maintenance of public order, as protected by the law.

2. No one may be compelled to make statements about his ideology, religion, or beliefs.

3. There shall be no official state religion. The public authorities shall take into account the religious beliefs of Spanish society and shall maintain the consequent relations of cooperation with the Catholic Church and other confessions."

The new Constitution represented a victory for Tarancón, who won a third term as president of the Episcopal Conference at its meeting in March 1978. The conservative bishops remained dissatisfied with his policy of "active neutrality" in the political process, with respect to both the Constitution and the electoral campaign. Their effort to elect a more conservative president who would give official backing to Christian Democrats failed to win more than thirteen votes. Moreover, for the first time, presidencies of a majority of the thirteen special commissions formed by the Conference were given to younger liberal bishops, in several cases even to auxiliaries.

Though the Church took no official stand on the national referendum for ratification, about sixty of the eighty bishops that made up the Episcopal Conference appeared to favor it, and only nine ultraconservatives directly opposed it. In January 1979, shortly after the Constitution had been signed into law by the crown, new agreements were negotiated between the Spanish state and the Vatican that recognized their mutual freedom in their respective spheres, completely ending the state's right of presentation. The accords provided for creation of a cadre of professors of religion, paid by the state, to offer voluntary religious instruction at all levels of public education. Official religious holidays were to be jointly determined by the Church and the government.

Ratification of the Constitution was followed by a new electoral campaign to choose Spain's first regular new democratic parliament early in 1979. This was approached with great anticipation by the non- and anti-Catholic left, who hoped to take advantage of the first major opportunity, since the Civil War, to win control of Spain. Both Socialists and Communists correctly anticipated that the new culture of materialism and mass secularization had deprived the political right of its primary base of religious reinforcement, and in fact the combined popular vote for all rightist groups declined further. Narcís Jubany, the progressivist and Catalanist cardinal archbishop of Barcelona, intoned during the campaign that "no political party can claim that its choice exclusively is the only valid reflection of the Gospel,"[10] and Communists were encouraged by survey results from the preceding elections which indicated that nearly half of nominally Catholic opinion now believed that it was at least theoretically possible to be both a good Catholic and a good Communist.

Such expectations were nonetheless exaggerated. The Permanent Commission of the Episcopal Conference, while avoiding any political endorsement, issued a statement warning that Catholics must reject "materialist ideologies of one form or another, totalitarian models of

---

10. *Cambio 16* (Madrid), Feb. 25, 1979.

society and violence as a political method,"[11] as well as the legalization of abortion, divorce, and restriction of the freedom of education. Moreover, a more detailed examination of Catholic voting behavior from the preceding contest revealed that the right, even though greatly diminished, still got the most heavily and exclusively Catholic vote. Most Catholics had voted for the centrist UCD and would do so again. While nearly half (43 percent) of the earlier Socialist vote had come from those who described themselves as regularly or occasionally practicing Catholics, only 15 percent of the Communist vote came from that group. A significant portion (about 45 percent) of the Communist voters could be identified only in the broad, vague terms of "non-practicing Catholic," but that degree of tenuousness still included practically the entire population and had little significance. In fact, both the Socialist and Communist votes declined in 1979, and the center-right remained in power for three and a half more years.

The Church had reason to be gratified with the new democratic regime. It provided the democratic institutions that so much of the clergy had been demanding and largely transformed the structure of Church-state relations along the lines that the Vatican had sought since 1968. The main issues of nineteenth-century clericalism and anticlericalism had at long last been laid to rest on terms that political opinion, both left and right, domestic and foreign, overwhelmingly agreed were enlightened and exemplary. Reaffirmation of the Church's prime concerns, however, was proving more difficult, for the culture of secularism that facilitated resolution of the Church-state controversy was showing itself to be much more difficult to deal with in the spiritual dimension.

---

11. Ibid.

9

Spanish Catholicism in the 1980s

BY THE BEGINNING of the 1980s Church spokesmen suggested that the crisis of the preceding generation of Spanish Catholicism was passing. They pointed to such factors as a flattening out in the decline of seminary students and in the rate of abandonment of vocations, coupled with a church building boom in some of the larger cities to provide new worship facilities for the greatly expanded urban population of the past two decades. It was sometimes claimed that the new stress on a personal and ethical approach to religion was producing a higher degree of personal devotion and fervor among the faithful, coupled with a growing attendance in certain regions.

The general theme was in the direction of "fewer but better," since it was impossible to deny the relative decline in religious identity among Spanish people as a whole and the drastic decline, both absolute and proportionate, of the clergy. Though surveys of various kinds have become fairly common in recent years, few if any of these inquiries into religious belief and practice have been thorough and systematic at the national level. In general, their findings indicate that by 1980 only about 80 percent of the Spanish population defined themselves as Catholic. Of these, fewer than 40 percent classified themselves as regularly practicing Catholics.[1] One national survey conducted in 1979 found that 82.8 per-

---

1. Perhaps the most systematic sample was that of the fourth *Informe sociológico* of the Fundación Foessa, published in 1981 with data from a cross-section of nearly 6,000 Spaniards. Of the approximately 80 percent who considered themselves Catholics, 7.82 defined themselves as "very Catholic," 29.2 as regularly practicing Catholics, 22.46 as "not very practicing" Catholics, and 19.5 as nonpracticing Catholics. Earlier, the Centro de Investigaciones Sociológicas had published data from a smaller national sample in 1978 in which 57.92 percent of the total categorized themselves as practicing Catholics and 30.81 percent as nonpracticing Catholics. *Revista española de investigaciones sociológicas*, no. 5 (1979), cited in *Vida nueva*, nos. 1348/49 (October 16/23, 1982), 30. These higher findings are not supported by other recent surveys, including those conducted by Church agencies.

A national study conducted in 1981 by the Comisión Episcopal de Asuntos Pastorales sampling nearly 7,000 found that 39.3 percent declared themselves practicing Catholics, 15.2 infrequent practitioners, 28.4 nonpracticing Catholics, 11.1 nonbelievers, and 6.0

TABLE 9.1
Senior Seminary Students in Spain,
1965–82

1965	8,000	
1970	3,500	(approximately)
1975	2,000	
1979	1,505	
1980	1,583	(beginning of term)
1981	1,686	
1982	1,728	

Sources: Guía de la Iglesia 1979; Vida nueva *1348/49* (*Oct. 16–23, 1982*), *19; Francisco Azcona, "El catolicismo español en cifras,"* Ecclesia *2098 (Oct. 23, 1982)*, 9.

cent of its sample expressed belief in God (77.1 of the men and 87.7 of the women), but with considerable difference according to age. Of those fifty-five years and beyond, 90.2 percent avowed belief in God, contrasted with only 75.6 of those between fifteen and thirty-four. Moreover, the proportion of genuine Catholics would appear to be considerably smaller than that of nominal Catholics or theists. Only 63.4 percent of this sample indicated belief in the Pope as the Vicar of Christ, and only 5.5 percent believe in the holiness of the Church itself.[2]

Church leaders have been encouraged by the fact that the number of senior seminary students, after reaching its low point in 1979, rose steadily during the following three years (see table 9.1). Moreover, it was pointed out that the ratio of ordained graduates to the total number of seminarians was also increasing slowly but steadily, indicating greater steadfastness and commitment among the current body of seminarians. These particular facts were undoubtedly encouraging, but the number of new ordinations represented only a modest increase over the very low figures of the late 1970s and were far from adequate to even maintain, much less expand, the current reduced size of the clergy.

Each year since 1968 the clergy had, with only the most marginal statistical exceptions, declined in numbers and increased in age. At the beginning of 1982, there were 23,039 diocesan priests enrolled in all Spain, but this figure includes many aged and retired curates, and some engaged in foreign mission work. Their geographical distribution has

believers in another faith (a high finding for Spain). Ibid. Other smaller surveys from 1979 and 1980 reported approximately the same results, finding the Catholic portion of the population to be approximately 80 percent.

2. *Comentario Sociológico*, no. 25 (1979), cited ibid.

varied little during the past generation, with the smallest proportionate number to be found in the largest cities such as Madrid and Barcelona and in several of the southern provinces. Only about 11,000 were *párrocos*, or parish priests, scarcely enough to cover half the 21,530 parishes in Spain, but to this total may be added thousands of sacerdotes religiosos, monastics who serve as priests. Some 500 were attached to the Military Vicariate as chaplains. Altogether, only 16,789 were listed as devoted wholly to their ecclesiastical duties, while 2,837 were fully retired and 2,861 partially retired.

The latter figures should increase rapidly, for the comparatively youthful clergy of the *contestataria* generation of the 1960s has become a middle-aged group. The average age of Spanish priests was approximately forty-nine years in 1982, distributed as shown in table 9.2.

During the three years 1975–77, the inclusive total of 845 secularizations exceeded the number of new ordinations by 131, not to speak of deaths and retirements. Though full data are not available for subsequent years, the deficit has persisted. In 1981, for example, 163 new ordinations exceeded the total of 135 secularizations, but fell far short of compensating for the 324 deaths among the aging diocesan clergy.

During the 1970s, as during the entire preceding century, much of the vigor in the Spanish clergy as a whole was provided by the monastic

TABLE 9.2
Age Distribution of the Spanish Clergy
at the Beginning of 1982

Age	Percentage of Total
Below 30	3.2
30–34	6.3
35–39	11.2
40–44	14.0
45–49	17.6
50–54	18.9
55–59	10.2
60–64	6.1
65–69	6.1
70–74	3.7
75–79	1.6
80 or over	0.7

Source: *"Datos sociológicos sobre el clero,"* Totus tuus *(Conferencia Episcopal Española, 1982), 60–61;* Vida nueva *1348/49 (Oct. 16–23, 1982).*

orders. Of all major divisions of Spanish ecclesiastics, only the male regular clergy were able to reverse the trend of declining numbers for most of that decade, yet their numbers also began to decline by its final years, and in 1982 stood at approximately 29,000.

The female orders, conversely, lost members much more rapidly during the 1970s. Among the active orders, 8,684 abandoned their vocations in 1971 alone. Between 5,000 and 8,000 renounced their vows during every single year of that decade save for 1978, when the number fell to 4,733. Though the female orders also gained many new members, their total fell from 80,242 in 1976 to 77,049 in 1980.

The regular clergy and female orders are primarily engaged in active religious, educational, and social work, and thus, in a highly urbanized Spain, are disproportionately concentrated in the larger cities (unlike the diocesan clergy). As of 1980, Madrid counted 340 residences of regular clergy and 765 of female congregations, while the corresponding figures for Barcelona were 241 and 672. Of 90 male orders in the country, only 6 were devoted to contemplative activities, compared with 33 of 254 female congregations. Approximately 10 percent of the male and 25 percent of the female orders were in the teaching profession. It was due primarily to their efforts that as of 1981, about 22 percent of all Spanish students in elementary, secondary, and professional schools (exclusive of universities) were still being educated in Catholic institutions.

The orders continue to play major roles in health care, even under the new social democratic welfare state. In 1981, according to church statistics, 45 percent of all registered Spanish mental patients were cared for in hospitals staffed or operated by the orders, who also administered three of the country's six centers for the severely mentally deficient. More than 42 percent of the elderly in nursing homes were also cared for in institutions maintained by members of religious congregations.

Altogether about 17,000 of the 29,000 *religiosos* are *sacerdotes*, or priests. As many as 9,000 of them may carry out various pastoral functions, and more than 3,000 are attached directly to parishes. On their grounds, the orders maintain approximately 8,000 chapels that are sometimes used for religious services for laity also. They are responsible in large part for the considerable religious publishing and broadcasting carried on in Spain, which in recent years has ranked fifth in the world in annual publication of religious titles. About 32 percent of the membership of male congregations and about 20 percent of all Spanish nuns are devoted full time to foreign missions, as ever primarily in Latin America. Finally, there are some 300 worker-monks in Spain who earn their livelihood as blue-collar employees and minister to workers.

Probably no region of Spain more graphically illustrates the recent changes in the role of religion and the structure of the clergy than Navarre, long the Catholic province par excellence. As recently as the 1960s, Navarre led the entire country in its percentage of religious attendance and ranked at or near the very top in the formation of new vocations. In that decade, however, the province began to undergo sudden large-scale industrialization, accompanied by a wave of immigration from other areas. This, along with the other alterations of the past generation, initiated a process of cultural change and secularization totally without parallel in Navarrese history. A survey conducted by Catholic sociologists in 1973 found at that point only 70 percent of Navarrese declaring themselves believers, a figure distinctly below the national average. Changes in cultural and political attitudes among the Navarrese clergy were just as pronounced as elsewhere. The rate of secularization was at least as high, and that of formation of new vocations seems to have dropped below the national norm.

Whereas there were 959 diocesan priests in Navarre in 1976, only 820 were registered by the beginning of 1983. During the seven intervening years, 143 died and 34 were secularized, the high point in secularizations for this period occurring in 1977 (none taking place in 1982). Only 6 new priests were ordained in the province and 22 others joined the ranks of the clergy there, leaving a seven-year deficit of 139. While the number of Catholic inhabitants per priest is still lower in Navarre than in Spain as a whole, the local clergy would appear to be increasingly handicapped in carrying out pastoral activities. By 1983, 2 out of every 3 Navarrese priests was over fifty, with an average age of fifty-seven. Twenty-one percent were over seventy, and only 10 in the entire region were thirty-eight or younger, indicating that the problem will rapidly become more severe. Many of active age were not engaged in regular pastoral activity. Seventy-seven were listed as engaged in foreign missionary work, and others held major offices in the Church in Rome or various parts of Spain. Two devoted their full time to careers in primarily Marxist parties, one of them—the well-known Víctor Manuel Arbeloa—as Socialist president of the Navarrese provincial parliament.[3]

Not the least of the Church's problems is financial, even though it still retains significant independent resources and has had the continued support of the new democratic regime. The last of the special Church-state accords of 1979 agreed that the present form of the state ecclesaistical subsidy would end in 1983, to be replaced by a voluntary tax

---

3. These Navarrese data come from the archbishopric of Pamplona, published in the *Diario de Navarra* (Pamplona), Feb. 4, 1983, and generously provided to me by Francisco J. de Lizarza Inda.

check-off system whereby only those desiring to contribute a portion of their taxes would have funds so allocated. The new arrangement is similar to that in West Germany and several other countries, but is accompanied by a safety-net provision that will protect the Church from any proportionate decline in support.

The evolution of the state subsidy in recent years has simply followed the general course of the Spanish national budget, parallel to the category of state employees (see table 9.3). By 1982 it amounted to an average of about 17,000 pesetas a month per priest, little more than two-thirds of the national monthly minimum wage. Ordinary ecclesiastical stipends in Spain have always been low, but in order to keep them at or slightly above the minimum wage, the Church in recent years has had to supplement the state subsidy from its independent income. Despite the major increases in individual income taxes under the democratic regime, no ordinary priest had been required to pay any tax, since after social security and insurance deductions, the basic salary has never reached the minimum of 350,000 pesetas per year at which tax liability begins.

According to P. Bernardo Herráez, financial director for the Conferencia Episcopal, the Church budget for 1983 amounted to approximately 11,300 million pesetas. The government ecclesiastical subsidy provided 10,377 million pesetas, as well as 45 million more for building maintenance. An additional 900 million came from separate diocesan income. The bulk of the Church's income—8,879 million—was transferred to the dioceses to pay the salaries of the clergy and meet other local expenses. The social security payments for the clergy amounted to 1,784 million more, and 490 million pesetas were spent for pastoral activity. Lesser amounts were allocated for organizational and patrimonial costs, and for the support of the ecclesiastical universities. A total of 76 million

TABLE 9.3
Evolution of the Spanish
State Ecclesiastical Subsidy, 1978–82
(in pesetas)

Year	Ecclesiastical Subsidy for Clergy, Seminaries, and Religious Expenses	Subsidy for Building Maintenance and Art Preservation
1978	6,178,740,000	35,900,000
1979	6,679,114,000	36,000,000
1980	7,589,555,000	36,000,000
1981	8,500,302,000	40,000,000
1982	9,265,330,000	45,400,000

Source: *Dirección General de Asuntos Religiosos, Ministerio de Justicia.*

TABLE 9.4
Evolution of the Monthly
Ecclesiastical Stipend in Navarre, 1973–82
(in pesetas)

Year	Monthly Stipend	Salario Minimo Interprofesional (Spanish Monthly Minimum Wage)
1973	7,500	5,657
1974	8,625	6,843
1975	10,000	8,516
1976	10,000	11,558
1977	15,400	15,208
1978	18,000	16,668
1979	21,000	21,048
1980	23,500	23,086
1981	25,000	25,975
1982 (January)	28,500	28,835
1982 (July)	30,500	28,835

Source: *Archbishopric of Pamplona, in the* Diario de Navarra *(Pamplona), Feb. 8, 1983.*

was spent on the bishops, each of whom—from the rank of cardinal down to auxiliary bishop—received a monthly salary of 61,600 pesetas (less than $500), plus two extraordinary payments of 50,400 pesetas each. The basic priest's stipend was 26,000 pesetas (about $200) a month.[4]

Despite the reality of a shrinking clergy—which will soon number only 16,000 active priests in a country of 40 million—and the danger of a reduced financial base, the primary problems of Spanish Catholicism in the 1980s are not entirely revealed by statistics alone. Whereas the Church remains quite conservative on a few key issues, the liberal reaction against the spiritual formalism and social conformity of earlier times continues to prevail among much of the clergy. Many apparently still agree with the predominant opinion of the late 1960s and 70s that religious language was irrelevant and inadequate for the contemporary public, and so a considerable number have replaced it with concepts and emphases parallel to the prevailing secular humanism of the non-Catholic intelligentsia. This creates the impression that a certain portion of the remaining clergy have limited conviction in their direct spiritual role. Many sermons address worthy issues such as community welfare, peace, brotherhood, and the common good but devote little time to primarily spiritual concerns and individual salvation. The comparison might have seemed ludicrous a generation ago, but by the 1980s the attitudes and pastoral approach of many of the Spanish Catholic clergy seemed not

4. Interview with P. Bernardo Herráez, *Cambio 16*, August 15, 1983.

dissimilar from those of liberal north Atlantic Protestantism. Of course, insofar as this was the case, Spanish Catholicism was scarcely unique within the Catholic Church as a whole.

One area in which the Church continues to play a somewhat controversial role is the Basque region. There the old Spanish national Catholicism of the Franco regime has been replaced by a proregionalist and Basque nationalist Catholicism under the new system of Basque autonomy installed in 1980. In view of the recent history and internal constitution of the clergy in the Basque provinces, this is not particularly surprising, and yet it has stood out as the sharpest exception to the Church's apolitical stance in Spain as a whole. Regional autonomy is generally blessed by the clergy in all districts, but even in Catalonia the local ecclesiastics have not been quite so partisan as in the Basque country. The clergy certainly played a major role in the later stages of the Basque resistance against Franco, and the Church leadership there was proud of the fact that the Basque population in general gave more evidence of continued religiosity than did that of almost any other major industrial zone of Europe. As Basque nationalism shifted sharply to the left in the 1960s and 70s, so did the political relations of the Basque clergy, who showed little reluctance to provide recognition, legitimation, and sometimes moderate support for even the new Marxist nationalist parties. It cannot be said that the Basque clergy have made a major effort to discourage terrorism by revolutionary nationalists against the new Spanish democratic regime. Marxist terrorists have often been given large public religious funerals, even though such ceremonies can, by the laws of the Church, be denied those guilty of killing their neighbors. A number of priests function as activists of the proterrorist political party Herri Batasuna. By the early 1980s appointments and promotions within the dioceses and monasteries of the Basque provinces were increasingly determined by the nationalist issue.

Possibly at the behest of the Basque Nationalist Party, a remarkable, and many said scandalous, collective pastoral was released by the three Basque bishops in April 1981. It took a strong stand in favor of Basque nationalism and autonomy, and for even greater freedom from central government. New legislation under discussion in Madrid that would coordinate and slightly reduce the scope of autonomy was denounced as unethical. Though the bishops condemned ETA, the principal terrorist organization, their position was unconvincing, and in fact suggested that ETA was to be compared with the reformed Spanish police. This touched off a public uproar and public protests from the major Spanish political parties.

In general, however, the tone of the Church became somewhat more

conservative during the early 1980s. The small right-wing minority protested the failure to support Christian democratic groups or to adopt a
more active stand in matters of religious concern. Even some liberal
Catholics began to wonder why the formerly puritan Church was not
more forthright in its commentary on the new culture of hedonism and
self-indulgence. It did take a strong position on certain issues, vigorously
opposing the legalization of divorce and abortion. These became rallying
points of Catholic opposition, though a moderate divorce procedure was
instituted in Spain in 1981. Another problem was the simple physical
security of church and other religious buildings, for the theft of artwork
had reached serious proportions during the past decade.

The pontificate of John Paul II has encouraged a more conservative
orientation. His remarks at the Conference of Latin American Bishops in
January 1979 repudiated what is called "liberation theology," which he
rejected for having little to do with either liberation or theology. John
Paul endeavored to bring to an end such phenomena as the election of a
parish priest as mayor of a Barcelona suburb on the Communist ticket. In
1980 Msgr. Dadaglio, the nuncio for the *apertura* since 1968, was replaced by the more conservative Msgr. Innocenti, who was to provide
more traditional guidance. John Paul showed himself particularly favorable to Opus Dei, whose work in central Europe had impressed him, and
late in 1982 raised the institute to the status of the first "personal prelature" in Roman Catholicism. The Pope's pastoral visit to Spain, spanning
ten days at the beginning of November 1982, drew enormous attention
and brought together by far the largest series of public crowds ever
assembled in Spanish history.

The Tarancón era in the leadership of Spanish Catholicism came to a
close in 1981. By that point the Cardinal was seventy-five years of age and
bound by a regulation that no prelate could serve more than three terms
as president of the Episcopal Conference. Overtly conservative interests
in the hierarchy were, however, thwarted once more, as Tarancón was
succeeded by the much younger and also relatively liberal Archbishop
Gabino Díaz Merchán of Oviedo. After the election of a new Socialist
government for Spain late in 1982, it became increasingly difficult for the
Church leadership to maintain fully the policies of neutrality and apolitic-
ism followed under Tarancón. New proposals to legalize abortion and
expand the state educational budget more rapidly than proportionate
subsidies for private education aroused more Church opposition than any
government measures since the closing years of the Franco regime.

Despite the enormous alterations of the past generation, much of the
external pattern of Catholic culture was nonetheless still recognizable
after 1980, even though reserved for special occasions. The innumerable

local religious festivals continued to be observed, together with the *romerías* (pilgrimages) and special activities that had always bulked so large in Spanish Catholic life. In the common effort to rediscover tradition that has occurred in various late-industrial societies, some of the traditional festivals that had died out were being revived. Whereas the extraordinary "Misteri d'Elx," Europe's last surviving late medieval mystery play, had never ceased to be performed each August save during the Civil War, local Easter Passion plays were being revived in several districts where they had been discontinued. Local devotions and shrines continued to survive and flourish in many areas, and there were still individual believers who displayed great intensity of devotion, such as Justo Gallego Martínez, the remarkable fifty-six-year-old farmer who has been engaged for years in the single-handed construction of a small cathedral in a country town near Madrid.

A survey of attitudes in ten European countries conducted by the European Value Systems Study Group in 1981 found that more people believed in the existence of God, the devil, and hell in Spain than in any other European land. Moreover—along with the French, Germans, and Italians—they placed the Church at the top of the list of institutions in which they had the most confidence.

CONCLUSION

THE DRAMATIC transformation of Spanish Catholicism that occurred in the 1960s and 70s was a product of the broadest social and cultural change. Though much of it stemmed from the influence of the worldwide Roman Catholic Church, the transformation was ultimately an internal process from the inside out, rather than a response to the kind of external assault launched by anticlericals in preceding generations. After largely withstanding two centuries of attack from without, the Church reformed itself drastically from within. The secularization of Spanish life that encouraged (and was further stimulated by) this great mutation rivaled the new industrialization of the socioeconomic structure as the most striking change in Spanish life during the second half of the twentieth century. The Franco regime, which had begun by effecting the most remarkable traditionalist restoration witnessed in the western world during the twentieth century, ultimately constituted the very final chapter in the millennium-long history of the traditional Spanish ideology.

The results of the Catholic transformation were paradoxical in the extreme. One of the two main institutional supports of the Franco regime became its most serious antagonist. One of the most conservative national churches in Europe underwent the broadest wave of liberalization, if only because it had further to go to liberalize. It implemented some of the new orientations in a bolder fashion than did certain other national Churches, convening the first joint assembly of priests and prelates in contemporary Church history in 1971. Yet it was not at first able to implement fully Vatican II's redefinition of the Church as the "people of God," with its emphasis on a broader and more autonomous role for the laity, because a radicalized laity was adopting ever more extreme positions, leading to a virtual breakdown of some of the Catholic Action activists groups.

It is not at all clear that the liberalization of the Church and its emanicipation from the state have produced the spiritual renewal in Spain that many proponents have claimed, or that this is not merely the ecclesiastical dimension of the general secularization of society which has

228

eroded traditional religion. Indeed, certain reformers in the Church have sometimes seemed as much the agents as the products or victims of secularization, to the extent that one North American anthropologist was able to carry out a study entitled "The Priest as Agent of Secularization in Rural Spain."[1]

At the same time, it is worth pointing out that the concept of secularization is itself sometimes used too broadly. As a turning away from traditional values and expressions of religion, secularization is an obvious fact, but the conclusion that this has led to development of a world view that is exclusively practical, skeptical, and given to objective material calculation is highly exaggerated. The contemporary secular world abounds in objects of reverence and worship that are personal, social, economic, or ideological in character. Desacralization of the cultural order has opened the way for new manias and fixations devoted to immanent objects and goals. Thus the "liberation theology" of the radical clergy is sometimes merely the obverse of the old socially and culturally embedded religion: instead of the sacralization of an existing Catholic society it has attempted to sacralize materialist, collectivist movements. Manuel Azaña, the twentieth century's most illustrious foe of Spanish Catholicism, saw things more clearly:

> The most foolish use that can be made of the Gospel is to adduce
> it as the text for political arguments, and the most monstrous de-
> formation of the figure of Jesus is to present him as a democratic
> propagandist or as a reader of Michelet or Castelar, or, who
> knows, as a precursor of the agrarian reform. No. The Christian
> experience, honorable deputies, is an awesome [terrible] thing, and
> can only be treated seriously.[2]

The conclusion that recent changes in Spanish Catholicism have necessarily freed "true religion" from culture or politics seems naïve in the extreme. Though some aspects of these alterations may be desirable in themselves, the transformation has stemmed from changes in the culture of the postwar era, whose values have been adopted second hand by religion. There is considerable evidence that a permissive, liberal, and indulgent society has succeeded in refashioning a permissive, liberal, and indulgent Church. Despite the talk about "prophetic religion," a more accurate description of transformed Catholicism might be "mimetic reli-

---

1. Stanley Brandes, "The Priest as Agent of Secularization in Rural Spain," in *Economic Transformation and Steady-State Values: Essays in the Ethnography of Spain*, ed. J. B. Aceves et al. (Flushing, N.Y., 1976).

2. Quoted in Pedro R. Santidrián, *España ha dejado de ser católica* (Madrid, 1978), 48.

gion." There has been little that is either original or prophetic about recent Spanish Catholicism. Much traditional baggage and some traditional values have been jettisoned, but whether a firm spiritual foundation has been retained, or a new one found, is less certain.

Bibliography
Index

Bibliography

CHAPTER 1

THE BIBLIOGRAPHY on Spanish Catholicism in virtually all periods is enormous. A general history of sorts was first attempted by Enrique Flórez and several collaborators in the massive *España sagrada*, 56 vols. (1747–1879), a vast compendium of all manner of information, legends, and uncritical data but a unique work for its time. More scholarly was the nineteenth-century study by Vicente de la Fuente, *Historia eclesiástica de España*, 2d ed., 6 vols. (Madrid, 1873–75). The most critical and up-to-date scholarly compendium consists of the six volumes edited by Ricardo García Villoslada, S.J., *Historia de la Iglesia en España* (Madrid, 1979–82).

Periodical literature is yet more vast. Two of the important scholarly journals are *Hispania Sacra* (Madrid, 1948–) and the *Revista Española de Derecho Canónico* (Madrid, 1946–). The *Diccionario de historia eclesiástica de España*, 4 vols. (Madrid, 1972–75) is also useful. On Portugal, see Fortunato de Almeida, *História da Igreja em Portugal*, 4 vols. (Coimbra, 1910).

There are several one-volume general accounts by foreign authors. Of these, Johannes Krinke's *Das christliche Spanien* (Hamburg, 1967) is superior to the older Jean Descola, *Histoire de l'Espagne chrétienne* (Paris, 1951), or Dom H. Leclerq, *L'Espagne chrétienne* (Paris, 1906).

There are several specialized Church histories dealing with ancient and medieval times, beginning with the Benedictine Pius Gams's scholarly *Die Kirchengeschichte von Spanien*, 3 vols. (Regensburg, 1880–82; Graz, 1956). Zacarías García Villada, S.I., *Historia eclesiástica de España*, 5 vols. (Madrid, 1929–36), stops at the eleventh century. Kurt Schäferdiek, *Die Kirche in den Reichen der Westgoten und Suewen bis zur Errichtung der westgotischen Katholischen Staatskirche* (Berlin, 1967), treats the early Visigothic period, but more central is the collection of articles by José Orlandis, *La Iglesia en la España visigótica y medieval* (Pamplona, 1976). A. K. Ziegler, *Church and State in Visigothic Spain*, (Washington, D.C., 1930), is an older study of an important topic. The best works on the two most famous personalities of early Hispanic Christianity are Jacques Fontaine, *Isidore de Seville et la culture classique dans l'Espagne wisigothique*, 2 vols. (Paris, 1959); *Isidor von Sevilla: Sein Laben, sein Werk und seine Zeit* (Cologne, 1962); and Henry Chadwick, *Priscillian of Avila* (Oxford, 1976).

Among the best recent studies on the early period are Justo Fernández Alonso, *La cura pastoral en la España romanovisigoda* (Rome, 1955); G. Martínez Díez, S. I., *El patrimonio eclesiástico en la España visigoda* (Comillas, 1959); José Vives, *Concilios visigóticos e hispano-romanos* (Barcelona-Madrid, 1963); Bartolomé Jiménez Duque, *La espiritualidad romano-visigoda y mozá-*

rabe (Madrid, 1977); Enric Llobregat, *La primitiva cristiandat valenciana* (Valencia, 1977); and J. N. Hillgarth, "Popular Religion in Visigothic Spain," in *Visigothic Spain: New Approaches*, ed. E. James (Oxford, 1980).

The two leading interpretations of medieval Hispanic culture and society are Américo Castro's *The Spaniards* (Berkeley, 1971), and Claudio Sánchez Albornoz's *España: Un enigma histórico*, 2 vols. (Buenos Aires, 1956). See also the latter's brief *El drama de la formación de España y los españoles* (Barcelona, 1977); *Américo Castro and the Meaning of Spanish Civilization* (Berkeley, 1977), ed. J. Rubia Barcia; and the critique by Eugenio Asensio, *La España imaginada de Américo Castro* (Barcelona, 1976). Thomas F. Glick, *Islamic and Christian Spain in the Early Middle Ages* (Princeton, 1979), provides an invaluable comparative ethnocultural study from a sophisticated social science perspective. Vicente Cantarino, *Entre monjes y musulmanes: El conflicto que fue España* (Madrid, 1978), is also useful.

The Mozarabs have been little studied. See Isidro de las Cagigas, *Los mozárabes*, 2 vols. (Madrid, 1947–48), and E.P. Colbert, *The Martyrs of Córdoba (850–859)* (Washington, D.C., 1962). F. J. Simonet, *Historia de los mozárabes de España* (Madrid, 1903; Amsterdam, 1967), and C. R. Haines, *Christianity and Islam in Spain 756–1031* (London, 1889), are older works of limited use. Richard Bulliet, *Conversion to Islam in the Medieval Period* (Cambridge, Mass., 1979), presents a stimulating revisionist analysis of the rhythm of conversion.

Spanish monasticism is the subject of a most extensive historiography. The best general works are Antonio Linage Conde, *El monacato en España e Hispanoamérica* (Salamanca, 1977), and Fr. Justo Pérez de Urbel, *Los monjes españoles en la Edad Media*, 2 vols. (Madrid, 1933). Maur Cocheril, *Études sur le monachisme en Espagne et au Portugal* (Paris, 1966), which deals especially with the Cistercians, is one of the best individual studies. Linage Conde's *Los orígenes del monacato benedictino en la Península Ibérica*, 3 vols. (León, 1973), is also superior. On the Cluniac reform, see Peter Segl, *Königtum und Klosterreform in Spanien* (Kallmünz, 1974).

Important work has been done during the past decade on the economic functions of monastic and other ecclesiastical domains. Among the best individual studies are J. A. García de Cortázar, *El dominio del monasterio de San Millán de la Cogolla (Siglos X a XIII)* (Salamanca, 1969); Salustiano Moreta Velayos, *El monasterio de San Pedro de Cardeña (902–1338)* (Salamanca, 1971); Eufemià Fort i Cogul, *El senyoriu de Santes Creus* (Barcelona, 1972); J. J. García González, *Vida económica de los monasterios benedictinos en el siglo XIV* (Valladolid, 1972); Jaime Santacana Tort, *El monasterio de Poblet (1151–1181) (Barcelona, 1974); Ermelinda Portela Silva, La región del obispado de Tuy en los siglos XII a XV* (Santiago de Compostela, 1976); V. A. Alvarez Palenzuela, *Monasterios cistercienses en Castilla (Siglos XII–XIII)* (Valladolid, 1978); and M. E. García García, *San Juan Bautista de Coria* (Oviedo, 1980).

F. J. Fernández Conde, *La Iglesia de Asturias en la Alta Edad Media* (Oviedo, 1972), provides a sound treatment of the first Spanish territorial church. The classic study of Church-state relations in the eastern kingdoms in Johannes

Vincke, *Staat und Kirche in Katalonien und Aragon während des Mittlelalters*, 2 vols. (Münster, 1931). Two recent key works on the Church in León are R. A. Fletcher, *The Episcopate in the Kingdom of León in the Twelfth Century* (Oxford, 1978), and Ludwig Vones, *Die 'Historia Compostellana' und die Kirchenpolittik des nordwestspanischen Raumes, 1070–1130* (Cologne, 1980), a careful and massively detailed study of the "Historia" and of Church politics in the age of Diego Gelmírez. For relations with the papacy, see Demetrio Mansilla Reoyo, *Iglesia castellano-leonesa y Curia romana en los tiempos del Rey San Fernando* (Madrid, 1945), and especially Peter Linehan, *The Spanish Church and the Papacy in the Thirteenth Century* (Cambridge, 1971). J. F. Rivera Recio, *La Iglesia de Toledo en el siglo XII* (Toledo, 1976), treats the new Church establishment in New Castile.

Derek W. Lomax, *The Reconquest of Spain* (London, 1978), is excellent and the only overall account of that decisive theme. On the topic of the crusade in a formal sense, see José Goñi Gaztambide, *Historia de la Bula de Cruzada en España* (Vitoria, 1958). The best case studies of Christian organization of conquered Muslims and their territory is the series on Valencia by Robert I. Burns, S.J.: *The Crusader Kingdom of Valencia*, 2 vols. (Cambridge, 1967): *Islam under the Crusaders* (Princeton, 1973); *Medieval Colonialism* (Princeton, 1975); and *Moors and Crusaders in Mediterranean Spain* (London, 1978).

There is an extensive literature on the most internationalized aspect of medieval Hispanic religiosity, the pilgrimages to Santiago de Compostela. The most extensive study is L. Vázquez de Parga, J. M. Lacarra, and J. Uría Ríu, *Las peregrinaciones a Santiago de Compostela*, 2 vols. (Madrid, 1948). Américo Castro presented his interpretation in *Santiago de España* (Buenos Aires, 1958).

Heresy in medieval Hispania was concentrated above all in greater Catalonia. See Jordi Ventura, *Els heretges catalans* (Barcelona, 1963), and Gabriel Alomar Esteve, *Cátaros y occitanos en el Reino de Mallorca* (Palma de Mallorca, 1978).

CHAPTER 2

GENERAL TREATMENT of the late medieval and early modern periods is provided in volumes 3 through 5 of the *Historia de la Iglesia en España*. Among general histories of Spain, J. N. Hillgarth's *The Spanish Kingdoms 1250–1516* (Oxford, 1976–78) is noteworthy for its presentation of religious affairs. Two fundamental works on state policy in Church affairs are Luis Suárez Fernández, *Castilla, el cisma y la crisis conciliar* (Madrid, 1960), and W. E. Shiels, *King and Church: The Rise and Fall of the Patronato Real* (Chicago, 1961).

Studies of the great Llull are numerous. In English, see E. Allison Peers, *Fool of Love: The Life of Ramon Lull* (London, 1946), and J. N. Hillgarth, *Ramon Lull and Lullism in Fourteenth-Century France* (Oxford, 1971). Among the best studies are Miquel Batllori, *Ramon Llull en el mon del seu temps* (Barcelona, 1960); Miguel Cruz Hernández, *El pensamiento de Ramon Llull* (Madrid, 1977); and E. W. Platzek, *Raimund Lull: Sein Leben, seine Werke*, 2 vols. (Düsseldorf, 1962–64).

236   *Bibliography*

There is also a considerable literature on late medieval reformism. The *Introducción a los orígenes de la Observancia en España: Las reformas de los siglos XIV y XV* (Madrid, 1957) is the product of a symposium. F. J. Fernández Conde, *Gutierre de Toledo, obispo de Oviedo (1377–1389)* (Oviedo, 1978), treats the career of a fourteenth-century reformer. Key works on the reforms of the Catholic Monarchs are Tarsicio de Azcona, *Elección y reforma del episcopado español en tiempo de los Reyes Católicos* (Madrid, 1960); José García Oro, *Cisneros y la reforma del clero español en tiempo de los Reyes Católicos* (Madrid, 1971); and G. M. Colombás, *Un reformador benedictino en tiempo de los Reyes Católicos: García Jiménez de Cisneros* (Montserrat, 1955). V. Beltrán de Heredia, *Historia de la reforma de la Provincia de España, 1450–1550* (Rome, 1939), deals with the Dominicans.

José Sánchez Herrero has presented new material on Church organization and religious reform in his *Concilios provinciales y sínodos toledanos de los siglos XIV y XV* (La Laguna, 1976) and *Las diócesis del Reino de León: Siglos XIV y XV* (León, 1978). José de Sigüenza, *Historia de la Orden de San Jerónimo*, 2 vols. (Madrid, 1907–9), remains the basic study of the most important of the new fifteenth-century orders. On the education of the clergy, see F. Martín Hernández, *La formación clerical en los colegios universitarios españoles (1371–1563)* (Vitoria, 1961), and for case studies of the social and economic dimension of monastic life in the eastern kingdoms, Ma. D. Cabanes Pecourt, *Los monasterios valencianos: Su economía en el siglo XV*, 2 vols. (Valencia, 1974), and Rosa Ma. Blasco Martínez, *Sociología de una comunidad religiosa 1219–1516* (Zaragoza, 1974).

The background of Spain's Jewish problem is presented in Luis Suárez Fernández, *Judíos españoles en la Edad Media* (Madrid, 1980), and Emilio Mitre, *Judaísmo y cristianismo: Raíces de un gran conflicto histórico* (Madrid, 1980). Antonio Domínguez Ortiz, *La clase social de los conversos de Castilla en la Edad Moderna* (Madrid, 1955), and B. Netanyahu, *The Marranos of Spain from the late XIVth to the early XVth Century* (New York, 1973), treat the situation of the Conversos. The best introduction to the Moriscos is the *Historia de los moriscos* (Madrid, 1978) by A. Domínguez Ortiz and B. Vincent. On their religious life, see Pedro Longás Bartibás, *Vida religiosa de los moriscos* (Madrid, 1915); M. J. Hagerty, ed., *Los "libros plúmbeos" del Sacromonte* (Madrid, 1980); and especially Louis Cardaillac, *Moriscos y cristianos: Un enfrentamiento polémico (1492–1640)* (Mexico City, 1979). D. Cabanelas Rodríguez, *Juan de Segovia y el problema islámico* (Madrid, 1952), studies a proponent of cultural comprehension and evangelism.

The earliest history of the Spanish Inquisition was written in 1598, but the first critical and scholarly study was Juan Antonio Llorente's *Histoire critique de l'Inquisition d'Espagne*, 4 vols. (Paris, 1817–18), which did not appear in Spanish until five years later and is now available in an English translation, *A Critical History of the Inquisition of Spain* (Williamstown, Mass., 1967). The most complete single scholarly account is, however, Henry C. Lea's classic *A History of the Inquisition of Spain*, 4 vols. (New York, 1906–7). The main work on the minuscule Spanish Protestantism and the Inquisition is still Ernst Schäfer, *Beiträge zur*

Geschichte des spanischen Protestantismus und der Inquisition im 16ten Jahrhundert, 3 vols (Gütersloh, 1902). The best Spanish Catholic studies are Bernardino Llorca's *La Inquisición en España* (Barcelona, 1946) and *La Inquisición española y los alumbrados* (Barcelona, 1936), and Manuel de la Pinta Llorente's *La Inquisición española* (Madrid, 1948) and *La Inquisición española y los problemas de la cultura y de la intolerancia* (Madrid, 1958).

Probably the most widely read single work is now Henry Kamen's *A History of the Spanish Inquisition* (London, 1965), an excellent, if occasionally tendentious, one-volume synthesis. Since its publication there has been a major flowering of Inquisition research, resulting in more scholarly publication during the past generation than in the entire preceding period since the demise of the Holy Office. The most original new volume of studies, presenting major quantitative data, is *L'Inquisition espagnole XVe–XIXe siècles* (Paris, 1979), edited by Bartolomé Bennassar. The results of a major international conference are presented in *La Inquisición española: Nueva visión, nuevos horizontes* (Madrid, 1980), edited by J. Pérez Villanueva. The best of the new regional studies are Ricardo García Cárcel's *Orígenes de la Inquisición en España: El Tribunal de Valencia, 1478–1530* (Barcelona, 1976) and *Herejía y sociedad en el siglo XVI: La Inquisición en Valencia, 1530–1609* (Barcelona, 1980); J. M. García Fuentes, *La Inquisición en Granada en el siglo XVI* (Granada, 1981); and Jaime Contreras, *El Santo Ofico de la Inquisición en Galicia 1560–1700* (Madrid, 1982). For Catalonia, see Eufemià Fort i Cogul, *Catalunya i la Inquisició* (Barcelona, 1973). Miguel Jiménez Monteserín has published a set of basic documents as *Introducción a la Inquisición española* (Madrid, 1980).

Case studies and monographs abound. Among the more interesting and useful are J. L. González Novalín, *El Inquisidor General Fernando de Valdés (1483–1568)* (Oviedo, 1968); Nicolás López Martínez, *Los judaizantes castellanos y la Inquisición en tiempo de Isabel la Católica* (Burgos, 1954), informative if somewhat biased; Julio Caro Baroja, *El Señor Inquisidor y otras vidas por oficio* (Madrid, 1968), a study of the inquisitors; John E. Longhurst, *Erasmus and the Spanish Inquisition: The Case of Juan de Valdés* (Albuquerque, 1950) and *Luther and the Spanish Inquisition: The Case of Diego de Uceda* (Albuquerque, 1953); and Maurice Boyd, *Cardinal Quiroga, Inquisitor General of Spain* (Dubuque, 1954). For the impact on science and literature, see Santiago Muñoz Calvo, *Inquisición y ciencia en la España moderna* (Madrid, 1977), and Antonio Márquez, *Literatura e Inquisición en España (1478–1834)* (Madrid, 1980). Gustav Henningsen, *The Witches' Advocate: Basque Witchcraft and the Spanish Inquisition (1609–1614)* (Reno, 1980), deals with the development of a critical and realistic attitude toward witchcraft. Pinta Llorente has investigated *Las cárceles inquisitoriales españolas* (Madrid, 1949); while Henry C. Lea also dealt with *The Inquisition in the Spanish Dependencies* (New York, 1908). For Portuguese comparisons, see Alexandre Herculano de Carvalho, *History of the Origins and Establishment of the Portuguese Inquisition* (Stanford, 1926), and A. J. Saraiva, *A Inquisiçao portuguesa*, rev. ed. (Lisbon, 1963).

In the study of religious dissidence, Marcelino Menéndez Pelayo's *Historia de los heterodoxos españoles*, 8 vols. (Santander, 1946–48), remains a classic, if flawed, work. Marcel Bataillon, *Erasmo y España*, 2 vols. (Mexico City, 1950), is a standard work; but see also José Luis Abellán, *El erasmismo español* (Madrid, 1976), and J. C. Nieto, *Juan de Valdés and the Origins of the Spanish and Italian Reformation* (Geneva, 1970). The chief study of one of the few noteworthy heterodox groups is Antonio Márquez, *Los alumbrados: Orígenes y filosofía (1525–1559)*, rev. ed., (Madrid, 1980). The main collection of works of Spanish Protestants is *Reformistas antiguos españoles*, ed. L. Usoz y Río, 24 vols. (1847–80; reprint, Madrid, 1980).

Walter Starkie, *La España de Cisneros* (Barcelona, 1943), presents a somewhat idealized view of the outstanding figure in the Spanish Church during the early sixteenth century, while J. I. Tellechea Idígoras, *El arzobispo Carranza y su tiempo* (Madrid, 1968) treats the most tragic hierarch of the era of Felipe II. One of the few helpful works on Catalan Catholicism during this period is J. Bada, *Situació religiosa de Barcelona en el segle XVI* (Barcelona, 1970). Albert A. Sicroff, *Les controverses des statuts de "pureté de sang" en Espagne du XVe au XVIIe siècle* (Paris, 1960), is the standard treatment of the "purity of blood" mania.

Such major themes as the Council of Trent and Counter-Reformation policies in general are poorly developed in Spanish historiography. The best and most recent study is J. M. Rovira Belloso, *Trento: Una interpretación histórica* (Barcelona, 1979). Constantino Gutiérrez, S.J., ed., *Trento: Un concilio para la unión (1550–1552)*, 3 vols. (Madrid, 1981), deals with only one aspect, while his earlier *Españoles en Trento* (Valladolid, 1951) presents a set of biographies. On Loyola, see Paul Dudon, *St. Ignatius of Loyola* (Milwaukee, 1949).

Charles R. Boxer's sardonic *The Church Militant and Iberian Expansion 1440–1770* (Baltimore, 1978) provides an overview of Spanish Catholicism's greatest enterprise. For the orthodox perspective, see Constantino Bayle, *España en Indias* (Vitoria, 1934), and Vicente Sierra, *El sentido misional de la conquista de América* (Madrid, 1944). The classic account of the Catholicization of New Spain is Robert Ricard, *La "Conquête spirituelle" du Mexique* (Paris, 1933). On Church organization and the dispatching of missionaries, see Antonio Garrido Aranda, *Organización de la Iglesia en el Reino de Granada y su proyección en Indias* (Seville, 1979), and Pedro Borges Morán, *El envío de misioneros a América durante la época española* (Salamanca, 1977). Basic works on the "struggle for justice" controversy are Lewis Hanke, *The Spanish Struggle for Justice in the Conquest of America* (Philadelphia, 1949); Manuel Giménez Fernández, *Bartolomé de las Casas*, 2 vols. (Seville, 1953–60); and Venancio Diego Carro, O.P., *La teología y los teólogos-juristas españoles ante la conquista de América*, 2 vols. (Madrid, 1944).

Evaluations of Spanish religious sensibility by two of the country's outstanding scholars are presented in Julio Caro Baroja, *Las formas complejas de la vida religiosa* (Madrid, 1978), and Salvador de Madariaga's idiosyncratic *Dios y los españoles* (Barcelona, 1975). Hilary D. Smith, *Preaching in the Spanish Golden Age* (Oxford, 1978), presents the best approach to sermons. William A. Christian, Jr., has recently published two highly original studies in religious anthropology: *Apparitions in Late Medieval and Renaissance Spain* (Princeton, 1981) and

Local Religion in Sixteenth-Century Spain (Princeton, 1981). Other useful works on diverse aspects include Francis G. Very, *The Spanish Corpus Christi Procession* (Valencia, 1962); J. R. Guerrero, *Catecismos españoles del siglo XVI* (Madrid, 1969); the composite *Corrientes espirituales en la España del siglo XVI* (Barcelona, 1963); J. A. Sánchez Pérez, *El culto mariano en España* (Madrid, 1943); and Javier Ibáñez and Fernando Mendoza, *María en la liturgia hispana* (Pamplona, 1975).

Otis H. Green, *Spain and the Western Tradition*, 4 vols. (Madison, 1964–68), is a major work on classical Spanish literature that reveals much of its religious dimension. José Antonio Maravall, *La cultura del barroco* (Barcelona, 1975), provides a broad cultural interpretation of the period. For religious drama, see Ricardo Arias, *Spanish Sacramental Plays* (Boston, 1980), and Henry W. Sullivan, *Tirso de Molino and the Drama of the Counter-Reformation* (Amsterdam, 1981). See also F. Márquez Villanueva, *Espiritualidad y literatura en el siglo XVI* (Madrid, 1968), and Raphael L. Oechslin, *Louis of Granada* (St. Louis, 1962), on one of the most original religious writers of the period.

The most recent history of Spanish thought, providing full attention to theology, is José Luis Abellán, *Historia crítica del pensamiento español*, 3 vols. (Madrid, 1979–). Melquiades Andrés Martín, *La teología española en el siglo XVI* (Madrid, 1976), is a leading work. Studies of major theologians include Venancio Diego Carro, *Domingo de Soto y su doctrina jurídica* (Madrid, 1943) and *El maestro Fr. Pedro de Soto y las controversias político-teológicas en el siglo XVI* (Salamanca, 1931); V. Beltrán de Heredia, *Domingo de Soto* (Madrid, 1961) and *Francisco de Vitoria* (Madrid, 1939); Antonio Molina Meliá, *Iglesia y Estado en el Siglo de Oro español: El pensamiento de Francisco Suárez* (Valencia, 1977); Friedrich Stegmüller, *Francisco de Vitoria y la doctrina de la gracia en la escuela salmantina* (Barcelona, 1934); and Gerard Smith, *Freedom in Molina* (Chicago, 1966). James B. Scott, *The Spanish Origin of International Law* (Washington, D.C., 1933), is a basic introductory work, and Cándido Pozo, *La teoría del progreso dogmático en los teólogos de la escuela de Salamanca, 1526–1644* (Madrid, 1959), is one of the more interesting studies in dogma. For the initial development of seminaries, see the first volume of Francisco Martín Hernández, *Los seminarios españoles* (Salamanca, 1964).

Studies of the Spanish mystics comprise a large library. Some of the more notable are J. M. Cruz Moliner, *Historia de la literatura mística en España* (Burgos, 1961); E. A. Peers, *Studies of Spanish Mystics*, 3 vols. (London, 1927); Pedro Sainz Rodríguez, *La espiritualidad española* (Madrid, 1961); Ernst Schering, *Mystik und Tat* (Munich, 1959); and Melquiades Andrés Martín, *Los recogidos: nueva visión de la mística española (1500–1700)* (Madrid, 1975). Some of the best works on Santa Teresa are those by Marcelle Auclair (New York, 1953), Robert Ricard (Paris, 1968), and Stephen Clissold (London, 1979); and on San Juan de la Cruz, those by F. Bede Frost (London, 1937), E. A. Peers (London, 1947), Léon Cristiani (Garden City, N.Y., 1962), and Gerald Brenan (Cambridge, 1973).

The most important work on seventeenth-century Spanish Catholicism is the first volume of Antonio Domínguez Ortiz's *La sociedad española en el siglo XVII*, entitled "El estamento eclesiástico" (Madrid, 1964). José Deleito y Piñuela, *La vida religiosa española bajo el cuarto Felipe* (Madrid, 1952), is an interesting descriptive account. Two case studies of state religious policy are Quintín Aldea, *Iglesia y Estado en la España del siglo XVII* (Comillas, 1961), and Rafael Rodríguez-Moñino Soriano, *Razón de estado y dogmatismo religioso en la España del siglo XVII* (Barcelona, 1976). J. R. Armogathe, *Le quiétisme* (Paris, 1973), treats the only heterodox theological current of the period.

The Enlightenment and Catholic reform in Spain has drawn attention from quite a number of French scholars. For many years the standard work was G. Desdevises du Dézert, *L'Espagne de L'ancien régime*, 3 vols. (Paris, 1897–1904), though somewhat inaccurate in detail. The principal study of the Spanish Enlightenment is Jean Sarrailh, *La España ilustrada de la segunda mitad del siglo XVIII* (Mexico City, 1957), though the best overall study of the reform era is still Richard Herr's *The Eighteenth-Century Revolution in Spain* (Princeton, 1958). For social change, Antonio Domínguez Ortiz, *La sociedad española en el siglo XVIII* (Madrid, 1956), remains fundamental.

The best summary of changes within the Church will be found in *Church and Society in Catholic Europe of the Eighteenth Century* (Cambridge, 1979), ed. W. J. Callahan and D. Higg. The basic works on Spanish Jansenism are Emile Appolis, *Les jansénistes espagnols* (Bordeaux, 1966); Maria Giovanna Tomsich, *El jansenismo en España* (Madrid, 1972); and Joël Saugnieux, *Le jansénisme espagnol du XVIIIe siècle* (Oviedo, 1975) and *Les jansénistes et le renouveau de la prédication dans l'Espagne de la seconde moitié du XVIIIe siècle* (Lyons, 1976). Alfredo Martínez Albiach has written three books on aspects of religiosity during the eighteenth and early nineteenth centuries. The principal is *Religiosidad hispana y sociedad borbónica* (Burgos, 1969), followed by *Etica socio-religiosa de la España del siglo XVIII* (Burgos, 1970?) and *Talante del catolicismo español* (Burgos, 1977). J. A. Ferrer Benimeli, *Masonería, Iglesia e Ilustración*, 4 vols. (Madrid, 1977), is the chief work on the Church and Masonry during this period. See also W. J. Callahan, *La Santa y Real Hermandad del Refugio y Piedad de Madrid, 1618–1832* (Madrid, 1980); Francisco Puy, *El pensamiento tradicional en la España del siglo XVIII (1700–1760)* (Madrid, 1966); Marcelin Defourneaux, *L'Inquisition espagnole et les livres français au XVIIIe siècle* (Paris, 1963); Francisco Martín Hernández, *Los seminarios españoles en la época de la Ilustración* (Madrid, 1973); Carlos Eguía Ruiz, *Los jesuitas y el Motín de Esquilache* (Madrid, 1947); Antonio Mestre, *Ilustración y reforma de la Iglesia: Pensamiento político-religioso de don Gregorio Mayans y Siscar (1699–1781)* (Valencia, 1968); Francesc Tort Mitjans, *El obispo de Barcelona Josep Climent i Avinent (1706–1781)* (Barcelona, 1978); and Rafael Olaechea, S. J., *Las relaciones hispano-romanas en la segunda mitad del siglo XVIII*, 2 vols. (Zaragoza, 1965).

CHAPTER 3

CHURCH AFFAIRS during the last years of the eighteenth century are treated in Francisco Martí Gilabert, *La Iglesia en España durante la revolución francesa*

(Pamplona, 1971). Two older works on the role of the clergy in the War of Independence are E. Paradas, *Las comunidades religiosas en la guerra de la Independencia* (Seville, 1908), and G. Jiménez Campaña, *Acción del clérigo español en la guerra por nuestra independencia* (Madrid, 1908), prepared for the centenary of the revolt against Napoleon, while E. Carro Celada, *Curas guerrilleros en España* (Madrid, 1971), is more recent.

Manuel Revuelta González, *Política religiosa de los liberales en el siglo XIX* (Madrid, 1973), deals primarily with the *trienio* 1820–23. There are four regional studies of scholarly merit for those years: Pío de Montoya, *La intervención del clero vasco en las contiendas civiles (1820–23)* (San Sebastián, 1971; Gaspar Feliu i Montfort, *La clerecia catalana durant el trienni liberal* (Barcelona, 1972); Joan Brines Blasco, *La desamortización eclesiástica en el País Valenciano 1820–1823* (Valencia, 1978); and the booklet by Francisco Candel Crespo, *Clero liberal y absolutista en la Murcia de Fernando VII* (Madrid, 1978). Pedro Antonio Perlado, *Los obispos españoles ante la amnistía de 1817* (Pamplona, 1971), studies the attitudes and formation of the episcopacy.

On the origins of "ultra" philosophy, see Javier Herrero, *Orígenes del pensamiento reaccionario español* (Madrid, 1973). The final struggles over the Inquisition are narrated in José Pérez Vilariño, *Inquisición y constitución en España* (Madrid, 1973); Martí Gilabert, *La abolición de la Inquisición en España* (Pamplona, 1975); and Luis Alonso Tejada, *Ocaso de la Inquisición* (Madrid, 1969).

The most active student of nineteenth-century Spanish Church history is José Manuel Cuenca Toribio. Two of his works, *Aproximación a la historia de la Iglesia contemporánea en España* (Madrid, 1978) and *Iglesia y burguesía en la España liberal* (Madrid, 1979), provide general discussion and interpretation, while *Sociología de una élite de poder de España e Hispanoamérica contemporáneas: La jerarquía eclesiástica (1789–1965)* (Córdoba, 1976) and *Sociedad y clero en la España del siglo XIX* (Córdoba, 1980) treat social background, elite structure, and social relations. His other studies include *La Iglesia española ante la revolución liberal* (Madrid, 1971); *Apertura e integrismo en la Iglesia española decimonónica* (Seville, 1970); *Don Pedro de Inguanzo y Rivero (1764–1836): Ultimo prelado del antiguo régimen* (Pamplona, 1965); and *Estudios sobre la Iglesia española del siglo XIX* (Madrid, 1973).

Another leading scholar of the period, Vicente Cárcel Ortí, has analyzed the *Política eclesial de los gobiernos liberales españoles (1830–1840)* (Pamplona, 1975) and published the *Correspondencia diplomática del nuncio Tiberi (1827–1834)* (Pamplona, 1976). Liberal doctrine has been examined by Jesús Longares Alonso in *Ideología religiosa del liberalismo español (1808–1843)* (Córdoba, 1979), and he has also provided the principal case study of Barcelona in this period, *Política y religión en Barcelona (1833–1843)* (Madrid, 1976). Studies on the disamortization of Church land are numerous; that of J. M. Mutiloa Poza, *La desamortización eclesiástica en Navarra* (Pamplona, 1972), provides more background than most on Church properties in a key region.

The only general study of the orders in this period is José Manuel Castells, *Las asociaciones religiosas en la España contemporánea (1767–1965)* (Madrid, 1973), but there is an excellent account of the suppression of monasteries by Manuel

Revuelta González, *La exclaustración, 1833–1840* (Madrid, 1976). For the elimination of the theological faculties, see Melquiades Andrés Martín, *La supresión de las facultades de teología en las universidades españolas (1845–1855)* (Burgos, 1976).

The only scholarly, book-length treatment of nineteenth-century Spanish religiosity is Baldomero Jiménez Duque's *La espiritualidad española en el siglo XIX español* (Madrid, 1974). J. A. Portero Molina, *Púlpito e ideología en la España del siglo XIX* (Zaragoza, 1978), is an interesting new study on the political and socioeconomic concepts of the clergy. Rafael García y García de Castro has compiled a collection of representative apologetics, *Los apologistas españoles (1830–1930)* (Madrid, 1935). Concerning Claret, the leading Church figure of the 1850s and 60s, a general biography is provided by Tomás L. Pujadas, *San Antonio María Claret* (Madrid, 1950), while Cristóbal Fernández, *El Beato P. Antonio María Claret*, 2 vols. (Madrid, 1946), offers more detailed treatment.

J. Pérez Alhama, *La Iglesia y el Estado español: Estudio histórico-jurídico a través del Concordato de 1851* (Madrid, 1967), and José de Salazar Abrisquieta, *Storia del Concordato di Spagna conchiuso il 16 marzo 1851, e della Convenzione addizionale al medesimo Concordato, stipolata il 25 agosto 1859* (Rome, 1974), are the chief studies of the concordat with the liberal regime. A brief comparative treatment of religious policy in modern Spanish regimes is provided by Juan María Laboa, *Iglesia y religión en las constituciones españolas* (Madrid, 1981); while Luis Gutiérrez Martín, *El privilegio de nombramiento de obispos en España* (Rome, 1967), contributes a broad overview of arrangements for the naming of bishops, traditional and modern. The basic works on Spanish relations with the Holy See during this period are Jerónimo Bécker, *Relaciones diplomáticas entre España y la Santa Sede durante el siglo XIX* (Madrid, 1908); E. de la Puente García, *Relaciones diplomáticas entres España y la Santa Sede durante el reinado de Isabel II (1843–1851)* (Madrid, 1970); and on the Roman question, Jesús Pabón, *España y la cuestión romana* (Madrid, 1972).

The fundamental work on the Church and the *sexenio revolucionario* is Cárcel Ortí's *Iglesia y revolución en España (1868–1974)* (Pamplona, 1979). There are two studies of the democratic parliament of 1869: Pedro Antonio Perlado, *La libertad religiosa en las Constituyentes del 69* (Pamplona, 1970), and Santiago Petschen, *Iglesia-Estado: Las Constituyentes de 1869* (Madrid, 1974). On the Basque country, see Francisco Rodríguez de Coro, *País Vasco, Iglesia y revolución liberal* (Vitoria, 1978) and *El Obispado de Vitoria durante el sexenio revolucionario* (Vitoria, 1976).

Statistical data on the clergy in this period are provided in Juan Sáez Marín, *Datos sobre la Iglesia española contemporánea (1768–1868)* (Madrid, 1975). C. Seco Serrano et al., *La cuestión social en la Iglesia española contemporánea* (El Escorial, 1981), presents a series of studies on diverse aspects of social relations in the nineteenth and twentieth centuries. The most extensive bibliographies will be found in Jesús Longares and José L. Escudero, *Bibliografía fundamental de la Iglesia en la España contemporánea (siglos XVIII–XX)* (Córdoba, 1979), and J. Cuenca and J. Longares, *Bibliografía de la historia de la Iglesia, 1940–1974: Artículos de revista* (Valencia-Córdoba, 1976). On Spanish Protestantism in the later nineteenth century, see R. M. K. van der Grijp, *Geschichte des spanischen Protestantismus im 19. Jahrhundert* (Wageningen, 1971), and Joan González i Pastor, *El protestantisme a Catalunya* (Barcelona, 1968). John D. Hughey, Jr., *Religious Freedom in Spain* (London, 1955), examines shifting standards of tolerance in modern Spanish regimes.

CHAPTER 4

THERE is no general study of the Catholic revival, which is approached by the existing Spanish historical literature in bits and pieces. Some of the most cogent work on the late nineteenth century may be found in the numerous articles by Fernando García de Cortázar, the most relevant of which to this main topic is "La Iglesia española de la Restauración: Definición de objetivos y práctica religiosa," *Letras de Deusto* 8:16 (July–Dec. 1978), 5–34. Jiménez Duque's *Espiritualidad española*, cited in the previous chapter, is also useful.

There are complete editions of the *Obras completas* of both Jaimes Balmes, 8 vols. (Madrid, 1948–50); and Juan Donoso Cortés, 2 vols. (Madrid, 1946). Works on each are numerous. The most complete biography of Donoso is Edmund Schramm, *Donoso Cortés* (Madrid, 1936), but John T. Graham, *Donoso Cortés: Utopian Romanticist and Political Realist* (Columbia, Mo., 1974), is probably the beat treatment of his thought. Among the better books on Balmes are José Corts Grau, *Ideario político de Balmes* (Madrid, 1934), and José Zaragüeta et al., *Balmes: Filósofo social, apologista y político* (Madrid, 1945).

Adolfo Muñoz Alonso, *Las ideas filosóficas de Menéndez Pelayo* (Madrid, 1956), treats the leading Catholic polymath of the century in Spain, while F. Díaz de Cerio, *Un cardenal filósofo de la historia: Fr. Zeferino González, O.P. (1831–1894)* (Rome, 1969), deals with the leading scholar among the episcopacy. For shifting cultural currents within Spanish universities, see A. Ollero Tassara, *Universidad y política: Tradición y secularización en el siglo XIX español* (Madrid, 1972).

There are two histories of the new Catholic universities: Carmelo Sáenz de Santa María, S. I., *Historia de la Universidad de Deusto* (Bilbao, 1962), and Nemesio González Caminero, *La Pontificia Universidad de Comillas: Semblanza histórica* (Madrid, 1942). Calasanz Rabaza, *Historia de las Escuelas Pías de España*, 4 vols. (Valencia, 1917), is a compendium on the devotional schools. There are numerous accounts of those engaged in new Catholic schools and programs during this period: J. M. Prellezo García, *Educación y familia en Andrés Manjón* (Zurich, 1969); J. Montero Vives, *Manjón, precursor de la escuela activa* (Granada, 1958); A. Torres Sánchez, *Vida del siervo de Dios don Manuel Domingo y Sol* (Tortosa, 1934); J. A. Hernán Sanz, *Mosén Sol* (Barcelona, 1970); Marcelo González, *The Power of the Priesthood: A Life of Father Henry de Ossó* (Barcelona, 1971); and J. M. Javierre, *Madre de los pobres: Sor Angela de la Cruz* (Madrid, 1969).

The religious attitudes of the literary elite are treated in F. Pérez Gutiérrez, *El problema religioso en la generación de 1868* (Madrid, 1975); and Brian J. Dendle, *the Spanish Novel of Religious Thesis 1876–1936* (Madrid, 1968). Fernando

244   *Bibliography*

Martín Buezas, *La teología de Sanz del Río y del krausismo español* (Madrid, 1977), examines the religious ideas of the leading anti-Catholic intellectual and pedagogical group; while Jesús Pabón, *El drama de mosén Jacinto* (Barcelona, 1954), explores the spiritual problems of the leading Catholic poet of the period.

José Andrés-Gallego, *La política religiosa en España, 1889–1913* (Madrid, 1975), is the leading study of Catholicism and politics in the late nineteenth century. M. F. Núñez Munoz, *La Iglesia y la Restauración 1875–1881* (Sta. Cruz de Tenerife, 1976), examines Church-state relations at the beginning of the new regime; while R. Sanz de Diego, *Medio siglo de relaciones Iglesia-Estado: El cardenal A. Monescillo y Viso (1811–1897)* (Madrid, 1977), deals with the role of a leading prelate of the period. On Integrism, see José Ricart Torrens, *Así era el Dr. Sardá y Salvany* (Barcelona, 1966); and the brief article by John N. Schumacher, "Integrism: A Study in Nineteenth-Century Spanish Politico-Religious Thought," *Catholic Historical Review* 48:3 (Oct., 1962), 343–64, unsurpassed as a scholarly analysis. Joaquín Buitrago y Hernández, *Las órdenes religiosas* (Madrid, 1899), is a treatment of the orders' legal status. The official collective pronouncements of the Church hierarchy have been collected in *Documentos colectivos del Episcopado español, 1870–1974* (Madrid, 1974).

Domingo Benavides Gómez, *Democracia y cristianismo en la España de la Restauración 1875–1931* (Madrid, 1978), is a general examination of the Catholic relation to social and political reform. For the earliest expressions of social Catholicism, see M. T. Aubach Guiu, *Los orígenes del catolicismo social en Barcelona en la segunda mitad del siglo XIX* (Valencia, 1971); and Florentino del Valle, *El P. Antonio Vicent y la acción social católica* (Madrid, 1947). Luis Palacios Bañuelos, *Círculos de obreros y sindicatos agrarios en Córdoba (1877–1923)* (Córdoba, 1980), examines another early effort at mobilization in Córdoba.

CHAPTER 5

JOSÉ ANDRÉS-GALLEGOS'S *La política religiosa en España, 1889–1913*, cited in the previous chapter, is the best general study of the religious issue in Spanish politics during the early twentieth century. The principal work on anticlericalism in Barcelona and the Semana Trágica is Joan Connelly Ullman, *The Tragic Week: A Study of Anticlericalism in Spain 1875–1912* (Cambridge, Mass., 1968; rev. and ex. ed., *La "Semana Trágica"*, Barcelona, 1972). Beyond these works there has been little study of Spanish anticlericalism. Julio Caro Baroja, *Introducción a una historia contemporánea del anticlericalismo* (Madrid, 1980), provides a brief cultural introduction to which J. M. Díaz Mozaz, *Apuntes para una sociología del anticlericalismo* (Barcelona, 1976), adds little. Two works of the period which despite their biases provided useful data and references are Luis Morote, *Los frailes en España* (Madrid, 1904); and "Máximo" (A. Salcedo Ruiz), *El anticlericalismo y las órdenes religiosas en España* (Madrid, 1908). See also V. M. Arbeloa, *Socialismo y anticlericalismo* (Madrid, 1973). José M. Sánchez, *Anticlericalism: A Brief History* (Notre Dame, 1972), provides historical perspective. John Devlin, *Spanish Anticlericalism* (New York, 1966), is a literary study.

Two very influential Spanish prelates in Rome are described admiringly in Antonio Ma. Barcelona, *El cardenal Vives y Tutó* (Barcelona, 1916); and J. M.

Bibliography 245

Javierre, *Merry del Val* (Barcelona, 1965). N. González Ruiz and I. Martín, *Seglares en la historia del catolicismo español* (Madrid, 1968), provides information on the origins of the ACNP. Two leaders in Catholic education during this period are treated in A. Sangüesa Garcés, *Pedagogía y clericalismo en la obra del P. Ramón Ruiz Amado, S.J. (1881–34)* (Zurich, 1973); and Domingo Mondrone, *El Padre Poveda* (Bilbao, 1965). Avelino Gómez Ledo, *Amor Ruibal o la sabiduría con sencillez* (Madrid, 1949), treats the leading Catholic philosopher of the era. María Jiménez Salas, *Historia de la asistencia social en España en la Edad Moderna* (Madrid, 1958), provides some information on charitable activities. Two regional studies are Josep Massot i Muntaner, *Aproximació a la història religiosa de Catalunya contemporánea* (Barcelona, 1973); and Santiago Díez Llama, *La situación socio-religiosa de Santander y el obispo Sánchez de Castro (1884–1920)* (Santander, 1971). *El padre Sarabia escribe su historia, 1875–1958*, ed. Pedro Santidrián (Madrid, 1963), is an interesting account by an "internal missionary" who began his work in this period.

Oscar Alzaga Villaamil, *La primera democracia cristiana en España* (Barcelona, 1973), treats the origins of Christian democracy, and an overview of Catholic trade unionism may be found in J. N. García Nieto, *El sindicalismo cristiano en España* (Bilbao, 1960), while Juan José Castillo, *El sindicalismo amarillo en España* (Madrid, 1977), treats all nonleftist syndicalism. The basic works on the CONCA are Castillo's *Propietarios muy pobres (La Confederación Nacional Católico-Agraria, 1917–1942)* (Madrid, 1979); and Josefina Cuesta Bustillo, *Sindicalismo católico agrario en España (1917–19)* (Madrid, 1978). Domingo Benavides Gómez, *El fracaso social del catolicismo español* (Barcelona, 1973), deals with the labor organizing of Maximiliano Arboleya. A more successful initiative is recounted in Jordi Nadal and Carles Sudriá, *Història de la Caixa de Pensions* (Barcelona, 1981). Colin M. Winston's work "The Catholic Right and Social Conflict in Catalonia, 1900–1936" is in press.

CHAPTER 6

THE BEST introductory survey of the conflict between the Church and the Second Republic is still José M. Sánchez, *Reform and Reaction: The Politico-Religious Background of the Spanish Civil War* (Chapel Hill, 1964). M. Fernández Areal, *La política católica en España* (Barcelona, 1970), provides a briefer summary that extends into the Franco period. The principal studies of the religious issue and the Republican constitution are Cesare Marongiu Buonaiuti, *Spagna 1931: La Seconda Republica e la Chiesa* (Rome, 1976); and Fernando de Meer Lecha-Marzo, *La cuestión religiosa en las Cortes Constituyentes de la II República española* (Pamplona, 1975). See also V. M. Arbeloa, *La semana trágica de la Iglesia en España (octubre de 1931)* (Barcelona, 1976); and F. Astarloa Villena, *Región y religión en las Constituyentes de 1931* (Valencia, 1976). E. Allison Peers, *Spain, the Church and the Orders* (London, 1945), is a defense of the Church by a leading British Hispanist.

The three leading biographies of the highest-ranking prelates under the Republic are Ramón Garriga, *El cardenal Segura y el Nacional-Catolicismo*

(Barcelona, 1977); Ramon Muntanyola, *Vidal i Barraquer, cardenal de la pau* (Barcelona, 1970); and Anastasio Granados, *El cardenal Gomá, primado de España* (Madrid, 1969). M. Batllori and V. M. Arbeloa have edited and published numerous documents from the papers of Cardinal Vidal under the title *Arxiu Vidal i Barraquer: Església i Estat durant la Segona Republica Espanyola*, 6 vols. (Montserrat, 1976–78).

The most extensive study of the the CEDA is José Ramón Montero, *La C.E.D.A*, 2 vols. (Madrid, 1977). A different perspective is presented in the first volume of Javier Tusell Gómez, *Historia de la democracia cristiana en España* (Madrid, 1974); and R. A. H. Robinson, *The Origins of Franco's Spain* (1970). Julián Cortés Cabanillas, *El bienio "santo" de la II República* (Barcelona, 1973), is an account of the conservative biennium. The only study of the leading intellectual and theorist of the Catholic right is Vicente Marrero, *Maeztu* (Madrid, 1955).

On Catholicism and Christian democracy in Catalonia during the Republic, see J. Massot i Muntaner, *L'Església catalana al segle XX* (Barcelona, 1975); the second volume of Tusell's *Historia de la democracia cristiana*; Hilari Raguer, *La Unió Democrática de Catalunya i el seu temps (1931–1939)* (Montserrat, 1977); and Varios, *La Federació de Joves Cristians de Catalunya* (Barcelona, 1972). Francisco Carballo and Alfonso Magariños, *La Iglesia en la Galicia contemporánea* (Madrid, 1978), provides extensive treatment of the Church in Galicia during the Republic, while José Fariña Jamardo, *La parroquia rural en Galicia* (Madrid, 1975), studies Galician parish structure in broad historical perspective.

The predicament of Basque Nationalist Catholics in the Civil War quickly generated an extensive bibliography. See particularly S. J. Gutiérrez Alvarez, *La cuestión eclesiástica vasca entre 1931–1936* (León, 1971); *Historia general de la Guerra civil en Euskadi*, vol. 5, *El clero vasco* (San Sebastián, 1981); and Juan de Iturralde (pseud. of Juan de Usabiaga), *La guerra de Franco, los vascos y la Iglesia*, 2 vols. (San Sebastián, 1978). Alberto de Onaindía, *Capítulos de mi vida*, I , *Hombre de paz en la guerra* (Buenos Aires, 1973); and Manuel de Irujo, *Memorias*, II, *Un vasco en el Ministerio de Justicia: La cuestión religiosa* (Buenos Aires, 1978), are important memoirs.

The definitive census of the persecution of the clergy will be found in Antonio Montero Moreno, *Historia de la persecución religiosa en España 1936–1939* (Madrid, 1961). Juan Ordóñez Márquez, *La apostasía de las masas y la persecución religiosa en la provincia de Huelva 1931–1936* (Madrid, 1968), recounts attacks on the Church in one province before the Civil War, while Ramiro Viola González, *El martirio de una iglesia: Lérida 1936–1939* (Lérida, 1980), describes the wartime persecution in part of Catalonia. Church policy during the breakdown of the Republic is defended in Angel García, *La Iglesia española y el 18 de julio* (Barcelona, 1977).

CHAPTER 7

GUY HERMET has presented a broad and systematic study of Church-state relations and Catholic politics under the Franco regime in his *Les catholiques dans l'Espagne franquiste*, 2 vols. (Paris, 1980–81). For a brief introductory, though somewhat one-sided, account in English, see Norman B. Cooper, *Catholicism and the Franco Regime* (Beverly Hills, 1975).

A spate of general works appeared in Spain immediately after the demise of the regime. Among the better ones were Rafael Gómez Pérez, *Política y religión en el régimen de Franco* (Barcelona, 1976); Santiago Petschen, *La Iglesia en la España de Franco* (Madrid, 1977); and Juan José Ruiz Rico, *El papel político de la Iglesia católica en la España de Franco* (Madrid, 1977). See also U. Massimo Miozzi, *Storia della Chiesa espagnola (1931–1966)* (Rome, 1967); Francisco Rodríguez de Coro, *Colonización política del catolicismo (1941–1945)* (San Sebastián, 1979); Manuel Tuñón de Lara, *El hecho religioso en España* (Paris, 1968); V. M. Arbeloa, *Aquella España católica* (Salamanca, 1975); Alfonso Alvarez Bolado, *El experimento del Nacional Catolicismo, 1939–1975* (Madrid, 1976); José Chao Rego, *La Iglesia en el franquismo* (Madrid, 1976); *Iglesia y sociedad en España: 1939–1975* (Madrid, 1977); and Melquiades Andrés et al., *Aproximación a la historial social de la Iglesia española contemporánea* (Madrid, 1978).

Hilari Raguer has written a general account of the Church during the Civil War, *La espada y la cruz (La Iglesia 1936–1939)* (Barcelona, 1977), as well as the principal study of Vatican policy in that conflict, "El Vaticano y la guerra civil española," in *Cristianesimo nella Storia* 3 (April, 1982), 137–209. Luis Aguirre Prado, *La Iglesia y la guerra española* (Madrid, 1964), presents the Franquist version, which may be contrasted with Ramon Comas i Madurell, *Gomá-Vidal i Barraquer: Dues visions antagòniques de l'Esglesia del 1939* (Barcelona, 1974), and Herbert R. Southworth, *El mito de la cruzada de Franco* (Paris, 1963). Ma. Luisa Rodríguez Aisa has prepared a critical study of *El cardenal Gomá y la guerra de España* (Madrid, 1981), while official pronouncements can be found in Cardenal Isidro Gomá y Tomás, *Pastorales de la guerra de España* (Madrid, 1955), and the collection *Iglesia, Estado y Movimiento Nacional* (Madrid, 1963). For the views of one of the few liberal Spanish Catholic intellectuals of that period, see José Bergamín, *Detrás de la cruz* (Mexico City, 1941), and *El pensamiento perdido* (Madrid, 1976). The polemic concerning Catholicism and Basque nationalism is extended into the postwar years in Julen Rentería Ugalde's rambling and disconnected *Pueblo vasco e Iglesia* (Bilbao, 1982).

Official Church-state agreements are presented in *Los acuerdos entre la Iglesia y España* (Madrid, 1980), ed. C. Corral and L. Echeverría; and the religious legislation of the Franco regime in A. Bernárdez Cantón, *Legislación eclesiástica del Estado (1938–1964)* (Madrid, 1965). See also Bernärdez Cantón's *El fenómeno religioso en España: Aspectos jurídico-políticos* (Madrid, 1972); and Isidoro Martín Martínez, *Eclesiásticos en organismos políticos españoles* (Madrid, 1973). Technical aspects of the Concordat of 1953 are treated in E. Fernández Regatillo, *El concordato español de 1953* (Santander, 1961); and Antonio Arza Arteaga, *Privilegios económicos de la Iglesia española* (Bilbao, 1973). By contrast, Aurelio L. Orensanz discusses expressions of popular religious devotion in *Religiosidad popular española, 1940–1965* (Madrid, 1974).

The most controversial sector within the Church during the Franco regime was Opus Dei, and the attendant bibliography has polarized around the extremes.

Salvador Bernal, *Mons. José María Escrivá de Balaguer* (Madrid, 1976), is a biography of the founder. The chief hostile accounts are Jesús Ynfante, *La prodigiosa aventura del Opus Dei* (Paris, 1970); and Daniel Artigues (pseud.), *El Opus Dei en España, 1928–1962* (Paris, 1971). Jean-Jacques Thierry, *L'Opus Dei: Mythe et réalité* (Paris, 1973), is much more favorable.

A defense of the regime's position on religious liberty is presented in E. Guerrero and J. M. Alonso, *Libertad religiosa en España* (Madrid, 1962); but terms of legal repression are examined in Lorenzo Martín-Retortillo Baquer, *Libertad religiosa y orden público* (Madrid, 1970). The plight of Spanish Protestants is described in Jacques Delpech, *The Oppression of Protestants in Spain* (Boston, 1955).

CHAPTER 8

THE FULLEST account of Catholic politics and Church-state relations during the era of Vatican II and after will be found in volume 2 of the work by Guy Hermet, cited for the previous chapter. Pierre Jobit, *L'Eglise d'Espagne à l'heure du Concile* (Paris, 1965), surveys the Church at the beginning of this period. Francisco Gil Delgado, *Conflicto Iglesia-Estado* (Madrid, 1975), presents an informative account of Church-state conflicts of the late 1960s and early 1970s, to which Rafael Díaz-Salazar, *Iglesia, dictadura y democracia: Catolicismo y sociedad en España (1953–1979)* (Madrid, 1981), adds little. Carlos Santamaría Ansa, *La Iglesia hace política* (Madrid, 1974), briefly expounds reformist policy; M. A. González Múniz lauds the ecclesiastical opposition in Asturias in *Clero liberal asturiano* (Salinas, 1976); and J. Castaño Colomer describes the main activist Catholic youth group in *La JOC en España (1946–1970)* (Salamanca, 1977). A. Sáez Alba, *La Asociación Católica Nacional de Propagandistas y el caso de "El Correo de Andalucía"* (Paris, 1974), presents a hostile account of a key lay association. The economic position of the Church is examined in Jean-François Nodinot, *L'Eglise et le pouvoir en Espagne* (Paris, 1973); and J. Castellá-Gassol, *¿De dónde viene y a dónde va el dinero de la Iglesia católica?* (Barcelona, 1975). *Der totalitäre Gottestaat* (Düsseldorf, 1970), ed. Michael Raske, is one of the more extreme treatments of the period.

Studies in Spanish religious sociology underwent considerable growth during the 1960s, led by Rogelio Duocastella and Jesús María Vázquez. Duocastella was a coauthor of *Análisis sociológico del catolicismo español* (Barcelona, 1967), and edited *Cambio social y religioso en España* (Barcelona, 1975). Vázquez wrote *Realidades socio-religiosas de España* (Madrid, 1967), and *Los religiosos españoles, hoy* (Madrid, 1973), and collaborated in writing *La Iglesia española contemporánea* (Madrid, 1973). Interesting regional studies are the Diocese of Bilbao's *Diagnóstico sociológico de los conflictos sacerdotales* (Bilbao, 1971); and A. Vázquez, J. M. Díaz Mozaz, and F. Azcona, *La vida cristiana ante el desafío de los tiempos nuevos: Estudio sociorreligioso de Navarra* (Pamplona, 1973). Though unsystematic, Paulo Iztueta Armendáriz, *Sociología del fenómeno contestatario del clero vasco: 1940–1975* (San Sebastián, 1981), presents considerable data. One of the most important documents of the period is Secretariado Nacional del Clero, *Asamblea Conjunta Obispos-Sacerdotes* (Madrid, 1971). Personal accounts of secularized and married ex-priests are given in *La gran desbandada (Curas secularizados)* (Madrid, 1977), ed. Angel de Castro; and *Los curas casados se confiesan* (Madrid, 1977), ed. Grupo de Redactores "Ekipo." The leading publicist of Marxist Catholicism is Alfonso Comín, author of *Fe en la tierra* (Bilbao, 1975), and *Cristianos en el partido, comunistas en la Iglesia* (Barcelona, 1977), among others. In *La secularización en España* (Bilbao, 1972), Jesús Jiménez Blanco and Juan Estruch provide a sociological study of secularization among university-educated professionals.

The last decade of the Franco regime produced a series of books on religious liberty and ecumenicism. Some that may be noted are José Desumbila, *El ecumenismo en España* (Madrid, 1964); José Jiménez Lozano, *Meditación española sobre la libertad religiosa* (Barcelona, 1966), a literary study; Jesús Amón, *Prejuicio antiprotestante y religiosidad utilitaria* (Madrid, 1969), based in part on survey research; Alberto de la Hera, *Pluralismo y libertad religiosa* (Seville, 1971), a legal study; Jaime Pérez-Llantada Gutiérrez, *La libertad religiosa en España y el Vaticano II* (Madrid, 1974); and Amadeo de Fuenmayor, *La libertad religiosa* (Pamplona, 1974). On contemporary Spanish Protestantism, see Carmen Irizarry, *The Thirty Thousand: Modern Spain and Protestantism* (New York, 1966); Manuel López Rodríguez, *La España protestante* (Madrid, 1976); and Juan Bta. Vilar, *Un siglo de protestantismo en España* (Murcia, 1979).

The most informative book on negotiations for a new Concordat is *Todo sobre el Concordato* (Madrid, 1971), ed. J. L. Martín Descalzo et al. See also N. López Martínez, *El Vaticano y España* (Burgos, 1972); J. M. Díez Alegría et al., *Concordato y sociedad pluralista* (Salamanca, 1972); and B. M. Hernando, *Iglesia-Esatdo, ¿luna de miel, luna de hiel?* (Barcelona, 1975).

The leader of the Spanish Church during the 1970s gives his version of events in J. L. Martín Descalzo, *Tarancón, el cardenal del cambio* (Barcelona, 1982). María Mérida, *Entrevista con la Iglesia* (Barcelona, 1982), presents a series of interviews with leaders of the episcopacy at the beginning of the following decade.

Considerable new work was done in Spanish religious anthropology during the 1970s, most of it published in articles. Perhaps the best book-length study was William A. Christian, *Person and God in a Spanish Valley* (New York, 1972). There were also new descriptive accounts of typical aspects of popular religiosity, such as Santiago Montoto, *Cofradías sevillanas* (Seville, 1966); Carlos Pascual, *Guía sobrenatural de España* (Madrid, 1976); and S. Rodríguez Becerra and J. M. Vázquez Soto, *Exvotos de Andalucía* (Seville, 1980). The work of Juan Sáiz Barberá, *El espiritualismo español y destino providencial de España en la historia universal* (Seville, 1977), may be noted as perhaps the final major statement of the traditional Spanish ideology, published two years after the death of Franco.

The periodic reference work for the Catholic Church in Spain is the triennial *Guía de la Iglesia en España*, last published in 1979. A general "Who's Who," including priminent laymen, was published a decade ago by Armando Vázquez, *Quién es quién en la Iglesia de España* (Madrid, 1972). Current activities may be followed in such Church periodicals as *Ecclesia* and *Vida Nueva*.

Index

Abd al-Rahman I, 6
Abd al-Rahman II, 6
Abd al-Rahman III, 12
Abortion, 59, 226
Acción Española, 163
Acción Social Popular (ASP), 142, 158–59
Action Française, 163
Adelelmo, San, 24*n*
Adoptionist controversy, 8, 9
Afrancesado, 73
Africa, 45, 55, 110
Agnosticism, 155
Aguirre, Cardinal, 142
Al-Andalus, 6, 7, 10, 12, 14, 23
Alarcón, Pedro Antonio de, 102
Alava, 14, 145
Alba, Duke of, 47
Alcalá de Henares, University of, 39, 40
Alcalá Zamora, Niceto, 94, 153–56, 164, 166
Alexander II (pope), 15
Alfonso II (king of Asturias), 8, 9
Alfonso III (king of Asturias), 11
Alfonso X (el Sabio, king of Castile), 21
Alfonso XII (king of Spain), 113, 114
Alfonso XIII (king of Spain): inauguration of Cerro de los Angeles, 106; and Maura, 133, 138; obeisance to papacy, 146; departure in 1931, 152; praised, 153; mentioned, 122
Al-Mansur, 14
Almería, Bishop of, 95
Almohads, 14–15, 20
Almoravids, 14, 18, 20
Alumbrados, 40
Amadeo of Savoy (king of Spain), 95, 96
America. *See* Latin America
Amor Ruibal, Angel, 140
"Amoral familialism," xii
Amortization, 65
Anales de Aragón, 42

Anarchism: anticlericalism in, 125–26, 133, 168; assassination of Eduardo Dato, 138
Anarchosyndicalism: anticlericalism, 137, 144; ideology, 150; mentioned, 142
Andalusia, 34, 60, 145, 184, 205
Añoveros, Bishop Antonio, 205
Anticlericalism: in the Middle Ages, 28, 29; weakness in sixteenth century, 58; of liberal governments, 76, 80–87, 127–30, 131, 135; effects on education, 79, 104, 139–40; propaganda, 82; against wealth of church, 85; legislation of Progressives, 89–90; separation of church and state, 93, 94; antireligious forms, 124–26, 149–50; riots, 127, 132–33, 147, 156–57, 164; defensive activity, 136–37; waning after 1912, 137; of revolutionary groups, 150; under Second Republic, 153–55, 158; in the Civil War, 168, 169–70; of extreme right, 204
Anti-semitism. *See* Minorities, treatment of
Apocalypticism, 10, 31
Apología del altar y el trono (1818), 75
Apostólicos, 78
Aragon, papal ratification of kingdom, 15, 35, 81, 145
Arana y Goiri, Sabino de, 112
Aránzazu, 197
Arbeloa, Víctor Manuel, 222
Arboleya, Maximiliano, 143, 146
Architecture: Asturian pre-Romanesque, 13; Mudéjar, 21; Gothic, 27; Antonio Gaudí, 102
Armada, 47, 52
Arnulf, Archbishop of Narbonne, 13
Artigas, Juan, 82
Asamblea Conjunta, 201–2
Asambleas Cristianas, 201
Asociación Católica Nacional de Jovenes Propagandistas (ACNP), 136–38, 147, 158, 184–85, 207

251

Devotional works, 44–45, 57, 105, 187
Deza, Archbishop, 39
Diagnóstico sociológico de los conflictos sacerdotales, 200
Díaz de Vivar, Rodrigo, 18
Díaz Merchán, Gabino, 226
Díez Alegría, José María, S.J. 211
Diferencia entre lo temporal y lo eterno y crisol de desengaños, 57
Dignitatis humanae, 195
Dilectissima nobis, 158
Dios, San Juan de, 51
Disamortization: legislation, 65, 74, 83, 87–88, 90; methods and economic effects of, 84–85; in return for bonds, 91
Discalced movement, 51
Divorce: in Mozarab society, 11; legalized, 156; abolished, 180; opposition of church, 226
Domingo de Guzmán, Santo, 30
Domingo de la Calzada, Santo, 24n
Dominicans, 30, 46n
Donoso Cortés, Juan, 100, 101
"Dos Ciudades, Las," 173
Drama, 42, 49, 52, 65, 59, 60, 102, 128, 227
Dress, 59, 140
Duero river, 27

East Asia, 168
Ecclesia, 184, 193
Editorial Católico, La, 137
Education: Muslim influences, 21; of common people in the Middle Ages, 30, 44–45, 53–54; expansion of higher, 39, 44, 51; decline, 56–57; improvements of the Enlightenment, 65, 69, 103–4, 219; restriction of church control of, 93–94; elementary and secondary school conditions, 104, 139, 156, 158, 186, 221; policies of radical republicans, 133; during Civil War, 172; under Franco, 179, 181–82; position of Opus Dei, 190; post-Franco era, 210–11, 216. *See also* Universities
Eíjo y Garay, Bishop, 184, 188
Electra, 128
Emperor, use of title by Spanish rulers, 10
England: comparisons with, 5, 52; relations with, 47, 48, 137
Enlightened despotism, 61, 64

Enlightenment, 62, 69, 71, 124, 150
Enrique y Tarancón, Vicente, 199, 205, 213, 216, 226
Ensalmadores, 59
Ensayo sobre el catolicismo, el liberalismo y el socialismo (1851), 101
Ensenada, Marqués de la, 64
Entente, 137
Episcopal Conference, 195, 204, 206, 214, 216, 223, 226
Erasmianism, 40, 68
Escarré, Aureli, 197
Eschatology, 9
Escobar y Mendoza, Antonio de, 57
Escrivá de Balaguer, José María, 190
España Sagrada, 68
Espartero, Baldomero, 86–87
Estado Católico, El, 177
Estado Corporativo, El, 177
Estado Nuevo, El (1935), 162
Estudio sobre la filosofía de Santo Tomás, 102
ETA, 112, 197–98, 225
Etymologies, 4
European Value Systems Study Group, 227
Evangelical Church, 98n
Evangelism, 31, 60, 69, 92, 97, 104, 182
Exaltados, 77
Exercises of San Ignacio de Loyola, 51, 181

Falange: Falange Española (FE), 162; Falangist student organization (SEU), 176; raised to official state party, 176; defined, 178; antagonism with church, 179, 181, 204, 207; criticisms of, 181; in Franco ministry, 185, 189; opposition to Opus Dei, 190. *See also* Fascism
Family: structure in the Middle Ages, 19, 22; among minorities, 32; marriage laws, 95–96
Faqihs, 20
Fascism: criticisms of, 159–60, 165; Italian, 162; and the Collective Letter, 175; use of Roman salute, 176; and statism, 184
Federación Nacional de Sindicatos Católicos-Libres, 143, 144
Feijóo, Benito Jerónimo, 62
Felipe II (king of Spain), 46, 47, 48
Felipe III (king of Spain), 55
Felipe IV (king of Spain), 56

Vélez, Rafael, 75
Verdaguer, Jacint, 102
Via crucis, 49–50, 56, 58, 66
Vincent, Antonio, 120, 121
Vich, 77
Vidal i Barraquer, Cardinal, 181
Viluma, Marqués de, 94
Vincent de Paul, St., order of, 88
Virgin Mary. *See* Marian devotion
Viscaya, 13–14, 108, 112, 169, 174, 198, 204
Visigoths: conversion to Christianity, 3, 4; failure of its elite, 5; violence of, 5; émigre, 7; church of, 8; court life, 10; mentioned, 63
Vitoria, Francisco de, 41, 43
Vives, Juan Luis, 40
Volksvereine, 141, 142

Waldeck-Rousseau, 127, 128
Wealth of the church: during Reconquest, 13, 27; landed patrimonies, 27, 28, 65
Weber thesis, 60
Welfare, 142–43, 145, 161, 221. *See also* Charity
Willughby, Francis, 59
Witchcraft, 37

Witizan clan, 5
Wittenburg, 40
Women: rights of, 19; slavery of, 19; veiling of, 21; concubinage, 29; names of, 57; education of, 104
Worker circles, 141
Worker organization, 141–46 *passim*, 184, 188, 193, 213
World War I, 137
World War II, 184

Xavier, St. Francis, 182
Xenophobia, 26

Yo creo en la esperanza (1972), 211
Young Maurists, 138–39
Youth groups: beginnings, 94; defense of Catholicism of, 113, 136–37, 138, 139, 163–64; fascism in, 160, 167, 176, 180; membership, 188; alliance with workers' organizations, 193, 198

Zamora, 204, 205
Zaragoza, 18, 83
Zorrilla, José, 102
Zurita, Jerónimo de, 42

DESIGNED BY BRUCE GORE
COMPOSED BY MODERN TYPOGRAPHERS, INC.
DUNEDIN, FLORIDA
MANUFACTURED BY THOMSON-SHORE, INC.
DEXTER, MICHIGAN
TEXT AND DISPLAY LINES ARE SET IN TIMES ROMAN

Library of Congress Cataloging in Publication Data

Payne, Stanley G.
Spanish catholicism.

Bibliography: pp. 233–249.
Includes index.
1. Catholic Church—Spain—History. 2. Spain—
Religious life and customs. 3. Spain—Church history.
I. Title.
BX1583.P29   1984   282′.46   83-25946
ISBN 0-299-09800-1